The Aesthetics of Equity

The Aesthetics of Equity

Notes on
Race, Space,
Architecture,
and Music

CRAIG L. WILKINS

University of Minnesota Press
Minneapolis · London

Parts of chapter 1 previously appeared as "Brothers/Others: Gonna Paint the White House Black," in *Anthology of Male Bodies*, Harington et al., eds. (Bloomington: Indiana University Press, 2002). Parts of chapter 2 previously appeared as "Beyond the Pale: Architecture's Authorization of Class and Racial Bias," *Blacklines* (December 1999): 14–16, 20. Parts of chapter 4 previously appeared as "The Space between Sight and Touch," *Dichotomy: Journal of the University of Detroit School of Architecture* 13 (Spring 2003). Parts of chapter 6 previously appeared as "(W)rapped Space: The Architecture of Hip Hop," *Journal of Architectural Education* 54, no. 1 (September 2000): 7–19; copyright 2000 by the Association of the Collegiate Schools of Architecture; reprinted with permission.

Published by the University of Minnesota Press
111 Third Avenue South, Suite 290
Minneapolis, MN 55401-2520
http://www.upress.umn.edu

Library of Congress Cataloging-in-Publication Data
Wilkins, Craig L., 1961–
  The aesthetics of equity : notes on race, space, architecture, and music / Craig L. Wilkins.
      p. cm.
  Includes bibliographical references and index.
  ISBN-13: 978-0-8166-4660-9 (hc : alk. paper)—ISBN-13: 978-0-8166-4661-6 (pb : alk. paper)
  ISBN-10: 0-8166-4660-0 (hc : alk. paper)—ISBN-10: 0-8166-4661-9 (pb : alk. paper)
  1. Architecture and race—United States. 2. Space (Architecture)—Social aspects—United
States. 3. African American architects. I. Title.
  NA2543.R37W55 2007
  720.89'96073—dc22   2007010801

Printed in the United States of America on acid-free paper

The University of Minnesota is an equal-opportunity educator and employer.

12 11 10 09 08 07   10 9 8 7 6 5 4 3 2 1

Produced by Wilsted & Taylor Publishing Services
Copyediting by Nancy Evans
Text design and composition by Yvonne Tsang

For my parents,
who both continue to
amaze and inspire me,

    and

for my Uncle Mickey,
who loved pen, paper,
and prose

Theory without practice has no value
Practice without theory has no purpose . . .

. . . and either without responsibility
has no place in architecture.

CONTENTS

PREFACE

Whatever reason you had for not being something, there's somebody who had that same problem and overcame it.
—*Barbara Reynolds*

It takes fortitude to be a man, and no less to be an artist. Perhaps it takes even more if the black man would be an artist. If so, there are no exemptions.
—*Ralph Ellison*

I want to be clear about the premise of this book up front: the discipline of architecture has both a systemic and specific resistance to African-Americans at every level. It can be seen in the entrance and graduation rates of students, where just nine years ago African-Americans constituted only 10 percent of the student body studying architecture, with a little more than 8 percent of that woeful number obtaining degrees. It can be seen in the constitution of the faculty teaching architecture, where African-Americans constitute a little more than 3 percent of that body, with historically black colleges and universities (HBCUs) accounting for two-thirds of all African-American faculty appointments. It can be seen in the number of registered architects, where just over 1 percent of all registered architects are African-American despite being 12.5 percent of the population. It can be seen in the makeup and material of published media, where to date there have been less than a dozen books in print documenting the work of African-American architects, one African-American architectural critic to have written for a major metropolitan newspaper, and zero African-Americans in editorial positions at the major architectural publications, in addition to the fact that articles in the most popular professional journals highlighting the work of African-American firms are few and far between—this despite a history of African-Americans in the building professions that dates back to the seventeenth century.[1]

For most African-Americans involved in the study and practice of architecture, it does not take long to realize that *something* is amiss: a comment here, a history class there, a dubious and/or obligatory "urban" design problem later on, scant support for scholarly pursuits, a less-than-desirable majority-office project assignment, a short-list snub, a questionable joint venture division of work, and/or a perfunctory firm interview all help to illustrate this dynamic. It takes a little while longer for many African-Americans to understand that the prevailing, underlying, and unyielding attitude of resistance they constantly encounter has less to do with their ability to teach or practice architecture and much more with something more slippery and elusive. Succinctly put, their "failure is not necessarily a failure to *know* something, but a failure to *be* something."[2]

This work aims to sketch an outline of what I have observed as both the structural and specific resistance to African-American participation in the discipline of architecture. My work in this area is informed by my participation in both the scholastic and practice provinces that constitute the architectural discipline, where I work not only to identify but also to penetrate this resistance to diversity in an effort to highlight both its systemic nature and the ways in which it operates specifically to impede African-American participation.

ACKNOWLEDGMENTS

First, I'd like to thank John Archer for both sharing and shaping my belief in architecture as a field worthy of critical study in the broadest sense. Much of what I discussed with John found its way into this book in one form or another and thus the work is better because of it. A much deserved and hearty thanks also goes out to John Mowitt, Robin Brown, Tom Fisher, and Todd Remington for demanding that I constantly think; Bill Morrish, Catherine Brown, and the Design Center for American Urban Landscape group (1996–99) for challenging me to act; Anna Scott, Lisa Aubrey, and Deidre Hamlar for graciously sharing their wit and spirit; Peter McAuley, Andrew Kincaid, Ole Gram, and Jen Downham for their late-night schedules; Steve Macek and Jackie Leder for their friendship; the cultural studies and comparative literature staff, colleagues, and students for making work fun; the Minneapolis coffeehouses Pandora's, Plan B, Bob's Java Hut, Blue Moon, Sister Moon, Muddy Waters, Spyhouse, and Dunn Brothers on Washington, as well as the Ann Arbor coffeehouse Portofino's for generously allowing me to sit and alternately zone out and write for hours on end; and, finally, my Washington, D.C., gang, who just let me be. Finally, I'd like to thank Christopher A. Smith, my partner-in-crime for many years, for sharing my experiences and concerns about the field we both chose to engage. Without the much-appreciated assistance of those above, this book simply would not have been possible. I trust you will see a little bit of yourselves in this work and I can only hope that when you do, I have done you justice.

ON THE ORGANIZATION OF THIS BOOK

The Aesthetics of Equity is organized in two parts, each with three chapters. The first part, "Architecture as a Noun," addresses the concept of architecture as a noun—a person, place, or thing—to highlight its current inert condition. As such, this section looks at the static, concretized understanding of architecture and deconstructs the systemic practices that have kept it from changing with the demands of a multicultural society. It examines the current condition of architecture from three specific sites of critique—*spatial*, as the manner in which we construct a very particular worldview for ourselves; *disciplinary*, as the manner in which we pass on that worldview to others; and *professional*, as the manner in which that worldview becomes embedded in the built environment—as a way to understand and reveal the hidden operations in each that impede the inclusion of diverse cultures in general and African-American participation in particular.

Chapter 1, "Space—Place," addresses the notion of power as it is embodied both abstractly and materially in the spatial organization of our built environment. I focus on the predominant Western notion of space that underlies the organization and perception of design and posit that space, as a critical element in the construction of identity and property, is racialized. The maintenance of this racialized space can currently be seen in the various ways state-authorized privatizations and policing of public space operate. I further argue that the seemingly "natural" decisions about space that authorize these and other biased spatial practices in the world are in actuality constructed on, legitimized by, and fundamentally invested in something equally naturalized but far less visible—*whiteness*—as the transparent and readily accepted requirement for desirable identity and spatial construction in our society.

In chapter 2, "Discipline—Person," I argue that the racialized dichotomies authorized by the spatial expectations of John Locke find their way into the academy, in both personnel and project. Through its historical alliance and service to an elite class, the profession has positioned itself as the primary, if not the only, authority on the architectural object, attempting to limit the discourse of architectural education and exclude public and allied professional discourses. This silencing of the academy in many ways allows the status quo (architecture's relationship to the elite) to go unexamined and subsequently perpetuate itself. This elite is defined in large part by its political, economic, social, and aesthetic desires, which are played out in the organization and form of space, place, and property; the discipline is the tool by which this organization is manifested, commodified, and institutionalized. From what I have observed, experienced, and investigated during my participation in both the academic and practice provinces of architecture, I sketch an outline of the manner in which this relationship to the elite has demonstrated both a structural and a specific resistance to African-American participation within the academy and in the process institutionalized class, racial, and spatial biases.

The final chapter of this part, "Architecture—Thing," takes Bill Hubbard Jr.'s observation that "when social structures give the lie to what a society says it believes, then architecture gets used as a tool in the management of the conflict"[1] as its starting point and examines how these racial and classist social structures operate in relation to society and the profession. Specifically, I look at the seeming disconnect between the profession—its presumptive function and concomitant legitimacy—and the society that authorizes its existence. Further, I examine the social structures within the professional arena, specifically in relation to African-Americans, where it seems that architecture as a management of conflict is most accurately read as a management of a conflict of *color*; exclusionary practices that work to render African-American practitioners invisible to both potential main-stream clients and colleagues.

In the second part, "Architecture as a Verb," I take a look at architecture as an action, state, or motion. Theorizing a new framework to address the shortcomings unveiled by "Architecture as a Noun," I ultimately suggest other possibilities for our shared environment. Again working from a critique of spatial, disciplinary, and professional domains, this section offers an alternative by rejecting the predestination and finality of the previous chapters and infuses its analysis with the concept of agency and active participation. "Architecture as a Verb" suggests that the worldview constructed in "Architecture as a Noun" can be changed to allow for a more fluid, inclusive, and mobile manner of engaging the built environment and offers a model for applying this hypothesis in an urban setting.

Beginning with chapter 4, "Space—Action," this part is concerned with what I have come to understand as problems with the Lockean notion of space. I begin by combining the positions of Henri Lefebvre and Michel Foucault that argue that space is a social construction—a relation between sites that are in turn defined by individual social relationships. I further incorporate arguments from Doreen Massey, Michel de Certeau, and others to theorize the construction of African-American subjectivities and identities via spatial appropriation and usage in opposition to what Lockean space allows. By interrogating the notions of *white* embedded in the naturalized spatial practices of society, I identify and analyze spatial strategies employed by African-Americans that resist spatial and political marginalization. Finally, I address the question of spatial construction specifically in the context of African-American inner-city spaces by engaging Foucault's heterotopia hypothesis, arguing for a third possibility for heterotopias, one that is specifically anchored in the urban environment and offers an alternative to the seeming inevitability of dead, vacant urban spaces, opening possibilities for the positive and substantive transformation of distressed urban spaces.

In chapter 5, "Discipline—State," I present a strategic outline designed to dismantle the systemic nature of the academy and the ways in which it operates to support class and racial bias and specifically to impede African-American participation, as discussed in chapter 2. I introduce, analyze, and synthesize several alternative models for thinking about architecture and disciplinary education that can form the foundation of new paradigms within the academy more amiable to African-American participation. Finally, I address the question of what a new architectural disciplinary model might look like and the advantages of working toward its adoption within the academy.

The last chapter in this part, chapter 6, "Architecture—Motion," theorizes very specific cultural influences in/on architectural theory, analysis, and creation. It specifically explores the potential of music and space being connected in a more profound and fundamental way than has previously been discussed. I assert that the construction of sound and its place in spatial production—and its concomitant effects on representations of such a space—radically changes the nature and understanding of the visual space in which we live. Specifically, I build a case around hip-hop music, identifying several principles of the genre that may be transferred into built form, theorize a manner in which an architectural manifestation can emerge from these principles, and present a model of such a manifestation. In this chapter, I am not so concerned with how music may or may not create a building, but with how music creates a spatial understanding that *results* in architecture, a fundamentally different search for an aesthetic paradigm of architectural and sonic production. In support of Tricia Rose's visualization that "[i]n the postindustrial urban context . . . hip hop style is . . . urban renewal,"[2] I outline a particular social relationship born in the hip-hop inner city that grapples with the question of space and identity. I illustrate how this social relationship manifests itself in a spatial emergence and renewal and, finally, discuss what such spatial recognition and renewal reveals about the future of the urban landscape and architecture.

ON THE ORGANIZATION OF THIS BOOK • xix

You have several choices on how to engage this material:

"Keepin' it real" (interdependent narrative): Read as a whole, *The Aesthetics of Equity* presents a comprehensive examination of architecture as a product that shapes and is shaped by culture and provides the reader with not only the background to the current crisis but ways in which to begin the process of dismantling many of the practices that have created it.

"Call-and-Response" (independent sets of concerns): *The Aesthetics of Equity* can also be read as a set of individual spatial, disciplinary, and/or professional concerns, depending on the reader's immediate interests. For example, each of the chapters in part I identifies causes and effects of particular conditions—and each has a corresponding chapter in part II that outlines a strategy to address the problematic conditions revealed in part I.

"Freestyle" (informal exchange): At the end of each chapter I include a portion written in the lyrical, expressive, and candid language of the hip-hop generation. This portion, titled "Remix," distills the work of the entire chapter by stripping away much of the theoretical, academic terminology and converts my voice into a more conversational but no less informative tone. This conversational tone is to ensure that the important concepts discussed are readily accessible to the typical student, young educator, and professional, each of whom are early enough in their careers to take the bulk of the strategies and practices outlined in the book and fully integrate them into their still developing architectural study and practice philosophies.

PART

I

Architecture as a Noun

noun (n) — a word or group of words
used as the name of a class or of a
particular place, person, or thing.

Space—Place

I

If you do what you've always done,
you'll get what you've always gotten.
—*Jackie "Moms" Mabley*

THE INITIAL CATALYST for my investigating the link between race, space, and architecture was something quite simple, really. Entirely commonplace, or so one would think. This particular type of incident had occurred in various forms and places so many times as to become at once both commonplace and unrecognizable. I no longer took much notice of it, and on the odd occasion when I did it was with a mixture of amusement and irritation. Sad to admit, but it is true. This time, however, something was different.

A female friend and I were heading into what could be arguably called the St. Peter's of conspicuous consumption—the Mall of America in Bloomington, Minnesota, just outside the Twin Cities of Minneapolis and St. Paul. As we entered the transept *(passing through one of its chapels—Macy's, I think)*, my friend smiled a contented smile. I think that she was in awe of the great cathedral of commerce and all its shiny discount outlet altars.

Several moments later, my friend—who happened to be Black—was struck by some religious experience at one of the altars *(Britches Great Outdoors, I think)* and was compelled to present an offering there to receive her gift of a wool hat and scarf set. Alas, she had no "gift to give" *(read: she was short on cash)* in return for the set, at which time she began to speak in, well,

3

shall we say ... tongues *(read: #@*&%@$!)*. So, on to an ATM that would allow the completion of her quasi-spiritual experience we went.

Upon arrival at the ATM, we joined several other "tongue-speaking" people in the thralls of their own personal commercial retail experience. We queued as best we could and waited our chance to pray *(for money)*. As our moment at the machine presented itself, a couple—who happened to be white—also approached the machine.

As my friend placed her card in the machine, the young lady—who was at least two feet away from the machine and behind us at the time—turned to her male companion with a look of combined astonishment, disgust, and indignation and said, "She jumped in front of us." I was amused *(and irritated)* and was about to dismiss it as yet another in a long line of such comments and attitudes, when my friend—her prayers having been answered *(read: her pockets fat)*—said, "Did you hear what she said?"

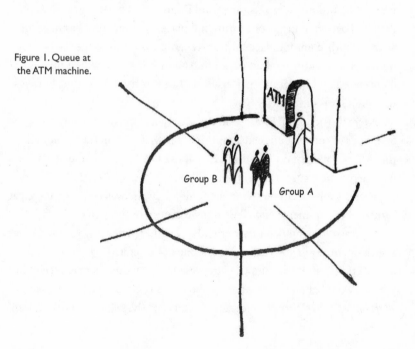

Figure 1. Queue at the ATM machine.

Did you hear what she said? Such a seemingly simple question, yet it filled my thoughts for the remainder of that day and led to my initial work in this area. Had I heard? What did I hear? And what does that have to do with space, architecture, and people of color?

Granted, I may be taking a micro event and extrapolating it into a macro condition, and forgive me if it seems like a stretch, but stay with me for a bit. A compelling analysis of this incident would argue that what occurred was nothing more than two sets of people (A & B) arriving at roughly the same moment at a destination limited in its capacity to only one set at a time. The inevitable consequence of this simultaneous arrival is that one set (set B) would be denied admittance to the very limited space. A reasonable explanation to be sure, except for the fact that it does not address the statement made by set B, "She jumped in front of us," which I think is telling.

Despite the fact that the position of set B relative to set A did not give them any more access to the ATM machine than set A, set B still felt that they were somehow denied their rightful, immediate approach to the machine. Why? What set of social and spatial constructs fueled such a statement? What set of assumptions about public space empowered the unlucky set of people to assume that their position—their *rights*—had been usurped? Where did this notion of space come from? Who has access to it? And what, if anything, does this have to do with the manifestations of the physical and spatial shape of the built environment, and the access—or lack thereof—of African-Americans to architecture, the discipline largely responsible for the shaping of space?

Such musings and investigations are nothing without conclusions. I shall try to answer the above questions in relation to architecture and African-Americans in the remainder of this book. An unnamed political pundit once remarked that to tear down a system is considered reactionary, but to tear it down and replace it with something else is considered revolutionary. It is my intention with this critique to fall somewhere in between—but not in the middle of—these two positions. Now here's where things get a bit interesting . . .

Culturally defined perceptions are often selfish

From birth, we are introduced to the phenomena around us through a set of sensory tools—i.e., sight, smell, sound, touch, and taste, to name a few. Through these tools, information about ourselves and the world around us is internalized—the data filtered through a framework of understanding that is largely culturally defined. In this sense, one can say that we are born into preexisting systems of perception and understanding and that we use these systems to create knowledge of both ourself and our world. In other words, we are taught to understand things and ourselves in particular ways, ways that are shaped by a specific cultural framework full of its own preconceived notions about the world at large (think Marshall McLuhan's famous phrase "the medium is the message"). Our eyes focus on particular things and our ears make sense of certain sounds because of the way we have been taught to see and hear. While this is undeniably true with all ways of discerning our environment, partly because the eye operates at a greater range than other available perception instruments, not to mention the fact that the visual world is arguably a much richer one—or at least a more richly developed one—most culturally constructed systems of understanding operate from a dominance of vision. Thus, one can safely conclude that for those fortunate enough to be in possession of all their sensory faculties, the strongest initial entry and connection to an understanding of the world is through a spatially defined perception of the world at large. However, as has been implied above, perception is not neural. Quite the contrary. Culturally defined perceptions are often selfish, or at least deeply protective, designed to ensure the long-term survival of the culture's worldview. As such, perceptions have an inherent tendency to categorize and differentiate, facilitating an endless supply of inclusive/exclusive hierarchies that those within the cultural framework employ when engaging the world. Ultimately, this "tendency to discriminate is extended into all the abuses of discrimination and privilege within a culture ... and into all the forms of competition within and between cultures" as well.[1] Thus, how we come to perceive the world around us is fundamental to how we come to see ourselves, others, and the relationship between the two.

According to historian Rhys Isaac, social relations are carved intaglio upon a society's living spaces, intervening in the historical dialogue concerning social relations.[2] Thus, "our worldview is a cultural pattern that shapes our mind from birth" and is to a large degree spatially enabled.[3] Put another way, the "where" of our sensory experiences in the world have a profound influence on our ability to create individual and collective identities—to become, know, and name who we are—primarily because "space comprises the social arena in which individuals reproduce or challenge their experiential boundaries of action and interaction."[4] It provides for us what Aspa Gospodini has referred to as a spatial membership, a type of place-based identity provided "to almost all individuals and social groups of [the same] society."[5] Space then—one's ability to perceive it, access it, etc.—becomes an essential element in the construction of identity and, concomitantly, entire societies as well. If that is the case, it is quite reasonable to assume that different societies might view space in different ways—a hypothesis that opens up some interesting questions.[6] For example, if space can be constructed differently across cultures, then perhaps it is not the universal, immutable, naturally occurring entity that we have been led to believe. And, if that is the case, just how is the current notion of Western space—under which the majority of the world operates—constructed? Upon what philosophical and ideological foundations are we building our own and collective identities? Why is it that we have been taught to perceive space in this manner and not another? And finally, who benefits from this spatial construction? For answers to these and other, similar questions, we must first revisit our current understanding of space and its origins.

Karsten Harries quotes Paul Weiss as saying that "architecture [is the] art of bounding space."[7] I dig this statement because it is poetic, clear, and epigrammatic; as brilliant in its simplicity as it is inspiring in its purpose. Architecture is about bounding space: capturing that most ethereal of concepts and creating from it that most concrete of things. Most architects reading this quote might feel more than a little pleased about the importance of their chosen profession and its ability to shape the built environment. That euphoria is short-lived, however, when attention is focused on the current state of our urban fabric. Faced with bounding fragmented and besieged urban spaces with the current architectural kit-of-parts can cause architects a rapid and maddening descent from that most rapturous high. Considering the nature of that descent in hopes of once again ascending to those rhapsodic heights, I have become increasingly convinced that current notions of space, rather than facilitating, actually impede solutions to long-standing urban conditions in any meaningful and substantive way. In our case, the power of American culture is embodied in a spatial organization that determines who will live where and why, and in physical manifestations that decide exactly what particular architectural forms will symbolize and why. These seemingly "natural" decisions are, in truth, anything but. They are in actuality constructed and legitimized upon the spatial foundations theorized by two influential Western philosophers; a framework initially conceived by René Descartes and later critiqued, modified, and further developed by John Locke.

A philosopher of immense influence, John Locke was fundamental to the development of the theoretical foundations by which we perceive and understand space, property, law, and government—four pillars of the American democratic experiment. His conceptual framework remains in use today and we will return to his work often in this document. As Alexander Boulton explains:

> It was Locke's achievement to describe a system of government in which the state, the rights of individuals and property formed a unity of interests. . . . By identifying the interests of property, the state and individual rights, Locke was able to embed the rationalism which was inherent in property relations within the structure of the state and a conception of individual rights.[8]

The influence of the concepts theorized by Locke is in no little part due to the fact that they were created and employed at a moment in human history when it was necessary to legally define and conjoin space, place, and property—enabling all sorts of poor conduct *(think colonial expansion)*. They have remained influential, owing primarily to the fact that his theories have fundamentally, materially, and substantively shaped Western civilization, especially in the areas of governance and property. For my project, though, Locke's theories are important for something less laudable but equally enduring and influential. The notion of space he puts forth is uniquely and fundamentally invested in something much less visible and far more problematic, especially within the current context of the urban core. Legal scholar Cheryl I. Harris has identified this something as an investment in " 'whiteness'—a characteristic that only white people have," that I will argue has become a transparent and readily accepted requirement for desirable spatial construction in Western society.[9]

An examination of whiteness

In this society, the white person has an everyday option not to think of herself in racial terms at all. . . . I label the tendency for whiteness to vanish from whites['] self-perception the transparency phenomenon. Because transparency is such a pervasive fact of whites['] conceptualization of ourselves, we have to be skeptical of ostensively race-neutral decision-making by white decision-makers.[10]

There is an increasing body of research that reveals how the construction of whiteness allows individuals to "benefit from a host of apparently neutral social arrangements and institutional operations all of which seem—to whites at least—to have no racial basis."[11] As examined in *American Quarterly* and *The Chronicle of Higher Education,* there is a growing group of scholars who are engaged in a complex study of our social framework that has as its foundation the examination of *whiteness*. This field has expanded over the past decade in part as a result of the work by intellectuals like Toni Morrison, who have long suggested that race studies must include a critical, self-reflexive body of work about whites that is antiracist, progressive, and based in substantial political, economic, and social evidence of historically perpetuated social inequalities. Scholars of *whiteness* represent a very diverse range of disciplines. Sociologists, historians, and anthropologists, as well as practitioners of ethnic, legal, cultural, and literary studies are bringing inter-disciplinary research methodologies, empirical data collection, and critical analysis to the study of *whiteness*.[12] Additionally, other professional fields have spoken to issues around *whiteness* as they appear in community orga-nizing, coalition building, and other forms of political movements. Some of those engaged in the study of *whiteness* include Michelle Fine, Depart-ment of Social Personality Psychology, The Graduate Center—City Univer-sity of New York; Andrew Hacker, Department of Political Science, Queens College, City College of New York; Linda C. Powell, clinical psychologist, Harvard University; David Roediger, Department of History, University of Illinois at Urbana-Champaign; David Theo Goldberg, Humanities Research Institute, University of California, Irvine; and Philomena Essed, Leadership and Change Program, Antioch University.

The dominant scholarly and legal arguments to emerge from this multi-disciplinary work position *whiteness* as a historically and socially produced concept that works to grant or deny different life opportunities. It is argued that *whiteness* is a form of cultural capital, similar to economic capital, and concludes that becoming aware of the advantage that *whiteness* provides is a necessary requirement to challenging it. For white people, race functions as a large ensemble of practices and rules that provide all sorts of small and large advantages in life. As such, *whiteness* is the source of many privileges and, to mask its benefits, *whiteness* is often discursively hidden within con-cepts like neutrality or universality.

Many (if not most) whites ignore white ethnicity and are not, in fact, even aware that they are doing so: *whiteness* is simply something one is; it is not analyzed, it is not felt, it is not a concern. It is base. Essential. It simply ... is. In other words, it is not that whiteness is just ignored, it is altogether unrecognized except, perhaps, when a white person is alone in a group of non-whites. George Lipsitz in *The Possessive Investment in Whiteness* argues that while "minorities" are able to see these unspoken privileges precisely because of their inability to access them equally and unconditionally, whites have a difficult time seeing and an even harder time acknowledging the privileges afforded by white skin color in the United States because for them, it has always been the case. It is the "natural" order of the world they inhabit.

It is a fact that the normative view of the world is almost entirely circumscribed by the system of beliefs imbued by the dominant culture, which in the end determines actions, behaviors, and motives. Whiteness studies reveals and illuminates the construction of a social structural framework in which assumptions, judgments, and decisions are made that generally support the image of all things white as the normative and anything non-white as the anomaly. The unquestioned assumption of neutrality in what is in truth a carefully constructed social view inevitably renders people of color not necessarily criminal, but suspect, for no other reason than being different, than for not being white. But if this is the case, how does this notion of *whiteness* operate spatially?

Locke posited that space preexists our knowledge of it; that, in a particular way, space is essentialized, visible only by the position of points, objects, or bodies, within it.[13] For him, our ability to know and fix the limits of space is defined by the relationship of bodies to one another. Through these relationships the boundaries of space become visible to us. The point where these bodies are at rest, determined by the relative position of two or more bodies, is what Locke calls place.[14] Space and place are dependent upon, and constitutive of, each other.[15] Lockean notions of space and place are definitive and discernible on a mathematical scale—*this* piece is *this* distance from *that* piece and is *this* long, *this* wide, etc. These concepts are illustrated in Figure 2.

However, Locke offers us something more profound in this construction,

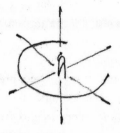 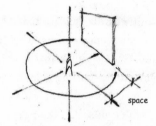

Space preexists.

Space is interrupted by objects. The location of the objects is called "place."

We employ sight and/or touch to gain knowledge of space.

Space can be perceived through the relation of a minimum of two points or places.

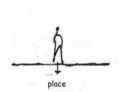 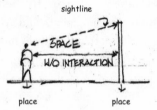

Figure 2. Diagram of Locke's fundamental concepts of space.

something that operates underneath the visible layer of Western space and plays a subtle but important role in both spatial and identity construction in America. The fact that space can be mathematically determined, thereby locating and delineating a specific place, provides not only the conceptual, but also the actual means for the locating and dividing of property (land). For Locke, bodies *define* space. They are essentially where Locke's space *ends*. As something that preexists and is "disrupted" by bodies, space is primarily empty, symbolic, establishing objects primarily in order to define itself. In short, space is understood in relation to place—a location—and place is the site, the locus of property.[16] Having established this essential, interdependent triad—space, place, and property—we can now further examine

Locke's notion of property authorized by this determinant relationship and the role it plays in the historico-cultural construction of both space and identity.

Clearing the site for his construction of property, Locke begins by positing that "God gave the world to Adam and his posterity in common . . . to make use of it to the best advantage of life and convenience . . . for their support and comfort of their being . . . nobody has originally a private dominion exclusive of the rest of mankind."[17] In his vision, land (the *world*, as he calls it) is provided by Nature *(God)* for the sustenance of humans *(mankind)* and no one person has more right or access to the land than any other person does *(in common)*. Nor does one control land solely, exclusive of others.

Locke now prepares the foundation of property by supposing that "every man has a 'property' in his own 'person.' . . . The 'labour' of his body and the 'work' of his hands, we may say, are properly his. Whatsoever, then, he removes out of the state that Nature hath provided . . . much as any one can make use of . . . life before it spoils, so much he may by his labour fix a property in. Whatever is beyond this is more than his share, and belongs to others."[18] Here, he proposes that humans have rights to and ownership of *(as property)* their own natural abilities *(person)*. A person's body and mind is one's alone and as an extension of this personal capacity, a person also has access to what he or she can rightfully, morally, ethically, and conservatively create or produce with the property of one's own person *(labour)*.

Furthering this line of reasoning, Locke constructs the foundational framework for property with the notion that it is labor that "put[s] a distinction between [what is produced] and the common . . . and removing it out of the state Nature leaves it in . . . hath fixed one's property in them."[19] Stated another way, Locke submits that a person owns what he or she can produce with his or her own labor. Having labored to create something, that something becomes one's property. One's labor has cemented one's interest in labor's result.

To complete the foundation of the justification of landed property,

Locke finishes the framework with this statement, the latter portion of which is exceedingly critical: "As much as a man tills, plants, improves, cultivates, and can use the product of, so much is his property. He by his labour does, as it were, enclose it from the common."[20] He concludes that ownership of the product of labor naturally extends to the ownership of the material employed to create that product, which in effect establishes the right to remove land from the common state in which it was originally situated. This is an important philosophical extension by Locke because in essence he has collapsed the product-of-labor—*resulting from the intrinsic property of the person*—and the place/material-of-labor—resulting from the extrinsic property of the common—into one. Thus, in the end, the fundamental principles of property are established: the *rights (entitlements) to have and/or to appropriate a thing or place,* in addition to the thing or place itself.[21] These rights included:

> [N]ot only external objects and people's relationships to them, but also all of those human rights, liberties, powers, and immunities that are important for human well-being, including: freedom of expression, freedom of conscience, freedom from bodily harm, and free and equal opportunities to use personal faculties.[22]

A claim to property can be secured as proprietary only by exercising these rights. Rights not exercised are considered wasted, thus forfeit, and in the case of land are subject to resettlement.[23] His notion of property—the exercising of rights and entitlements *over* a thing—can be seen exercised in the relationship between Blacks and whites in eighteenth-century America.

> Central to Locke's political philosophy, and to our own, is his attitude towards slavery. His ideas on slavery form the model and the vocabulary for virtually all the social and political relationships described in his writings—and to eighteenth, nineteenth and twentieth century conceptions of government and the state.[24]

Alexander Boulton further explains that

> [f]rom these examples it should appear that virtually everyone was in-
> cluded within Locke's civil society, but such was not the case. For the
> purposes of determining those who were "obligated to obedience,"
> nearly everyone qualified; but many people were simultaneously, ei-
> ther explicitly or implicitly, excluded from full participation in civil
> society. Most notably, Locke's new vocabulary of political and so-
> cial relations established new categories which marginalized women,
> children, the inhabitants of other lands (especially the "waste" lands
> of America), and slaves—all who became part of a large "invisible
> population."[25]

Locke's conflation of intrinsic and extrinsic property ultimately becomes problematic. Considering what he theorizes as the basic human
right to property, there was (is) little difference between Blacks and whites,
save one: Race. And it is by this single characteristic that Locke excludes
one group from freely accessing space and property while empowering another. African-Americans were legally defined as property primarily—if not
solely—because they were *Black*, while whites were not property because
they were white. Blacks were *objects* (property), while whites were *subjects*
(owners), part of the civil society, and therefore enjoyed access to property.
Locke takes particular care to make this distinction clear when he writes:

> [T]here is another sort of servants, which by a peculiar name we call
> them slaves, who being captives taken in a just war, are by right of
> nature absolute dominion and arbitrary power of their masters . . .
> and being in the state of slavery, not capable of any property; cannot
> in that state be considered as any part of civil society; the chief end
> whereof is the preservation of property.[26]

For Locke, the "exclusion of slavery from the social order was the basic requirement for freedom."[27] The knowledge of being "not-Black" and
therefore not subject to becoming property and, with that assurance, the

expectation that one's rights—one's very identity—will be recognized and protected, permeates the foundation of a Lockean idea of space in the form of *whiteness*.

> Because the system of slavery was contingent on and conflated with racial identity, it became crucial to be white; to be identified with white; to have the property of being white. Whiteness was the characteristic, the attribute, the property of free human beings.[28]

Chief Justice Roger B. Taney confirms Harris's assessment in the Dred Scott decision of 1857, when he writes for the court that the Black man—slave or freeman—"had no rights which the white man was bound to respect; and that the negro might justly and lawfully be reduced to slavery for his benefit."[29] The implicit fundamental principle of space and property is that only free people had the right to access it—and as Locke and law make clear, only people who could lay claim to being unequivocally, irrevocably, completely free were white.[30] Currently, the relationship between Black and *white* bodies is no longer defined legally by a master/slave dynamic. But, and this is crucial, that does not mean (a) this relational *(and therefore, spatial)* conceptualizing is dead, and (b) some new form of relational *(and therefore, spatial)* hierarchy has not taken its "place."[31] On the contrary, evidence of the existence of such a hierarchy can be gleaned every single day. Recent events on the highways of Maryland, Florida, and New Jersey highlight the fact and mechanisms of racial profiling as a way to control the rights of African-Americans to what most people take for granted—access to public space. In addition, while a crisis of color—DWB (Driving While Black)—is being played out publicly via the automobile to the point that successive Presidents Clinton and Bush have decried the practice, there is also cause for us to look beyond the highway for further evidence of the racial and spatial profiling of our shared realm. The recent Supreme Court decision striking down Chicago's anti-loitering law makes visible the existing specter of what many had considered long-dead legal efforts to limit access to public space based on race. Such efforts have their genesis in the slave patrols created by early European colonizers of the Americas, which were appropriated, modified, and employed by various governmental and nongovernmental organizations in the American South and are clearly anchored in Lockean constructions.[32] In fact, the legacy of that history was so obvious that the court specifically and accurately recalled that such general anti-loitering ordinances were once common, thinly veiled attempts to keep or displace African-Americans from certain towns and neighborhoods. The City of Chicago's attempt to invoke this well-established tactic of denying the constitutional rights of people it considered suspect is just another indication of the manner in which such illegal policing of people of color has become much more common and widespread, so much so that the mere sight of more than one black man is cause enough to disturb "normative" space.[33] And lest this be seen as a recent strategy aimed only at African-Americans, Raúl Homero Villa suggests a broader historical application of such spatial practices against others who have non-white status:

> As in the previous era, the administrative and spatial regime peaking in the late 1920s and early 1930s was built on a concerted urban plan of physical displacement of *mexicanos* from the expanding downtown administrative and industrial districts, along with their corollary ideological and symbolic displacement from the historical and cultural geography of the city.[34]

These are but a few of the most egregious examples of the innumerable indisputable everyday demonstrations that remind us of the continued existence of an overt—if not blatant—racialization of space. It is inarguable that in Western culture, the power of *white*—the body of *white*—maintains a place on the American stage as its most important, historic, and immovable actor. As a result, *whiteness*—as the normative condition—becomes embedded in the foundation of, and is critical to, the determination of desirable space, place, and property. In this case, this spatial *whiteness* is located in the political, social, and economic concerns of the dominant culture and can be seen in the current manifestations of the city: White flight from city neighborhoods—and the concomitant effect of middle-income people of color's desire for the same; negative reinvestment in predominantly Black neighborhoods; the past phenomenon and current repercussions of urban renewal and "sundown towns"; and boundaries both physically real—the Cabrini Green and Robert Taylor homes in Chicago—and mentally real— the eight-mile thoroughfare in Detroit; Back Bay Boston; Bensonhurst, New York; Southeast Washington, D.C.; Houston's Third and Fifth Wards; New Orleans lower Ninth. We can see this demonstrated perhaps most clearly in the nation's capital, where the visual boundaries of space are distinctly marked by the grand and noble gestures to the principles owed to no civilization or culture but the *white* cities of Athens and Rome, from which the symbols of our national architecture have been appropriated; the *white* marble on the *white* Capitol; the *white* temple *White* House; the tall *white* Freudian gesture in the center of *white* male patriarchal power, its origins carefully *white*washed. In a city where homelessness and poverty are hardly new(s), the appropriation of land and space for the purposes of doing nothing should be understood in its proper context. In a city that is predominantly Black, the power and (perceived) purity of *white* reigns supreme.

Lockean space is a space of no motion, no resistance, a "framework that locates the body within a static space and time."[35] It is a dead space, a space that fossilizes identity and thus renders space less than pliable for political engagement and identity construction for African-Americans. When viewed from the dominant spatial perspective, the issue for African-Americans becomes this: What happens when the relational foundation of space has to navigate between aspects of identity and rights, or, in other words, when Locke's space is defined by a single white body and a single Black body? What is typically observed is that the white body, while recognizing the Black body because it is necessary—as a relational point—to define their own (place in) space, at the same time is hostile to the Black body's right to be in the space.[36] The operation of Locke's space/place relationship creates and situates identity *(your [Black] place is always in relation to my [white] place)* and also places the emphasis on the importance of "knowing your place" to the construction of that identity *(my [white] space is the standard by which your [Black] space is judged).*[37] This is at the heart of why set B was so upset during the encounter at the Mall: My friend and I didn't remain in our place and by not doing so, we immediately brought set B's privilege —B's identity—into question.[38] It was a small, but perhaps inevitable, clash of worldviews. The direct result of this spatial rationalization for African-Americans can perhaps best be understood by an analogy based on the following passage by Henry Shue:

> I am a pebble, the world is the pond I have been dropped into. I am at the center of a system of concentric circles that become fainter as they spread. The first circle immediately around me is strong, and each successive circle is weaker. My duties are exactly like the concentric circles around the pebble: strongest at the center and rapidly diminishing toward the periphery. My primary duties are to those immediately around me, my secondary duties are to those next nearest, my tertiary duties to those next, and so on. Plainly, any duties to those on the far periphery are going to diminish to nothing, and given the limited resources available to any ordinary person, her positive duties will barely reach beyond a second or third circle.[39]

If this passage is—as intended—an illustration of American cultural and social relations, then Shue's first circle can be understood in American society as being singularly occupied by the Euro-American man. Predicated upon a particular notion of history, the white male has emerged, justifiably or not, front and center in the theater of American identity formation. Not only has his brotherhood assigned itself top billing, but it has also assumed the playwright's authority to define the subject positions of remaining actors as it sees fit—and how it sees fit is always to its advantage. Satisfied with the impermeability of the spaces of power that reinforce their authority, white males have unilaterally secured this central position by a variety of ideological means on the American stage, where a singular notion of male emerges that simultaneously embraces and protects their own guild and excludes *other* actors from leading roles.

Further observation reveals that Shue's second circle is occupied by the Euro-American female. The both overtly and covertly disseminated ideology of the white woman as the ultimate paradigm of female subjectivity in American culture exists despite the white male's failure to resolve her assigned dichotomous subject positions as both worshipped and worshipper; queen and worker bee.[40] Awash with patriarchal and paternalistic platitudes, the image, position, and power of the white woman has been—comparatively speaking—just to the right and slightly behind that of the white male; fitting for one who will bear and nurture heirs to the power and authority inherent in this construction of national color.[41]

An equally distorted image of the African-American woman can be found in the third circle.[42] It is clear that the bodies of Black women have always been a benign, somewhat controlled—and controlling—fetish of both white men and women alike. Conflicting images of the African-American female as surrogate child rearers, confidants, welfare mothers, (un)willing mistresses, and sisters in the struggle for economic, social, political, and spatial equality constitute past and present notions of Black female subjectivity essentially as *"Black Back-Ups."*[43] Stuart Hall has suggested that the partnership between past and present is an imaginary construction and clearly, such fossilized views of the Black female are principally products of a (D. W.) Griffithized ideological imaging of the past, produced through a lens leveled on the Black female body that has never quite been in focus.[44]

Relegated to the fourth circle in this hierarchy we find the African-American male. The naturalized image of the brutal, base, highly sexualized, aggressive, animalistic, angry male is constantly broadcast through airwaves—and hairwaves—to an all too receptive public.[45] Resisting being situated in the fourth circle—the visually transparent and peripheral spaces of society—Black men have historically attempted to make a separate, different circle in Shue's pond; a deeper, more reaffirming impression in the cultural sea. From public auction to Public Enemy, from Reverend King to Rodney King, from H. Rap Brown to gangsta rap sound, every attempt by Black men to make the transparent visible has been met with various and often violent forms of resistance outside and inside their community.

Historically, men have always gathered space around the issue of identity—at the office, in the bar, on the ball field—and American nationalist culture has positioned males—read *white* males—as its principal spatial conquering hero. The result of this privileging is that for Black men, "self-representations of black masculinity in the United States are historically structured by and against dominant (and dominating) discourses of masculinity and race, specifically (whiteness),"[46] or, as Fanon succinctly states "not only must the black man be black; he must be black in relation to the white man,"[47] a relationship that defines Lockean *place* and is clearly acted out in Lockean *space*. Locke's space, by positioning the body as solid, impenetrable, the place where space *ends*, represents space as the between, the left over, the undisturbed. As he puts it "[s]olidity is so inseparable for the Idea of the Body . . . [and] Space is not Body."[48] Lockean space is anti-body. Bodies never occupy space, but become definitive markers as to what and where space *is*. Lockean space dichotomizes and polarizes the predominant understanding of space by legitimizing its inherent *whiteness* as THE desirable defining factor—and the implied non-whiteness of space as undesirable. Locke's space is incompatible with the project of Black identity construction, as its very tenants—the fixed, the *end*, the disruption—all work to deny African-American access to space. Three precious little words—learned at an early age to be employed for primarily selfish reasons by the dominant culture—*"That Black man . . ."* have historically been enough to make this point about access painfully clear. Enough to make the seemingly permanent, unequivocally temporary. Enough to strip away the illusion of spatial empowerment and to render visible the temporality of Black access to Locke's space. Enough to completely dichotomize space again, again and again. Enough to keep the Black body in its *place*. Whether it falls from under the colonizer's multi*colored*, but not multi*cultural*, flag, or from the lips of the Scottsboro women, Charles Stuart, Susan Smith, or any hundred of other Ellisonian[49] moments that fill the day of every member of the Fourth Circle fraternity, the utterance *"That Black man . . . "* is enough to immediately and immeasurably diminish Black space to nothingness. In this paradigm, Black (access to) space is always temporary, exposed, and objectified. It is a space where everyone knows their *place* and that *place* is based on an absolute relationship to *white*; a relationship that becomes abundantly clear the moment a collective agency attempts to define Black male identity *against* this *white* spatial backdrop—in spite of the very visible signs of what—and where—America's males should be.

At a moment where the focus on the Black male body as an object of fascination, pleasure, and fear is raised to the level of obsession, Black men and women have historically been required to employ material culture in transformative spatial strategies of survival, so much so that it has become "[in] the context of 'place making', [that] blacks form their individual and collective identities," rejecting the spatial imposition of separation strategies based on color*less*—not color*blind*—definitions of identity.[50]

In the spatial partitioning of our shared environment and its physical manifestation, architecture has a history of, and is currently being used to, perpetuate this spatial and racial dichotomy in what I have come to describe as spatial profiling—the physical and material process of locating social relations and social practices in space based on historical, political, cultural, and economic exercises of hegemonic power. Lockean space dichotomizes and polarizes the predominant understanding of space by legitimizing its inherent whiteness as the defining factor of environmental desirability, informing us that any other space created in this system will inevitably be measured against its original—white—paradigm and will always be found wanting, no matter what its construction and/or similarities.[51] Consciously or not, the desirability of space is fundamentally and intimately informed by race. We pay a lot of attention to the color of space under the guise of desirability. Many if not most white, and, to an alarmingly increasing degree, African-American people "think danger is black, brown and poor, and if we can just move far enough away from 'those people' in the cities we'll be safe. If we can just find an 'all-American' town, life will be better, because 'things like this just don't happen here.' "[52] Thus, the public gathering spaces of Black men are not understood in any real, tangible manner, but habitually known to America through proxies and substitutes, where Black bodies are "centralized in [a] faceless space, peripheral [even] at the social center."[53] Black male public space, residing "somewhere between the too visible and the not visible enough," is known and fossilized by (white) America through film, TV, census tracts, crime statistics, newspapers and magazines—places where white male aggression is displaced.[54] This kind of coloring of space supports the notion that episodes of violence in Arkansas, Oklahoma, Colorado, and Virginia—the "here" where such things don't happen—are problems to be solved, and thus retain their spatial desirability, while similar events in Chicago, New York, and South Central, Los Angeles—the location of "those people"—are pathologies to be endured, and thus their undesirability is confirmed.[55] The fact that " 'here' is about the only place these kinds of things do happen" has little to no barring on the desirability of space or the practice for spatial profiling.[56] Danger remains largely, if not solely, a condition of color and the evidence of its effect is inarguable: African-Americans rarely enjoy the benefit of space, as they are historically and routinely rendered "visually transparent, peripheral, part of the landscape, ready to be moved, cleared and discarded for spatial use and improvement" or to remove "danger."[57]

> [S]pace is an arena where the black male is thought of as the bogeyman, a volatile predator, ready to pounce on anyone caught slipping. The idea that he might be concerned about his safety is regarded as a ridiculous notion. Yet, it is often he who is unable to pause and relax without physical, psychological, and other non-verbal harassment when almost any movement is viewed with suspicion.[58]

Cultural critic bell hooks has eloquently concluded in regarding Black bodies in public space that "[o]ur very presence is a disruption."[59] For hooks, "disruption" is a dynamic that can be observed whenever a person of color enters into any space that is predominantly white. Journalist Brent Stapes adds:

> In that first year, my first away from my hometown, I was to become thoroughly familiar with the language of fear. At dark, shadowy intersections, I could cross in front of a car stopped at a traffic light and elicit the thunk, thunk, thunk, thunk of the driver—black, white, male, or female—hammering down the door locks. On less traveled streets after dark, I grew accustomed to but never comfortable with people crossing to the other side of the street rather than pass me.... Black men trade stories like this all the time.[60]

Arthur Symes's statement that "[t]here are no 'Architectural problems' per se, they are a part of society as a whole"[61] has its origins and relevance in this immediate and unquestioned validation of the *whiteness* of any space by public or private police, store owners and operators, developers, architects, planners, economists, or politicians—you may add to this list at your leisure—that presents African-Americans with the fiction that they are destined to live where the physical, emotional, and intellectual remnants of the hostilities of the early twentieth century, the civil disturbances of the middle twentieth century, and the indifference of the late twentieth century come together to convince them that their lives are environmentally predetermined. As a result, many continue to live their lives based on false realities; expectations of possibilities are stunted, deformed, and eventually die, stillborn. It is part of the responsibility of design professionals and stewards of the built environment—those charged with the shaping of space and place—to develop alternatives to the current spatial perception within the discipline, particularly if the current employment of that perspective is socially detrimental. The cold, hard fact of the matter is that the "built environment is anything but an innocent landscape; its sensual pleasures are constituted through economic, social, and political forces that are hardly benign,"[62] and regrettably, what Whitney M. Young said to the architectural profession over thirty years ago is still painfully true: architects "share the responsibility for the mess we are in . . . in terms of the white noose around the central city. We didn't just suddenly get this way. It was carefully planned."[63]

If the connection between how this privileging of *whiteness* operates inside what we do as architectural educators and professionals is still unclear, consider the words of architectural historian and critic Bruno Zevi. He posits that "[u]ntil we have learned not only to understand space theoretically, but also to apply this understanding as a central factor in the criticism of architecture, our history, and thus our enjoyment, of architecture will remain haphazard."[64] Zevi's statement must be carefully considered, because it makes plain the importance of an overlooked but fundamental issue and demonstrates that the architectural discipline's structural resistance to diversity is not intractable:

> Architecture . . . does not consist in the sum of the width, length and height of the structural elements which enclose space, but in the void itself, the enclosed space in which [the public] lives and moves . . . that space which . . . can be grasped and felt only through direct experience, is the protagonist of architecture. To grasp space, to know how to see it, is the key to the understanding of building.[65]

If place is a mode of space and is also the location of site, then place can be understood as existing at the nexus of abstract space and concrete property. It is the physical, legible manifestation of space and property. It also then follows that if place is constituted by a racialized space and is the location of property, then that racialization is embedded in, and dispersed through, property. Finally, if architects are in the business of space-shaping and place-making, without a critical examination of this relationship, they will remain complicit in the racialization of the built environment.

The powerful determinant of race in affecting every aspect of the built environment has a long history. The spatialization of race relations—a social act of structural racism that rests at the core of the dominant culture's practice of planning and building—needs greater theoretical analysis combined with activist practice to overcome uneven development.[66]

The architectural silence on the influence of *whiteness* "as a framework to categorize people and understand their social locations" helps to sustain a white spatial privilege that begins with "the assumption that to be white is the 'natural condition.' "[67] If we are to have any real discussion about the impediments to full representative African-American architectural participation, we must acknowledge and understand that at the heart of the common understanding of space—key to the creation and production of architecture—is a fundamental spatial privileging of *whiteness* that is a primary part of the foundation of the architectural discipline and start from there. Space—and subsequently, architecture—is surely more diverse than that.

Remix

So, yo … in short, here's the dealio. My girlie and I broke out for the mall and we were trippin' on all the folks just starin' at me—I'm a rather big brotha *(6' 4", dreaded and about 250)*—when she decides she wants to buy a lil' sumppin' sumppin'. Checkin' her pockets, she's finds out that she is low on chedda, so we head for one of them auto banks. We slide up to the joint a little bit before another couple who happen to be white and the chick starts buggin' *(but not too loud)* 'bout how we just bum-rushed them—all indignant and shit *(obviously, she ain't never been "jacked" before, 'cause we were definitely in front of 'em)*. Well, I just ignored her crazy ass, but my girlie heard all that shit. So we got our money in spite of all that low-level drama and when we left, she turns to me and says, "Did you check that shit out?" So of course, this gets my dome to runnin' about what the f——just happened …

Remember that Locke cat I was talkin' about earlier? I started thinkin' 'bout him and all the shit he said in the past. He says a couple of things that we should check out 'cause people are still diggin' on this vibe today. First, he says that we should call the emptiness between point a and point b "space" *(really, he says that space is all around us, but because it is so big, you need some kind of reference point just to feel it).* Okay, so yo, if you can see space, you can figure out a way to mark it off; in other words, you can measure space. Now, what you use to measure it don't really matter, so it can be whatever you want. For example, if you wanna tell someone how to get from here to there, you might tell them it's so many miles, or it might be easier to say it's so many lights. Either way, the important thing is that you have just figured out a way to divide, define and communicate space, dig?

Okay, now, because you can divide space, you can also divide land the same way, 'cause if you think about it, land ain't nothin' but space on the ground, knowhatI'msayin? But so what? Why would anyone wanna divide land? So you can determine which piece is mine and which is yours, fool! So you can cop that shit; own it. This is one of the things the courts call property—divided land. That divided land is my *acquired* property. How do I prove it is mine, that I own it? Because I do something with it—I work it, improve it—build a house or some other shit. For Locke, that was the initial way to own land. If you made a claim that some piece of land was yours but you didn't do anything with it—like grow food, raise cattle, or sump-pin'—well somebody else could just come, punk you, take your shit and you couldn't do a damn thing about it. *(That's how the Indians got played in the courts—on the rare occasion when they got there. Punk-ass judges kept sayin' they didn't "do" anything to the land, so they didn't "own" it—at least accordin' to Locke and the law—and somebody else just came and took what they thought was theirs and got away wid that shit. Welcome to Amerikkka, y'all.)*

Na, back in the day, in order for a man to truly *represent (to be able to vote, hold office, make decisions, get your respect in the law, etc.)* you had to have you some property—some land—otherwise you were gonna get diss'ed ... Alot. A whole lot. Na, I'm gonna come back to this point in a minute.

Now, land isn't the only property you can acquire, right? You can get a horse, a house, clothes, hell, you can get a lot of stuff, and that would be your property, too. Na, back in the day, you could also acquire people as property. Thems was called slaves—and slaves were nuttin' but Black folk. In fact, they were slaves *because* they were black. Na, Locke is okay with all of that—other kinds of property and all *(although he was primarily concerned with his crib)*, but he also said that property can't own property. That makes some sense, 'cause your car can't buy its garage, your soda cannot buy its own refrigerator nor can your clothes buy their closet. But check this, that also meant that slaves could not own shit.

Now, there is another kind of property that he doesn't talk about, but it's there. It's the stuff that you are made of—the stuff that describes you. How tall you are, your ability to use your brain, your arms, legs, color of your eyes, etc. That what we'll call *innate* property, and back in the day, this kind of property couldn't be bought. *(Today, though, if you got the chedda, you can buy all this and then some—think bleachin' creams, extensions and colored contacts and you got it.)*

So, to be a serious playa, you had to have some land. But to have some land, you couldn't be property, so, it was very important to have—at least— the *innate* property of "whiteness," so you could have a chance at claimin' some *acquired* property. In fact, it was probably the most important thing, 'cause no matter what other kind of innate properties you possessed *(intelligence, height, strength, good looks, whatever)* if it included "blackness," you were just shit out of luck.

Okay, so check this. Over 350 years ago, when Locke's theories were teaching people how to view space, only white people could claim ownership of *acquired* property *(which is really just space and land)* primarily because the *innate* property of "whiteness" made them free from being property themselves. If blackness made you property, whiteness kept you from being property. So there is a kind of "I-am-the-shit" attitude that is embedded in how we first learned to see space, dig? Now today, that "Blackness makes you property" shit has been purged from our legal system. On the other hand, it has only been fifty years or so since the struggle for the civil rights of African-Americans has been fully engaged, and that "I-am-

the-shit" mentality still exists at some level among many—if not the majority—of people of European descent. At the very least, we can agree that there
is a BIG difference—economically, spatially, physically, etc.—between the
majority of spaces where white people live and the majority of spaces where
Black people live, yes? No shit. Always has been, and residents growing up
in these different spaces develop decidedly different views of the world and
their place in it based in part on their access to space. In other words, if you
think you can live anywhere, you do. If you think you can't, you won't. You
stay put, thinkin' what you got is all you gonna get.

Architects have contributed to both ways of seeing the world. Brother
Whitney told 'em so over thirty years ago that *we didn't just suddenly get
this way. It was carefully planned.* And I would add planned and *executed!*
As people whose job is to shape space, to ignore this reality is to perpetuate
it; and that's the bullshit. No lie.

Holla if ya hear me.

2 Discipline—Person

A comparison of models indicates that the philosophical or worldview of the educator is largely responsible for shaping the components of each method and the expectations of the role of the architect in society.

—*Karen Bermann*

THE DOMINANT HUMAN KNOWLEDGE SYSTEM suggested by the work of the Enlightenment arbitrarily separates knowledge into small, discrete, elite areas of expertise *(e.g., mathematics, literature, biology, sociology, architecture, etc.)* and formally institutionalizes that knowledge into "contingent organizing schemes that distinguish knowers, knowledges and truths" that we presently call disciplines.[1] Intended to provide specific knowledge and intellectual skills, disciplines are the frameworks by which we produce and organize the knowledge that makes sense of our world.[2] For the record, the *Oxford Encyclopedic English Dictionary* defines the term as:

> Control or order exercised over people ... the system of rules used to maintain this control ... the behavior of groups subjected to such rules ... adversity as used to bring about such training ... a branch of instruction or learning ... punishment.[3]

I have always found it telling, apt, and more than a bit frightening—particularly when thinking about architecture from the perspective of an African-American—that *knowledge, control,* and *punishment* are all defined by the same word. When engaging non-African-American colleagues about

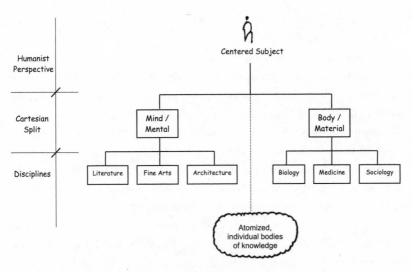

Figure 3. Cartesian-supported disciplinary framework.

the architectural discipline, I often wonder exactly which of these interpretations they are employing in their interactions with me.

In architecture's long and fascinating narrative, the institutionally trained architect is a fairly recent character—only about 150 years old or so. Prior to 1671, there were no schools of architecture per se. Before then, to become an architect—which means "chief builder" in Greek—one became an apprentice in a particular craft *(masonry, carpentry, etc.)*. After learning and practicing that craft for many years in conjunction with ancillary work in the other trades involved in the building process, the most talented and accomplished apprentices become recognized as masters in their particular area of knowledge in addition to being fairly conversant in all other aspects of building. These architects knew enough not only to partake in the construction—focusing on the practices and materials that they were proficient in—but also to supervise the trades in which they were not an active member. They understood how a structure was constructed inside and out and they participated in the entire process. The trades of the Greek and Roman periods grew into the guilds of the medieval period, from which the architect emerged until the time of the Enlightenment—a period that fundamentally altered the study and practice of architecture.

Prior to the sixteenth century, knowledge about the world was understood to be given from the heavens, interpreted and disseminated by the church. In what can be loosely called the old cosmology, the church was also the institution that educated those lucky enough to receive formal instruction. In that educational system, the Bible was the ultimate authority on the truth and the church was the ultimate authority on the Bible, not only because most people were illiterate, but also because it was considered to house the "experts" on the text and its meanings.

Enter Copernicus (1543) and Galileo (1609). They put forth the radical and heretical notion that the sun, not the earth, was the center of the solar system. This was in complete contradiction to the position held by the church, which supported its interpretation on the foundation of the Bible's infallibility. The ensuing battle between faith and science brought the church's hold over knowledge into question; the battle is still being fought today, most visibly in the debates over intelligent design. Suddenly *(well, maybe not so suddenly),* the church's knowledge was viewed as unreliable, and . . . if they were wrong about one thing, why not all things? Breaking the church's hold on the truth, this philosophical shift loosely marks the beginning of a new cosmology, sometimes referred to as the Age of Reason or the Enlightenment period. The new cosmology ushered in a fresh paradigm of thinking where there was no longer a universal belief in, or support for, the notion of knowledge being handed down from above; myth, superstition, ritual, and guesswork were no longer acceptable ways of interpreting, discussing, and being in the world—reason would reign supreme in understanding the world, and the belief that reason and science could be taught would dictate the construction of the educated man.

Since the church did not operate within the new science and reason paradigm, there was a need to create and validate other institutions to teach the new ways of knowing. These institutions became the secular universities; during this period of the institutionalization of knowledge, the master craftsman architect gave way to the humanist artist architect. What this meant to the notion of the architect was twofold:

> [E]ver afterward architects were removed from the constructive process; but [it also] meant that they were freed from working only with established conventions to pursue intellectual exploration and creative artistry.[4]

Through this process architecture became a discipline as we know it, leading to the establishment of The Royal Academy of Architecture in Paris in 1671 as the first institution created for the education of architects. Arguably, the first school of architecture in the United States was established at the Massachusetts Institute of Technology in 1865.

Disciplines construct a knowing subject

> Knowledge is never a neutral entity. Rather, as any commodity, it is a social construct, produced and distributed according to particular voices situated in relations of power for particular ends.[5]

It has been persuasively argued elsewhere that disciplines are formed around political and economic interests of the ruling class as a way to control and perpetuate knowledge and privilege. The purpose of this boundary work is primarily to define the area of expertise around a specific knowledge base and ultimately control the definition of the object of study by creating and policing its margins. Disciplinary boundary work is concerned with the regulation of its knowledge, object, and members in the interests of the discipline—and concomitantly—in the interests of the ruling class, which during the Enlightenment period was educated, wealthy, upper/middle class, heterosexual, male, and white—a constitution that has changed little over the centuries. Furthermore, the institutions that were under the control of this class and protecting its interests were theological, familial, legal, political, cultural, financial, commercial, and educational—again, quite similar to our current society. Finally, it should astound no one that these interests and institutions are the often unspoken, but fundamental foundational elements of disciplines in general, and the architectural discipline in particular. By setting their own standards and regulations of how, who, and what a discipline will consider relevant to its object of study and its field of expertise, disciplines include and exclude people and knowledge and determine who obtains expert status and what they will be responsible for once they have obtained that status. These interests, once located and grounded within a disciplinary institution, are bounded and protected primarily on the basis of the claim to expert knowledge. In this scenario, to become an expert it is essential to conform to the dictates of the discipline or, in other words, to become "disciplined" to ensure professional, judicial, and legislative protection. This is accomplished through particular disciplinary practices that teach the initiate to accept and act accordingly within the boundaries discursively set by the discipline, to view the object of that discipline as natural, and to replicate this view in their everyday interactions with the world at large without question. They come to see this way of acting in the world as natural and historical. Disciplines delineate and produce bodies of knowledge, define responsibilities, and reproduce and promote expert status by inculcating, as Kathryn Anthony says, "the values, virtues, and desirable ways of behaving that are communicated in subtle ways in every field."[6] Disciplines construct a knowing subject through disciplinary practices that socialize and replicate people and knowledge, creating a particular type of knower. This is the seed from which professions—and professionals—grow. Professions, for our purposes, shall be defined as "a calling requiring specialized knowledge and often long and intensive preparation, including instruction in skills and methods as well as in the scientific, historical, or scholarly principles underlying such skills and methods."[7] Wasserman further states that professions provide services "without which the quality of our lives and our well-being would be diminished or even at risk."[8] I will come back to this theme later in this chapter, but for now, I wish to return to the discussion of disciplines and their shaping of particular types of subjects. Historically, the discipline of architecture has accomplished this through a unique form and location of educational propagandizing—the ateliers of the past and the design studios of today —where most of its attitudes and perceptions become embedded in the studio.

In the educational paradigm of architecture, the studio is the primary site for the gathering and dispensing of discipline-specific architectural knowledge; as such, what "is taught in design studios plays a strategic role in the political socialization of students."[9] This system of education comes directly from the Ecole des Beaux-Arts in Paris, where students were divided into classes—ateliers—that were led by a Head. Students were presented a design problem by the head. Upon completion, the head and others—the jury—evaluated the solutions to the problem. The studio is where the students' architectural—and concomitantly, world—value system is developed, monitored, adapted, corrected, validated, or rejected. Currently during the educational experience, the disciplinary practices of the academy most common to the architectural initiate include, but are not limited to:

- Valuing rational, independent, and objective modes of thinking over experiential, collaborative, and subjective modes (rightly or wrongly, the former are more closely associated with men and the latter with women)
- Encouraging the ideology and pedagogy of the studio to take precedence over other studies; classes that offer a way of seeing the world outside of the architectural disciplinary perspective—anthropology, sociology, political science, economics—are almost nonexistent
- Implicitly, if not directly, encouraging the neglect of classes, activities, and sometimes personal relationships outside the discipline as the unfortunate, but inevitable and unavoidable result of being a "serious" student
- Intentionally or unintentionally displaying marginalizing attitudes in the studio; e.g., discouraging a student from going home to sleep or

staying at home to work, or allowing peers to ignore, marginalize, or ridicule a student for being culturally or intellectually different

- Determining, with little or no input from the actual producers of the material, what to show *(e.g., plans, perspectives, axons, sections, elevations, etc.)*, how to show it *(e.g., scale, alignment, lettering, size of paper/boards, number of models, etc.)*, where to show it *(e.g., gallery, conference room, desk, etc.)*, when to show it *(e.g., individually, collectively, first, last, etc.)*, and how long to show it *(e.g., presentation and critique time limits, etc.)*
- Implicitly encouraging students to invest an inordinate amount of self-value in what is said about a project and to believe that one's identity and value as a student, as a potential architect, and as a person is ultimately determined by how well one conforms to the culturally specific value system embedded in the discipline through student awards, faculty recognition, higher level of attention and critiques, etc.
- Perpetuating a subjectively determined, publicly judged system of merit, where individuals are required to present their design solutions to a panel of already disciplined experts for review, critical comment, and judgment of the ultimate value of their work based on a culturally specific set of values.

Ultimately, after prolonged, intimate, and intense engagement with these and other disciplinary practices, the subject emerges as a particular type of knowing practitioner: a person who sees the world through the discipline's prism. The disciplined architectural subject emerges as the artist, humanist, and expert professional; the classic modern example of a praxis where sacrifices are made to the artistic vision of the architect, who claims expert knowledge of the humanities, aesthetics, and beauty, as well as the physical and social sciences; a subject who is blissfully unaware that this process of becoming was anything but neutral and is unable to disassociate from, or even substantially locate, much less address, the political and economic concerns firmly established in the discipline's foundation and now, within themselves.

The disciplined subject emerges as a person trained to service the elite.

Paulo Freire wrote that all education has an intention, a goal, which can only be political, and the education of the architect has historically and currently served the elite in a variety of institutionally ideological and material ways:

- Educationally, it is responsible for producing those who will manifest the concerns, wealth, and power of the ruling class in the physical world
- Commercially, it shapes the physical environment to the will of economic efficiency
- Culturally, it supports a version of aesthetic beauty primarily defined by values that serve the political interests of the ruling class
- Financially, it replicates the dominant/subordinate relationship of patron/artist forebears

Two discourses, unable to coexist

Spaces developed by the disciplined architect to protect the ruling class "depend on conforming to the dictates of the [global] capital of metropolitan economies,"[10] where the appropriation and manipulation of space becomes an instrument of power relations. As the studio is positioned as the model for architectural practice, the conditions of the profession have assumed primacy in the discursive practices that operate within it. The studio becomes the site where the "skills and methods" of the profession and "high standards of achievement and conduct" are maintained "by force of organization or concerted opinion,"[11] facilitating a "socialization that too often reinforces and sustains the dominant interests of contemporary society."[12] In other words, the disciplinary practices within the studio are designed to ultimately produce a disciplined subject that is applicable to the practice of architecture as defined by the profession. The influence of the narrowly constructed professional ideology is pervasive, as it at once limits the ostensibly broader discourse of the academy and excludes public and allied professional discourses as much as possible while positioning architecture as both an art and a science.[13] Such authority over the discourse of architecture allows the profession a primary position in determining the identity of the architectural object. When the discourse of the academy comes in contact with that of the profession, its fraternal twin often dismisses or subjugates it.

So, how does the profession enforce its control over the educational discourse of architecture? In a very Althusserian fashion, it assumes control of the knowledge bases that we employ in the discipline.[14] It takes what Wigglesworth perhaps inaccurately calls objective and reifies it with education, linking the subjective with practice:

> In the area of objective knowledge, professional institutions dominate the epistemological foundation of architecture by an appeal to the scientific and instrumental bases of learning.[15]

Wigglesworth illustrates the reification of objective knowledge in the discourse of architectural education by linking learning, which is done in the academy (as opposed to practice, which is done in the profession) with scientific discourse and its epistemology of implied impartiality, reliance on empirical observation, and, most important, quantifiable results and applicable research. These results are controlled (evaluated/judged) at sites of professional institutions, not the academy, illustrating that the primary purpose is to produce practitioners. This less-than-subtle reification of education with scientific ways of learning, which include research and scholarly pursuits, is revealed as disingenuous and self-serving by the growing argument in the academy that centers on repositioning the development and cataloging of architectural knowledge away from the historically and architecturally self-referential personal perspective toward a holistic, contextual, and cross-disciplinary inquiry. There is a decided lack of respect or even acknowledgment within the profession for this type of endeavor, whatever public face the profession may attempt to show. Unlike the disciplines of medicine and law—on a par with which architecture continues to place itself—there is less respect for architectural research and scholarship and those who do it than there is for the practitioner. As a result, the discipline of architecture has been slow to develop a professed and professionally called-for objective body of knowledge with which it can evaluate itself.[16] The lack of this broad, research-based foundation, many academics contend, directly contributes to the current devaluation of the profession within a broader cultural and academic context. Outside of static historical mapping and cataloging of architectural artifacts, according to the academic position, objective architectural contextual knowledge is almost nonexistent, and the lack of this broad empirical, or even historical credibility, it is argued, brings unnecessary challenges to the validity of the discipline. At present, empirical research is replaced by subjective design and criticism presented as justification ex post facto, if justification is presented at all. "In the realm of subjective knowledge, the conceptual framework for practice maintains its hold by appealing to the unassailability of artistic creativity, defining the artist as a medium of inspirational purity."[17]

There is a clear appropriation of concepts embedded in art and other subjective discourses—"unassailability of artistic creativity" and "inspirational purity"—by the architectural practice/professional discourse, as opposed to the so-called objectivity that is located in the academy. This perpetuation of subjective criteria serves the profession well since it paves the way to design stardom—the thoughtful geniuses who rarely ever err— and is a result of Immanuel Kant's influential theory of aesthetic judgment on the humanities in general, artists in particular, and architects specifically.[18]

In Kant's writings, particularly in his three critiques (*Pure Reason, Practical Reason,* and *Judgment*), he persuasively argues for the pursuit of the good, the true, and the beautiful, in which the true is the ultimate object of knowledge, the good the ultimate object of action, and the beautiful the ultimate object of judgment. A full discussion of Kant's aesthetic theory is beyond the scope of this argument, but in brief he argues that aesthetic judgments—the result of judgments of taste—must have four key distinguishing features:

1. They are disinterested.
2. Such judgments are universal.
3. Such judgments are necessary.
4. Based on the application of these aesthetic judgments, the beautiful appears to be "purposive without purpose."

I focus here only on what is immediately germane to my investigation—his conclusions about the creation and judgment of the beautiful. In Kant's philosophical writings, the beautiful is determined as that which universally and necessarily gives disinterested pleasure without knowledge of an object's function, through an aesthetic analytical process. It differs, consequently, from his notions of the agreeable and the useful, as the beautiful is—in fact, it must be—devoid of politics, interest, or even knowledge of purpose. This disinterest confirms the universality of any subjective claim of the beautiful.

> In a sense, [aesthetic judgment] is a matter of a constant negotiation between individual and the community for warrant to have made aesthetic claims. As we explained with reference to universality, judgments involve a concern with their own origin and application ... but this reflection is fallible, so we need some other criterion by which to confirm our reflection and so claim success for our judgments ... [and] for Kant such confirmation must come from other subjects.... The community of taste is essential to confirming the subject's actual judgment of taste, and the very structure of judgment therefore is a constant negotiation between individual and community; and given that the community is constantly developing—that the ideal is "always in progress"—that search for universality and communication is constantly changing with the community.[19]

If claims to the beautiful—as Kant posits—are about the subject and not the object, then we can conclude that the claim to universality is about the subject's relationship to—and communication with—other subjects. This is important, because Kant uses this subjective relationship to address the notion of the origin of the beautiful and its claim to universality through the case of fine art and his understanding of genius, and it is this conclusion that is critical to the study and practice of architecture.

Kant's conception of genius—a human activity conducted by the rational will to create beauty—is comparable to the classic Aristotelian one, which stresses judging the object that is produced, not the process by which it is produced nor the producer of the object. For Kant, the primary property of genius is originality—the ability to produce something for which there are no existing rules.[20] He argues that the relationship between the production and the result is at best tangential, if not completely arbitrary to the value of the object itself. Whether it is produced accidentally or intentionally, we should judge it the same. The fact that the production of the object is dislodged from the object manifest is the reason, Kant argues, that no single determinate rule is appropriate—there are infinite ways in which genius can manifest—which means there can be no objective understanding of the production of genius. Perhaps one cannot be taught to design, but one can be taught the (objective) tools needed to design. What is created from there is based on one's own aesthetic judgments, or, more specifically, one's level of genius. So-called objective knowledge remains in the titular province of academia, and subjective knowledge—genius—lies in the province of the practice.

Now, here's the interesting dilemma for the architectural profession.

If genius is about subjectively producing new rules, then, once produced, these rules become rather useless as praxis for individual creativity. The most their materiality can demonstrate is what creating new rules can produce, for by working from these now-existing rules, one will never reach Kantian genius. In short, to produce genius, one must create new rules *(even if it means rejecting the appropriate)*—and not be held accountable for how that is done. Now, if we equate the notion of genius with the notion of de-sign expert, or, in architectural parlance, design superstar, the desire of the designer *must* be to master the aesthetic; to be always involved with creative innovation; to constantly do the new. The genius is *required* to eschew ac-cepted rules and to create not only the new, but also something that can-not—by definition—be understood by objective means. In this manner, the function, economics, and politics of the object are all rendered immaterial to the aesthetic product. So why bother to investigate or even teach its eco-nomic and political implications? It is immaterial to the production of the object, which of course, as positioned by the professional discourse, is what architecture is really all about. In effect, the designer is *obliged* to eschew the social, economic, and political in their quest to top the previous design or designer. This is the prevailing view of current architectural production and, more specifically, of design education and criticism. From this hidden foundation architects lay claim to and legitimize their disciplinary design expertise and professional superstar status in the public arena. This founda-tion also unduly exacerbates the crisis of legitimization the discipline cur-rently faces by dissuading the academy from aggressively pursuing research agendas that might contradict this position *(e.g., participatory design, behav-ioral research, etc.)*—especially those areas that might call into question the over-dependence on the designer-as-hero as the discipline's primary, if not sole, justification of its lofty social position.[21]

What is significant about this particular series of maneuvers is not only that it has repressed the independent, disparate, search-for-truth discourse of the academy—whose disciplinary contribution is not always a physical or even theoretical design—but that it has also almost rendered allied dis-ciplines and the public completely silent; a condition some see as less than advantageous.

The key problem lies with the privileged role assumed by the profes-sion in this attempt to direct the values, goals and public face of ar-chitecture. Strategies devised by the profession to effect professional closure have elevated neither the status nor the influence of the architect in public life.[22]

Within the architectural profession, a degree of hierarchy excludes architectural educators from contributing fully to the definition of architecture and architect—*from the position of the academy*—although they are charged with producing the raw material for the perpetuation of the profession. The term commonly used by the profession when discussing education is "training"—recalling both vocational and traditional, pre-disciplinary discourses. But, the profession has not done this alone; the academy has been complicit in the subjugation of its discourse.

> Educators have commonly justified the practices of architectural schools (and their own reluctance to change them) by pointing to both the demands and the rewards waiting in the "real world."[23]

Again, the discourse of professionalism is prominent, particularly in referring to rewards waiting in the "real world." Employing the practice term professionalizes education, allowing the primacy of profession over education to remain in place. Educators, by positioning the university apart from the real world, assert—by default—the primacy of the world outside of it: the realm of the professional. The statement implies that the goal of architectural schools is to produce subjects prepared for the real world *(i.e., traditional architectural practice),* thereby granting enormous power to the profession(al practices) over education(al practices). In essence, what is illustrated is that the disciplinary practices of architectural schools in preparing and presenting subjects to the profession produces a collection of new initiates who believe that the ultimate realization of the architectural identity is to achieve the "naturally" defined status of Kantian genius. To do anything less is to be less of an architect, if an architect at all.

A primary obstacle to reversing this hierarchy is the fact that architects and architectural critics, as observed by Cornel West, "do not have the historical and analytical training to do [cross-disciplinary] analysis."[24]

The academy is ill-equipped to dismantle the profession's hold over the discourse of architectural education because, to paraphrase Freire, all education can legitimately be termed political. In other words, to quote Cornel West:

> This . . . leads us to the crucial issue of the political legitimacy of architectural critics—namely why are they trained as they are, how are they reproduced and what set of assumptions about history, economics, culture, and art inform the curriculum and faculties that educate them?[25]

One answer is that such training has not been advantageous to the architectural profession, content as it was/is to have the academy produce architects in the current definition of practice.

So where would a critical perspective emerge to untangle the professional hold over the academy, if it is to emerge at all? Has it emerged already and is it being systematically silenced? Chrysler sees the latter when he states that:

> [w]ithin the university, new political formations organized by feminists, people of color, gays and lesbians, and "post-colonial" subjects from the Third World are challenging a curriculum that continues to define professional expertise in relation to the history and theory of a self-actualizing, white, heterosexual, Euro-American male consciousness.[26]

These educators attempt to confer upon the university real-world status; to remove it from the ivory tower and place it within the realm of the public, within society, the body that authorizes the architect's professional status. Key to this move is the investment in the term "political"—which mobilizes a set of real-world discourses. As architectural philosophy, inquiry, and criticism have become almost insignificant to anyone outside the profession, a new architectural perspective has become to some, a political necessity. By politicizing the site of the university—through its new political formations—these educators work to reposition the university to challenge and transform the current definition of the architectural professional, allowing new debates on architecture—and consequently, architect—to be recognized by the discipline.

Why, then, isn't more of this oppositional work going on? Such work has received little notice and legitimacy outside of academic circles, where those allied with the discipline's goals tightly control the dissemination of information, ideas, and objectives embodied in the profession. The control of information emphasizes a more insidious problem that academics face in pushing forth an alternative agenda. This barrier hinders the acceptance of their position by the professional entity, has exacerbated the subjugation of academic architectural perspectives by the profession, and has little to do with philosophical positions and everything to do with the political ideologies of gender, race, and power.

Seen through the production-oriented, patriarchal professional perspective—which has traditionally been recognized by society as the definition of what an architect is—those who have primarily chosen teaching and research over practice are seen as noncontributors or, worse, as failed architects. The historical legitimacy bestowed upon the singular practice version of the architect as the discipline's only valuable area of production and the proponents of this position have given certain cultural status and power to those who engage primarily in practice. This power has been welded with impunity within the discipline and ensures that the practice version of the architect remains in this primary position.

Those who have chosen academia as a way to contribute to the discipline have needed to find new ways of obtaining power and voice.[27] In the discipline of architecture, particularly in academia, women have been more adept at finding an alternate path to some type of power. One of the more favorable paths has been the development of a body of work that is cross-disciplinary in its nature and application. Unfortunately, this contribution is often disregarded by the old generation of educators and practitioners as rhetoric; sound and fury, signifying little, if not nothing. This is the underlying gender issue that poisons the discipline's well.

Parallel to and sustaining the gender issue is the current cultural questioning of difference and the appropriateness of the fundamental position that the white male has assumed in society. The structural patriarchy of a decidedly white, male profession is being examined by those struggling with unresolved issues of class and race, and one can expect the profession to be slow to ingenuously question its position. Typically it has been left to those who reside outside that power to begin to demystify it. Many women and people of color are in a position to do this work, but often encounter resistance to their inclusion on faculties, as evidenced by the fact that:

> Thirty years after the dawn of the civil rights era, architecture remains among the less successful professions in diversifying its ranks—trailing, for example, such formerly male-dominated fields as business, computer science, accounting, law, pharmacology and medicine.[28]

Dr. Sharon Sutton observed some time ago that those outside traditional power structures are motivated to find roles that will bring about change. In this context, change is tantamount to imbuing one's existence with value in the greater society. I believe Dr. Sutton's assertion speaks to a principal reason why many, but certainly not all, African-American students begin the study of architecture: to effect change. However, it also highlights a plethora of obstacles that may inhibit these students from achieving the change they desire through the study and practice of architecture, the principal obstacle being that:

> [Students] must feel culturally and historically linked to excellence in order to excel. You must feel deeply culturally obligated to perform in order to feel free to reach your finest performance. In order to feel historically, culturally obligated to contribute to society, you must be made strong by *your contributions already made.*[29]

Ralph Wiley spoke directly to the question of the readily accepted, sup-posedly "natural" development of the architectural discipline's culture, at-titudes, and theories. Architecture is often considered by most disciplines as a reflection of culture; because it is a physical expression of what we as a society think and feel, it can more accurately be described as a diary of society.[30] The authors of this diary—its gatekeepers[31]—pen the commonly accepted entry of what is considered historically and culturally significant and valuable in the built environment. It should come as no surprise that these gatekeepers—and subsequently the stories they write—have white protagonists. At the time of this writing, only 3.2 percent of faculty in the discipline of architecture are African-American, with approximately 4.1 per-cent full time and 2.4 percent part time. Of the total full-time architectural faculty that are African-American, only 3.9 percent are tenured. However, these numbers are slightly skewed. If we remove the 7 HBCUs, where 65 percent of all African-American professors are employed, the remaining 111 schools accredited by the National Architectural Accrediting Board report-ing in 2004 show that African-Americans make up just 1.6 percent of the faculty and 1.7 percent of the tenured faculty. By the same token, at the time of this writing African-Americans make up 23 percent of the faculty of all disciplines at American institutions of higher learning with approximately 15.1 percent full time and 8.8 percent part time. Of the total full-time faculty, 4.8 percent are tenured.[32] Lee Mitgang, coauthor of the Carnegie Founda-tion report entitled *Building Community: A New Future for Architectural Ed-ucation and Practice*, succinctly summarizes and contextualizes this lack of representation, stating that "[t]the race record of architecture education is a continuing disgrace, and if anything, things seem to be worsening," citing that the numbers of African-American educators in architectural schools have been decreasing over the past five-year period.[33]

Not surprisingly, as defined and guarded by its appointed gatekeepers, the architectural diary mentioned above—inarguably the cultural and his-torical link to excellence introduced by Wiley—is held as the exclusive privi-lege of the dominant culture, so much so that:

[African-Americans] are not seen by most White people as being within the same value system—a convenient blindness that allows them to think what they like and make it come true. Most White people cannot see [African-Americans] the same way they see themselves.... Worse, they don't realize that this is a result of how they were educated in schools and universities.[34]

The current system of education was created to educate and instill that all-important cultural obligation into the progeny of the dominant culture. Hence, all the resistance to multicultural *discussion,* much less *education,* which is primarily based on the widespread thinking that affirming diversity threatens disciplinary unity.[35] To receive the full benefits of the system, *other* users must have their values and desires modified or subjugated to that larger cultural objective, which remains veiled but legitimized and active under the auspices of the universal or the natural. The importance of having African-Americans on the faculty to counter this ideological subjugation and fulfill a cultural obligation to students of color cannot be overemphasized:

African-American faculty are needed and choose careers in academia because: (1) they serve as role models for African-American students; (2) they teach and understand within the context of the experiences that are shared by African-Americans; and (3) students need to have the presence of people who believe in them and expect them to succeed and do well.[36]

Unfortunately, "with only tepid support from the profession, and with recent anti-affirmative action federal court rulings clouding the picture even further, schools of architecture are throwing a party to which few in the minority community are likely to come any time soon,"[37] and when they do come, they are subjected to the immense and intense disciplinary practices specific to African-American educators in institutions of higher education which include, but are not limited to:

- A level of isolation that has African-American faculty feeling like an "X" in a field of "O's," a solo status at majority institutions that is often both patronizing and ostracizing[38]

- An assumption that African-American educators are the representatives of their people on all issues or that "Black" issues are—by their very nature—their issues. This marginalizing dynamic allows the other, typically majority, faculty to remain silent on and divest themselves from the hard work necessary to confront difficult issues *(e.g., issues of diversity and equal access)* because "X" will do it and if they don't, it must not be important. It also has the additional disadvantage to African-American faculty of allowing majority faculty to effectively "tune out" of the discussion or debate when these issues are consistently argued by the same one or two individuals. It is the "here-they-go-again" or the "one trick pony" syndrome.[39]

- More attention paid to scholarly production—and, to a lesser degree, academic service—as a manner of retention and tenure and little or no attention paid to the faculty support necessary to reach tenure. For example, the majority of African-American faculty are solicited to provide the "black" perspective on numerous committees *in addition to* research, teaching, and advising loads. Service on these committees tends to distract from doing research and ultimately is weighed as less important for tenure, but failure to serve is seen as being noncollegial or antisocial and adversely affects the perception of the faculty member and their work production.[40] Rare is the occasion that majority faculty are required to be the voice of their people.

- Exaggerated high or low expectations due to the fact that at most institutions their selection as faculty may be a pioneering event. While this is not limited to African-Americans—all new hires, majority and marginalized, face this phenomenon to varying degrees—it does place the performance of African-American faculty under a much sharper lens, as they are positioned to bear the burden of an entire underrepresented group. If they fail, it is much more likely that it will be perceived as a group failure rather than an individual failure by administrations, who are typically majority. As one faculty member put it, somewhat facetiously, it removes their "right to be mediocre," a privilege that majority faculty can—and often do—exercise.

• Subjective performance criteria that by its nature and the constitution of the reviewing committees becomes much more problematic to measure equally across the faculty body due to what has been identified in studies as "aversive racism."[41]

• Having a particular research agenda considered tenure worthy. Historically, focusing research on African-American issues, like correcting the historical omissions of knowledge sets of the discipline of which the researcher is a member, often reinforces the marginality of African-American faculty.[42]

• Difficulty in finding sources for publication and validation, where the success level of the search and submittal process can seem to be inversely proportional to the level of African-American focus of research agendas in architecture.[43]

Current architectural paradigms and pedagogy are produced within this culturally obligated, aesthetically depoliticized educational system, and thus the study and practice of architecture is retained as an instrument used for control in the production of environments.[44] Because of the primacy of the aesthetic—which "appear[s] to mark distinctions between things [but] turn[s] out to mark distinctions between people"[45]—it is also an instrument for control of the production of practitioners as well. The gatekeepers have so institutionalized their cultural and professional legitimacy in this educational system that not only is the question of disciplinary values, their propriety and pertinence not addressed, it is difficult to even perceive an extension of cultural bias, if not blindness. Put another way:

The dominant group believes that their version of reality and the "truth" is right and objective. As a result, "they are incapable of seeing the world from another point of view" and "they don't see the racism that is there." This blindness to racism plays a role in many situations.[46]

For example, in addition to the disciplinary practices outlined previously concerning African-American faculty, blind practices specific to the experience of the African-American student include, but are not limited to:

- Remote or nonexistent presence of architecture/architects in most African-American communities. The discipline is viewed as not having an influence or impact on the daily lives of most African-Americans. Architecture has little—if any—"juice" or power to change economic, political, or social conditions.[47]
- Little audiovisual material or actual role models and illustrations of tangible success in architecture in general, but almost nil concerning African-American successes in particular, are made available to inspire and excite students to pursue careers in the design professions, particularly architecture—historically thought to be inaccessible to African-American children.
- Generally inadequate, indifferent, patronizing, or culturally insensitive curriculum and career counseling.[48]
- When presenting their work to a jury, African-American students receive more interruptions than all other students, male or female, are given less time to present than all other students, and the comments made on their projects tend to be very general, tepid, condescending, and not very useful. Often, the composition of the juries themselves is lacking a person of color.[49]
- The prevailing attitude of studio instructors is, for the most part, not to empathize with influences that drive non-Eurocentric cultural concepts, and often to discourage with silence a student's pursuit of a different path of inquiry. Architectural educators are hesitant to give culturally influenced conceptual development standing, for fear of

according power to this line of inquiry, which they have little access to or control over.

- Questions of validity are succinctly summarized by the statement that often, particularly in architecture, to use a phrase of Gloria Joseph, "it takes whiteness to give even Blackness validity." Typically, when culturally—and particularly racially—influenced concepts are developed and manifest themselves in a product for debate, African-American students are given the impression that such work is not worthy of in-depth discussion.[50] They are therefore left to conclude that such exploration is meaningless when based in a cultural knowledge that is particularly, but not exclusively, theirs.

Ahrentzen and Anthony observe that "[g]enerally, white male architects are treated as if their sex and race were utterly irrelevant to their work," which when viewed objectively is proven to be quite the contrary.[51] The same can be said for architectural education, which gives little emphasis to developing a comprehensive understanding of underrepresented cultures.[52] It is far too easy to complete the formal education of the architect without exploring any culture other than European.[53]

A structure that has shaped the academy and profession

To conclude, the architectural profession has been carving out smaller and smaller positions in society and it has done so in relative secrecy. Now, as other related cultural concerns have brought this defection to the attention of society, the traditional boundaries of the architect—and with it, architecture—no longer exist and society at large has no idea where the new boundaries have been established, a position seemingly confirmed by the statement that, "[t]o the outside world, the architectural profession seems incredibly insular and, compared to many other fields, archaic."[54] A redefinition of these boundaries is long overdue. This reexamination signals the moment that the discipline of architecture in general should be compelled into a concerted effort to close the real and perceived gap between professional artifact and academic knowledge and, in the process, it must take this opportunity to address its disciplinary political and social shortcomings as well.

Specifically, with respect to African-American participation in the discipline, a review of the current structure of the architectural discipline will reveal a structure that has helped to shape an academy—and profession—that:

- Supports a Eurocentric worldview of white male interests that don't necessarily address the concerns of many in society—particularly African-Americans—to any great degree
- Supports the dissemination of images of good, great, and indifferent that are gendered and color*less*, but not color*blind*
- Isolates difference in both the academic and professional sites
- Appeals to a largely upper-middle-class segment of society
- Is expensive—both financially and personally—to pursue
- Requires much education, offers little initial reward, and a more limited opportunity for future reward in comparison to other professions

These are but a few of the very basic structural problems that impede equal access to the opportunity of an architectural career for African-Americans and "raise serious questions about the lack of diversity in architectural education today."[55] As it stands, architecture as a discipline is just not a very attractive option to members of marginalized communities. For many educators, being a member of a population that is regarded as having a lower status in the larger professional society as well as in the university, coupled with the lower-ranking status of most African-American faculty in majority colleges and universities, compounds any decision related to remaining in a profession where the rewards are both few and far off.[56] Many students, coming to the discipline from economically challenged situations, can ill afford the time, the expense, or the low initial return on the investment spent pursuing the study and practice of architecture when very real and specific cultural/racial obstacles exist, immediate relevance and impact is questionable, and other options may be available. These restrictions on educators and students limit the number of diverse human elements entering the discipline, giving no impetus to the discipline to change its foundations, boundaries, or practices in any way—particularly when change is embodied in the body of African-Americans who are typically most adversely affected by the decisions made and executed by the ruling class in the built environment. All of which makes the lack of participation in architecture by people of color seem natural, when, of course, it's not.

Society has arrived at a point in time where significant cultural investigations are occurring and disciplines are reevaluating and realigning their perspectives, shaping and being shaped by a transforming global society. The hostility toward African-Americans in the architectural discipline should be unacceptable for anyone serious about the study and practice of architecture. From my position in both the academy and the profession, this marginalization brings the discipline of architecture into question with a sense of urgency. Architecture's representation of the world around us includes little of marginalized cultures in our society, and based on such an exclusionary text, the validity of current architectural paradigms should come under rigorous review.

Remix

Okay, so check it. We have these divisions of study called disciplines that were first established way, *way* back in the day. These divisions have been added to over time, but how the original categories were first determined is anybody's guess. I mean, somebody—we'll call them the "enlightened"—decided that to be an educated man, you needed to know math, Latin, and such. Hell, it could have been anything, but since these cats had the juice, they made the rules. The point is—most folk didn't have shit to say about it.

Before these "enlightened" jacked the scene, the church made the rules —but they slipped up and got caught frontin' 'bout the rotation of the earth and some other stuff, and their game got real raggedy. Folks began to think they were lyin' 'bout a lot of shit, and they decided they couldn't truss 'em. Then the "enlightened" *(self-proclaimed scientist and shit)* bust on the scene rappin 'bout some different ways for why things were as they were, dig? And here is how they played that game: They said that anyone could know anything if you just study it scientifically. Basically, they were sayin' that even the dumb and poor could learn. Now before, only the folk the church deemed down *(priests, bishops, cardinals, and the lucky nobles and royal folk)* had access to knowledge—and the church was still the last word on what was and wasn't the real deal. Now here come the "enlightened" sayin' y'all can do this shit yo' self—to hell wid' them other folks tellin' you. Find out for yourself. Snap!—who wouldn't jump at that? And to help get started, they divided up the world into these disciplines so that they could be studied, and the place to do all this studyin' was in the University. Eventually, architecture got its own little category, and this meant that the old, traditional way of becoming an architect—by bustin' yo' ass workin' on the cheap under some cat you had to call "master"—was on the way out. Droppin' science in school was in.

Now we got these categories—decided by the "enlightened" *(all of which typically had fat pockets)*—that for a brotha to represent, he had to study one *(or more)*. Now, not only did the "enlightened" get to determine the divisions, they also got to determine what goes into the divisions. In other words, they get to set up the game *(what will be played)* and the rules *(how it will be played)*—and they set it up so that they hold all the cards and can't lose. No shit—who wouldn't? So they determine the game and the rules—which of course determines who wants to play. And those that want to play are typically just like them. If not, they will be after playin' the game for a while, wid' no chance of winnin'. The "enlightened" way *(that keeps 'em in ice and chedda)* becomes their way, so while they may think that they are playin' a game for their own benefit, in reality, they are doin' just what the "enlightened" want them to do, 'cause the rulers will always win if you play by their rules. The sad part is that these dumb-asses don't know any better, but don't hate the playa; hate the game. And, for the most part, it is still that way—which of course, means that you yourself may be gettin' played by studyin' architecture as well. How? Well, check this out.

When you decide to study architecture, you quickly find that most important—where you spend most of your time—is the design studio. So what happens in the studio? You'll be "disciplined," bitch. That basically means that you are told to do and say something over and over again until you just buy that shit. These things that you are told to do are called "disciplinary practices"—'cause they practice disciplining your ass with them. In the end though, if they are successful, you discipline yo'self. You are kinda "programmed"—and that program ain't always (in fact almost never is) to your advantage. It is to the advantage of somebody else to have you doin' things that you don't think about. So, in the studio, you are "disciplined" by "practices" to:

- Instead of "think for yourself," you are really taught to "think by yourself." Teachers don't encourage group projects, dig?
- Think of studio as the most important—if not the only—thing you have to do, in or out of school. If you try to roll wid' a "I'm-not-tryin'-ta-hear-dat" attitude—folks will call you out. They will think you are frontin' 'bout being a down student. And even if you accept all that other shit, you will still be dogged if you don't stay in the studio all night, even if you are working at home. Folks wanna see you suffer for your art.
- Na in the studio—although you are told to do independent, creative thinking—most of the time you are told what to do, how to do it, where to do it, when to do it, and sometimes who to do it with. Again, you can try "I'm-not-tryin'-ta-hear-dat" shit, but your professors are gonna spank-that-ass when it comes to gradin' time, dig?
- Puttin' a whole lotta weight—most of the time, too much weight—on what folks think and say about your work. It is easy to internalize that

shit, like, if they don't like my work, they don't like me. It ain't true, but try tellin' that to some folk. Instead of askin' "What's wrong with the criteria?"—you know, tryin' to dig why and how these folks are buggin'—you ask "What's wrong with me?"

So what happens to somebody who subjects themselves to five, six, even seven years of that in school? They become converted. At some point, you either accept it, get out, or snap. This is what they call the "disciplined" person *(or subject)* 'cause you have been disciplined *(programmed)* to think that this is okay, that this is normal. And what exactly are you acceptin'? Well, whatever they want you to—or, to be more to the point—what they have disciplined you to accept. And that is the golden rule, of course: He who has the gold, makes the rules.

Okay, so why do we do this crazy shit? If it is this easy to see, then why not change? Well, 'cause some folk are gettin' paid in this system, and fat pockets don't want nobody different to wear the pants, dig? So, they gotta keep this shit on the down low. And they do that by controllin' who gets into the schools, the requirements for students and teachers, who gets to teach, what, how, where, and when they teach, the magazines about architecture, and just about anything else you can think of. Basically, they control what people think when they hear the words "architect" and "architecture." How often do you see anyone—in the classrooms *(studio or lecture)* or administrations *(dean, assistant dean, department heads or chairs, etc.)* of architectural schools, in the papers, in the magazines, in the museums, in library lecture series, on the radios, in the movies, you could go on and on—who ain't white and male? You think that shit is natural? Fool! That shit ain't by accident. Black architects—and Black folk in general—are gettin' straight played.

So the architectural schools explanation goes like this: *"Well, hell. We ain't got enough Black folk to fill these positions. You know, they just not comin' to study architecture—and when they do, they just fail. Maybe they just ain't got what it takes. We want more, but it just seems too hard for them."*

B-U-L-L-S-H-I-T! They don't start—and when they do, don't finish—'cause they get dogged in school. You don't believe me? Keep readin'.

In addition to the shit I outlined above, here is some shit that happens to nobody but Black folk in architectural school. Nobody. Check this crazy shit out:

- First, African-Americans never see architects when growing up—not Black ones anyway. Why? Well, there aren't a lot of them, true, but those that are gettin' paid don't get in the paper or magazines, they don't get invited to the grade, high schools, or the universities to teach, they don't get interviewed on the radio or get books published about them. They get nothing. So ... they just stay invisible, dig? So, Black folk grow up thinking that architecture ain't got no "juice" to fatten pockets, to change the conditions in the 'hood—or anywhere else, for that matter. Architecture? That's just some art shit that white folk do—like Mr. Brady on the *Brady Bunch*. Oh ... and Wesley Snipes in that Spike Lee joint.
- Second, say you get past all that and make it into college to study architecture. What happens more than it should, is that you will get some cheesy counseling *(both formal or informal)* about classes and you will take other classes that are NOT situated in a world you are familiar with. Check out how many architectural history classes will talk about Paul Williams, Vertner Woodson Tandy, Hilyard Robinson, or Clarence Wigington. Those are just a few of the older brothas who should be included in the canonical timeline. But you *will* hear—and see—a whole lot of folk that don't look nuttin' like you. Bet on it. Why is that? And all your classes are like that. But you ain't supposed to say anything 'bout that 'cause, that is just the way things are. B-U-L-L-S-H-I-T. It's that way for no other reason than some folks want it that way—and work to keep it that way.
- Snap! You still here? Okay, fine. We'll fix that. Come on into the studio where we can really f—— wid' yo' silly, hard-headed ass. First, your

teachers don't know much about your background or your concerns, so they are just gonna typically ignore all that and give you some concerns—their concerns, which of course, ain't got nuttin' to do with you. If you point that out, then you are "ghetto-izing" yourself. "You have to open your mind to the rest of the world," they'll say. *(Of course, you are the only one who has to do that—not the teacher, who don't know shit about you.)*

- Still here? Gonna show your work, huh? You sure? Fine. Let's see it. You can expect to get interrupted more often than anyone else, have the jury spend less time on your project than anyone else, and make some bullshit comments that don't help very much—that is, if they don't completely ignore your work altogether. Finally, don't expect to see any Black folk on your jury. Your teachers don't know any—otherwise, they would have invited them, right? I mean, what other reason do they have for not having Black folk there?

Maybe you might spot an Black instructor if you look hard enough, but not more than one, and for damn sure not often. Why? Well . . . they too have issues to deal with, like:

- If they are lucky enough to be recognized for their abilities, more than likely Black faculty will be the only "one" in their department. Try being the only "one" of anything—and see how long before you get tired of that shit.
- As Neo *(the "one")*, white folk assume that anything "Black" is their responsibility. Which lets white folk off the hook—they ain't gotta deal wid' anything "Black" 'cause the "one" will do it. Of course, they never learn anything different—'cause they never have to deal with real difference. The "one" gets them off the hook. And . . . if they take up the "Black" thang, the white faculty can—and will—ignore you. Why? 'Cause they can.
- Okay, say the "one" takes up the "Black"—oh, excuse me, it's now called "diversity"—thang. So they go to all the meetings and sit on all

the committees and "represent" the people and the department. That shit takes up a lot of time that they could be doin' other shit, but dig it, somebody is gonna appreciate this when it comes to gettin' paid, right? So when it comes time for a promotion, the "one" hasn't written or built a lot—hell, they haven't had the time! Compared to other folk, the "one" hasn't done as much. But—and here's the kick in the ass—other folk have been allowed to do more BECAUSE the "one" was doin' what the other faculty *wouldn't* do. Snap! But they get promoted and the "one" is out on his/her untenured ass.

- So back to the promotion thang. Often when African-American faculty get hired, they gotta be the sharpest, the smartest, the strongest, etc. You know, "Super Nigga," ready to leap tall assumptions in a single bound, 'cause if they can't, well that means that ALL Blacks can't. So, if the "one" fails, they don't just f—— it up for themselves ... they f—— it up for e-v-e-r-y-b-o-d-y! Nobody but the "Super Nigga" gotta deal wid' people sweatin' 'em that much, na-wha-I-mean? I mean, why can't the brotha or sista be just a "nigga"? Why they gotta be super all the time?

- Okay, say these Super Nigs actually decide not to have a life *(sleep, eat, clean, etc.)* for a few years so they can do all the writin' folks are gonna wanna see when it comes time to get fatta pockets. And let's say the writin' has got to do with their interests—and perhaps those interests happen to do with some Black shit. *(Like this book—which wasn't easy to get published and I can tell ya, ain't gonna win me no new friends in high places.)* Ain't a whole lot of books, papers, magazines, etc. that are gonna be tryin'-to-hear-that. And, even though they did all the writin', nobody wants to put it out, ya dig? So ... whose fault is that? Well ... no matter whose fault it is—that's Neo's ass as far as watchin' pockets gettin' fatta.

So ... dig it. Here's the deal. The way the schools of architecture are set up today f——ks wid' a brotha/sista—student and teacher—by presenting a picture of the future in architecture that looks a little something like this:

- A worldview is hostile to Black people, and consequently, their issues
- Ignores in books, mags, and classrooms the contributions that Black folk have made to the profession back in their day and today
- Plays both students and practitioners in and out of school way too close, sweatin' 'em in ways other students and teachers ain't gotta deal with
- Is full of white folks—privileged white folk—and, 'cause they don't see nothin' wrong wid' that, ain't workin' too hard to change it
- Costs a shit-load of cash to pursue
- If-and-when you graduate, don't immediately pay a whole hell-of-a-lot

And they tell you that this shit above is *"just the way it is—it's always been this way—it has to be this way."* Don't you believe that bullshit for a minute. For the benefit of a select few, it was made this way. And for the benefit of many others, it has got to be unmade.

3 | Architecture—Thing

The design culture—cultivated in the academy; perpetrated by
critics; and promoted by design publications, awards programs,
even paper sessions like these—has an ambivalent relationship with
the public. Why, given our dependence on clients and communities
for support and approval, do we often seek freedom from them?
Why do our notions of good design differ so much from that of
the public, and what are the consequences of that difference?
—*ACSA News*

IT IS MY CONSIDERED OPINION that this particular moment of globalization[1] has placed the architectural profession at a critical point in its long and
storied history. It has highlighted, even exacerbated, a curiously complex,
historical internal and external struggle to retain a position of substantive,
not symbolic, significance in today's increasingly colonized, homogenized,
and commodified society. Leo Marx succinctly characterizes this conflict,
embodied by the opposing views of architecture as a private commodity/
privilege or a public service/necessity, when he states:

> Star turns or commendable rehabilitations—that is the choice the
> profession offers its young aspirants today. The polarization is well-
> nigh total. At one pole is the discourse of necessity and utility . . .
> plain, stripped-down, affordable single-family houses in an urban
> setting. At the other pole is the discourse of art and celebrity . . . a
> perfect expression of the delightfully varied and rich sensuous life
> available to the privileged in America today.[2]

These apparently mutually exclusive conditions lead one to ask: *By what framework will the value of the discipline's cultural contribution be evaluated?*

The profession has attempted to respond to the ever-increasing complex cultural constructs of liability and litigation by narrowing the scope of work and responsibility expected from architects. Retreating into the ideological realm of Kantian aesthetics in an effort to legitimize its practical product, the profession has focused—through awards, media recognition, public opinion, and superstar status—on one less-than-comprehensive (albeit indispensable) aspect of architecture: design services. As Kim Dovey states:

> The claim for the autonomy of architecture rests upon a separation of form from instrumental function. And it also rests implicitly upon a broader Kantian aesthetic of universal judgment, Kant's transcendental aesthetic is an a priori judgment which is at once both universal and subjective.[3]

More than at any other moment in recent history, architects are freer—theoretically, at least—to pursue design as personal ideology, since now the outline of what an architect is expected to do, and will do, during the project has been increasingly weighted toward design only. While throughout history this modus operandi has never been far from the architectural core, positioning the architect as "aesthetic expert" only results in the belief that she or he is no longer expected to substantially contribute anything beyond the imaging phase of the project, even if willing and able to do so. It is easy to envision that the conclusion of such a process will be that the architect will eventually become purely a provider of design expertise—and then only for those who can afford it—inconsistent with the role of the professional in society. The practice of architecture—and the architect—is *(or should be)* too important to be limited to only one facet of the building process, but the fact that "this happy if complacent aesthetic discourse is rewarded with most of the lucrative commissions"[4] is an indication of the profession's complicity in its own prostitution. Silence, in this case, is truly golden . . . or perhaps platinum.

The dilemma presented by the narrowing of the professional scope of responsibility is that in the process, the study and practice of architecture is giving birth to disciplines and professions that develop primarily *because of* its discarded responsibilities at the same time it is whittling itself into oblivion because of *the lack of* responsibilities. By default or design, since the end of World War II, architects have increasingly allowed the commodification of their work by others, reinforcing the "architecture as product" argument. However, the technical skills of the architect are no longer *necessarily* required to complete the modern building process as now "we have engineers who design buildings, and construction managers who take over the management of the project."[5] Thus design becomes not one of the things, but the only thing that the architectural profession offers. This process is well under way, further exacerbated by the desire of capital to be heard in a global market.[6] In the rush to limit the responsibility that certainly has historically been part of the concern of architects, this narrowing of professional responsibilities leaves the practice of architecture open to questions of professional legitimacy from a skeptical and increasingly alienated public. Much of that skepticism arises from the discipline's close alliance with—if not slavish dependence on—a class-based elite who supply the financial fodder for their ideological indulgences. Unlike the disciplines of law and medicine, one must remember that much as everyone *thinks* they have a sense of humor, everyone *thinks* that they have a sense of design creativity, and it is foolish to believe that they are willing to pay for the privilege of being told otherwise. The question I am forced to ask as I watch this divestiture of position and responsibility is this: *As the discipline whittles itself into irrelevance, what does this mean for current and future African-American practitioners?*

Despite the fact that "African American architects and their buildings have always been invisible,"[7] they have and continue to establish interesting and productive practices across the United States. Still, despite their historical and contemporary success, we should not lightly gloss over the reasons for that invisibility. African-American practitioners are faced with several very real systemic obstacles that are specific to them as a professional group. I will outline only three of these obstacles, primarily because they are so interdependent. They are, in no particular order: (1) a lack of an acknowledged historical place within the profession; (2) a decided lack of opportunity to excel within majority-owned firms; and finally (3) institutional bias, shown in a lack of recognition of architectural excellence as individual practitioners. I will further illustrate how the current professional position, both internally and externally, adversely affects African-American practitioners in ways that do not exist for their non–African-American colleagues.

1. A lack of an *acknowledged historical place within the profession*—a connection to excellence that is assumed by most of the dominant architecture community.

"Are there any African-American architects? We can't find them." is a comment often heard when people gather to consider architecture. Now, a myriad of conditions contribute to the illusion of invisibility around African-American architects; far too many to go into here. Admittedly, some have been created by African-Americans themselves. For example, the initial edition of the celebrated *Encyclopedia Africana*—a project begun by W.E.B. Du Bois and completed by noted Harvard scholars K. Anthony Appiah and Henry Louis Gates, Jr., almost a century later—which purports to comprehensively cover the exploits of the African Diaspora, unforgivably contained no entry for the category of "architect." No entry whatsoever. Imagine the outcry had the category of doctor or lawyer been omitted, yet, for architect, hardly a peep—or an apology—was heard. Further, one might also point to the fact that those African-Americans who have the desire and ability to employ an architect don't look often enough to the African-American architectural community to provide those services. But, don't get it twisted. I want to be very clear that this, of course, is not a requirement, and I am hardly arguing for a balkanization of professional design services along color lines. That would be foolish. Still, the lack of opportunities seized by the African-American service and consumer communities in this area demonstrates a certain amount of apathy on the part of both the practitioner and the potential client pool that must be examined. My point is that as both a cultural and professional group, African-Americans bear some responsibility for their seeming invisibility in the field of architecture. Having said that, I will show that many of the conditions that contribute to that invisibility, and certainly the most significant ones, exist through no fault of their own. They are institutional in nature and, indeed, have deep historical roots. In fact, history is where I'd like to begin.

For any profession to justify its control over a specific body of knowledge—be it medical, legal, architectural, etc.—establishing a notion of history, and a progressive history at that, is imperative. For the public, the belief that what the profession offers is a time-honored, ever-increasing, and essential service is key to its willingness to allow the monopoly to continue; for the professionals, the belief that what they do is not only all of the above, but also both specific and special, is critical to attracting future practitioners to perpetuate the profession. This is a point I will return to later in this book, but, put another way, in the legal arena, without Charles Houston there would be no Thurgood Marshall. Without Marshall there would be no *Brown v. Board of Education of Topeka*. In medicine, without Charles Drew there would be no blood transfusion. Without transfusions, there would be fewer people around who might possibly read this book. In each case, the ability of the professional to perform that *special* act was in large part a *cumulative* effort. It built on a past knowledge base—a history, if you will—to reach that necessarily transformative moment that in theory is why professions exist. But, equally as important as having a professional history is the dissemination of that version of history. Through this dissemination we as a public learn to trust professionals. History—the place where the expectations and aspirations of the public and the profession conflate—becomes both the repository of the past and the promise of the future. We hold both past accomplishments and future aspirations in the body of our professional practitioners. History is where the heroes and heroines are acknowledged, emulated, and, one dares hope, advanced. The profession of architecture is no exception; in fact, it might be more the rule than most. Yet within its historical narrative, architecture has paid little attention to the presence of, much less the contributions of, African-American practitioners. Bradford Grant, chair of the Department of Architecture at Howard University School of Engineering, Architecture, and Computer Science, has accurately observed that historians "have not yet incorporated African-American contributions to American architecture into their work or into architecture curricula."[8] Given what history means to sustaining professions, the importance of this omission cannot be overstated.

Now, one might reasonably remark that the omission is not an omission at all; it is simply the result of the natural course of events and nothing more. Perhaps African-American architects simply have not yet created work worthy of note; there may be no Houstons, Marshalls, or Drews within their ranks. However, Vincent Scully, professor emeritus at Yale School of Architecture and one of the discipline's preeminent historians, disagrees. He writes that it is "obvious that a good many black architects have been very good architects indeed—a great many of them in relation to their number,"[9] which at the very least renders the previous supposition debatable, and probably false. Thus, some other reason must account for the fact that even today, a cursory review of the syllabi, debates, and images that constitute the typical history survey course of the nation's architectural schools, not to mention professional seminars and conferences, will routinely be found lacking any mention of names like Julian Abele, chief designer of Horace Trumbauer and Associates, who designed much of Duke University; Hilyard R. Robinson, whose Langston Terrace Dwellings in Washington, D.C., won several design awards as well as high praise from Lewis Mumford in the 1930s; Vertner Woodson Tandy, who with his partner, George Washington Foster, designed St. Philip's Episcopal Church in New York City and the mansion of Madam C. J. Walker; Clarence "Cap" Wigington, the first African-American municipal architect in the nation, who designed an array of public buildings in St. Paul and six of the fabled Winter Carnival ice palaces of the 1930s and 1940s; and Paul R. Williams, who designed homes for

Tyrone Power, Frank Sinatra, the iconic tower at Los Angeles International Airport, and who was called the most successful Negro artist in the United States by *Life* magazine in 1950; architects who produced work deserving of a place within the chronology of architectural history. Yet within the annals of architecture, the work of these and other African-Americans continues to be—to borrow from James Baldwin—evidence of things not seen.[10]

Furthermore, I think we all can agree that architecture, whatever else it may or may not be, is a highly visual profession. Buildings, neighborhoods, and cities are all created through the interventions of designers, and the resulting objects and landscapes, when done correctly, can certainly be called works of art. In fact, it would not be a stretch to say that this is indeed what the architect strives to create with every commission: art. But the art world is no place for the uninitiated. It is not a place the majority of the public enters without a guide, without some assistance to make sense of what they see. The media and other methods of mass communication play an important role in forming public opinion about what is architecturally significant. However, forms of mass dissemination—which include journals, magazines, newspapers, books, museum exhibits, public lectures, films, and the like—that pay attention to the works of African-American architects are underwhelming at best. To date, fewer than a dozen books have been printed documenting the work of African-American architects, one African-American architectural critic has written for a major metropolitan newspaper, and zero have held editorial positions at the major architectural publications, while stories in the most popular professional journals that highlight the work of African-American firms are few and far between. None of this is by accident. None. More than simple oversight, this is the result of a deliberate, almost willful ignorance. In this day and time, it is unconscionable that many architects, whom I have found generally to be some the brightest and well-read people around, cannot name four or five African-American architects who have a substantial body of work, or even a few of their most prominent commissions. Yet within both the academy and the profession, this is the rule, not the exception. As a further example of this erasure, take the current employment and currency of the design buzzwords "New Urbanism" and "Community Design."

Architecture—which has a long history of being used to perpetuate spatial dichotomy and marginalization—has since the 1960s overtly viewed the urban condition as an inevitable illustration of the pathologies of its residents, becoming a place to mitigate, not to cultivate. As such, architecture and urban design are not viewed as having the power for social *change*, just social *control*, not only of space, but of identity and basic humanity. Many of the architectural interventions in the urban environment from the late 1960s to the early 1990s demonstrate this phenomenon all too clearly. Fortunately, there have been a few committed architects, mostly African-American, working in the same urban sites that nurtured both the Black Power and Black Arts Movement (BAM) of the 1960s, who had a different view of the urban. Rooted in the ideological foundation that refused to accept that African-Americans were without power over their identities and environment, these architects and architectural collaboratives worked to empower marginalized people by helping them to recognize the value of the social, political, and economic capital in their spatial environment and employ its physical manifestation—architecture—to develop and create spaces that represent this power. The feminist critic bell hooks elaborates on why such an active engagement of space was historically critical to the Black community at the time:

> Many narratives of resistance struggle from slavery to the present share an obsession with the politics of space. . . . Indeed, black folks equated freedom with passage into a life where they would have the right to exercise control over space on their own behalf, where they would imagine, design, and create spaces that would respond to the needs of their lives, their communities, their families.[11]

The process and product of these architectural collaboratives were embedded in the self-help, self-defining, pro-Black principles of the Black power/Black arts movements of the time. Their situating architecture as a product of participatory design processes and activities helped them address and record the struggle for Black identity born out of inner-city social relationships with the built environment. Architect and historian Richard K. Dozier writes concerning the catalyst for these young activist-practitioners:

> With the continued development of the community workshop, an even greater need emerged: not only did urban communities desperately need the technical resources supplied by the workshops, they also needed that deep sensitivity to interpret accurately and to communicate their desires. With the rise of urban advocacy emerged the full-time urban technician who could interpret accurately the communities' needs: The CDC.[12]

Architecture for these activist-practitioners was viewed as a community-empowering cultural product; a product employed against an erasing oppressive spatial paradigm embodied in the inhumane housing projects of Pruitt-Igoe, Cabrini-Green, and Robert Taylor that authorized and sanctioned the wholesale movement of people and erasure of communities. Many of these activist-practitioners were survivors and, to a certain degree, beneficiaries of the urban rebellions of the time and their objectives were inarguably shaped by these events. In addition, this was also a moment in American history where African-American students were able to access higher education—particularly majority colleges and universities and especially Ivy League institutions—en masse (relatively speaking). Particularly conscious about employing their talents in African-American communities upon graduation, these young architects had a sense of urgency that led to the establishment of community design, planning, and educational organizations:

- the Black Workshop in New Haven
- the Black Architects' Collaborative in Chicago (which existed at the same moment during the 1960s as the BAM organization AfriCobra)
- the Architects Renewal Committee of Harlem (ARCH) (located in

the same site as Amiri Baraka's Black Arts Repertory Theatre/School [BART/S])
- the Urban Workshop in Los Angeles (which, along with the Afro-American Association and the work of Maulana Karenga, represented sites of resistance and self-empowerment in the Los Angeles African-American community)

Unfortunately, this important contribution by African-American architects in the development of educational and professional architectural theory and practice has been conveniently and insidiously erased, forgotten, and finally appropriated by nonprofit (Association for Community Design [ACD]) and for-profit (Congress for the New Urbanism [CNU]) communities alike—a process that once again dislodges the African-American practitioner from any professional or disciplinary position within the architectural teleology or any benefit from their painstaking and groundbreaking work.

It is curious that, with many of these groundbreaking practitioners still working in the profession, the "official" history of community design was written by Rex Curry, director of one of the more prominent CDCs, the Pratt Institute Center for Community and Environmental Development in Brooklyn, and currently considered one of the elder statesmen in the field. This version of the CDC history for the ACD's Web site and updated for the Association of Collegiate Schools of Architecture (ACSA)'s *Sourcebook of Community Design Programs at Schools of Architecture in North America* completely erases the African-American initiative and influence that cata-lyzed and energized this movement throughout its inception and beyond. For example, Curry's account of the CDC makes several curious claims about moments of CDC significance and as a result leaves huge gaps in the story of the CDC movement and its participants:

Although community design practice began as early as 1964 (with the Architect's Renewal Committee of Harlem—ARCH), a national network was not established until nine years after Young's address. In June 1977, the directors of community design centers met formally for the first time at the AIA's national headquarters in Washington DC, and incorporated the following year.... The first survey of community design was done in 1970 by the Community Design Resource Center, School of Architecture and Planning at MIT.... Roughly fifty Community Design Centers (CDCs) were listed in the MIT project. Coincidentally in May of 1971 The Association of Collegiate Schools of Architecture published a directory that found 67 centers. And, in that same year 74 centers could be found in the 1971 CDC Listing—Community Design/Development Centers, published by the CDC Director—Community Services Department of the AIA. ... Subsequent directories were produced when the Community Design Center Director's Association (CDC/DA) was formed in 1978. The CDC/DA Survey 1987 found just 16 design centers. What happened?[13]

While Curry's account acknowledges the existence of the Architectural Renewal Committee of Harlem (ARCH) in 1964, his history effectively begins with the 1970 survey of CDCs, as if what transpired between those two moments is of no consequence to the CDC movement; as if the movement itself did not gain legitimacy until its first survey was conducted in 1970, if not the 1977 meeting at the AIA headquarters. This appropriation of CDC history by the ACD is deeply troubling. What has been inexplicably erased are the early years of the CDC movement, which was, in large part, spearheaded by practitioners of color. For example, note the different perspective on the CDC movement provided by Dozier in the AIA publication entitled *Community Design Centers Information*:

1965—Urban Workshop in Watts, California, is established by two young black architects. First CDC to be operated as a full-time professional firm.... Their skills were used in developing a communications system for the community explaining various aspects of urban renewal, urban planning, and transportation networks. The major objective of the Urban Workshop was to eliminate the negative structural characteristics and growth dynamics of communities in South Central Los Angeles as a base from which to design and implement new approaches to community and regional planning.... 1966 ... the Urban Planning Studio is established as New York's second CDC; the first Puerto Rican CDC ... [its] major goals were to establish a process whereby interdisciplinary teams including community members, students, and trainees as well as sociologists, economists, lawyers, architects, and planners could work for the total environmental control of East Harlem. Also, to help increase the number of indigenous architects and planners in East Harlem and to help professional schools recruit Puerto Rican and black students.... 1967 —Architects Workshop in Philadelphia is established and becomes the first AIA charter-supported CDC.... Sept., 1968—Black Workshop at the Yale School of Architecture is formed—the first all-black group of architecture students to organize in a major white school. The Black Workshop's thrust was developing an architectural curriculum that would deliver the resources of the university to the community, as well as provide a way to educate black architects to social reality.... Oct., 1968—AIA establishes the Task Force on Equal Opportunity chaired by David Yerkes as a response to Whitney Young's charges.... April, 1969—Task Force on Equal Opportunity issues "Guideline for Community Design Centers." The AIA's first document on CDC's answered questions about the conflict of the CDC and the profession.... March, 1970—AIA sponsors the National CDC Conference at Howard University, Washington, DC.... June, 1970—AIA hires Vernon Williams, graduate architect from Chicago, as CDC director.... While in Chicago, Williams' experience included CDC work with the Black Architects Collaborative.[14]

What the ACD document—which is widely considered the official history of CDCs—erases is the first CDC developed as a professional office; the first CDC created by Latino activist-practitioners; the first all-black group of architecture students to organize a CDC at a majority school; and the first African-American hired by the AIA as a professional staff member (head of its CDC department). In short, there are numerous important moments within the time frame of the official ACD/ASCA history that mark significant, if not critical, contributions by people of color in this area of the profession of architecture that were simply left unacknowledged. One must wonder, to employ Curry's plaintive wail, "what happened?" in his own narrative—or, more important—*why* it happened.

This erasure is not limited to the community-based nonprofit arena. It is prevalent on the larger commercial professional playing field as well. In the for-profit arena, the CNU has appropriated many of the principles originated, developed, proposed, and promoted by the architects and communities working in the original CDCs as their own creation—or at the very least, as its intellectual property. Of the fourteen principles "developed" for inner-city neighborhood design published in conjunction with the U.S. Department of Housing and Urban Development entitled *Principles for Inner City Neighborhood Design: Hope VI and the New Urbanism,* at least eight of the detailed definitions incorporate core objectives with little or no acknowledgment of the original CDCs: Safety and Civic Engagement, Economic Opportunity, Neighborhoods, Infill Development, City-wide and Regional Connections, Mixed Use, Dwelling as Mirror of Self, and, last but not least, Citizen and Community Involvement.[15] The CNU is just one more example of professional organizations that have become active in community development not necessarily out of any particular understanding of classic professional responsibility or even legitimate concern for the urban environment, but because funds have been made available for this type of work. The following passages from Dr. Richard K. Dozier and architect Charles Smith—who were both involved in the beginning of the CDC movement and have been connected to it in various ways over the last thirty-plus years—demonstrate that the profit motive has all but erased the African-American presence in an area that they pioneered. Dr. Dozier writes:

As the urban panacea programs developed with the new community participation aspects, communities soon realized that without technical resources, they had little, if any, effective input or control over their communities' development.... Few communities saw architecture and planning as effective means of voicing their concerns about their own control mechanisms. But architecture and planning were the vocabulary of the new 20-year, long-range planning documents presented to them by the local planning authorities. And in order to have input into these plans, the communities had to organize and acquire these skills—this new vocabulary. They readily learned that without technical expertise they were unable to develop alternate plans or negotiate effectively for changes in existing plans.... Thus, the need for a full-time community technical advocate developed.[16]

Unfortunately, while there has remained a need ever since, any effort to respond to that need on anything other than an ad-hoc basis had been dormant for at least a decade. It has currently reemerged with a sense of urgency, but now with a completely different face. Charles Smith, an original member of the Black Architect's Workshop formed in Chicago in the late 1960s, noted this phenomenon in a conversation with me in January 2001:

A good case in point. Public housing in Chicago is getting ready to go through a mass transformation, matter of fact, throughout the nation. There was an RFP [request for proposal] put out just recently which we submitted for. They're trying to select architectural firms or architects for community advocacy, so that, when the plans come before these advisory councils, they'll have some technical expertise on their staff who are being paid by, paid by the . . . ah . . . I think it is the MacArthur Foundation, that will allow them to have people there who can review those architectural drawings and development packages so they can understand what it is those people are saying they're gonna get when they tear down all their high-rises. And they need that technical expertise.

But there were no architects running around saying, "I'll volunteer for you ... I'll do this for you through the community design centers," so the MacArthur Foundation and groups like that had to put some monies there to make people get interested. Now the problem is, although we submitted over three weeks ago, we haven't heard one word, one way or another, whether or not we were selected.

The criteria is gonna be "who's making the selection?" And when they make the selection, how many African-Americans or minorities are gonna be selected to provide that kind of consultation, or are they gonna do the traditional thing, go right back to the status quo? ... And I suspect, just my suspicion again, because I haven't heard anything saying, we received your package, we're reviewing it, because they said to us that they needed to make ... a decision right away, that that's what's going on. I don't beg folks to hire me.[17]

Indeed.

Still, concerted efforts have been made for some time to address the textual and visual omissions, and there are indications that these efforts have not been in vain—that the tide may in fact be slowly but inexorably changing. Textually, the National Organization of Minority Architects (NOMA) has been in existence for over thirty years and, like the American Institute of Architects (AIA), has recently begun to publish its own professional journal. The Center for the Study of the Practice of Architecture has published two separate volumes of *The Directory of African American Architects*, identifying thousands of African-American architects registered to practice in this country. Several new works that focus on African-American architects and their work are being published, in addition to general books written by African-American scholars. *African American Architects: A Biographical Dictionary, 1865–1945*, edited by Dreck Wilson and Dr. Wesley Henderson, is an invaluable resource that I hope will become indispensable for survey courses around the country. Visually, the 2006 exhibit highlighting African and African-American architectural visionaries, "Architecture: Pyramids to Skyscrapers," was curated by Wilson at the Museum of Science and Industry in Chicago. In 2004, Studio Museum of Harlem curator Thelma Golden organized the exhibit "Harlemworld" and invited more than a dozen black architects to participate. It was the first such endeavor since the 1993 and 1994 traveling exhibits "Design Diaspora: Black Architects and International Architecture 1970–1990" curated by Carolyn Armenta Davis, and the "African American Architects and Builders" organized by the late Vinson McKenzie, respectively. These are believed to be the first major shows featuring African-American architects since the Harmon Foundation artist awards—which included the work of such African-American architects as Hilyard Robinson, Louis Bollinger, Paul Williams, and John Lewis Wilson—ended in the late 1960s. Finally, in the institutional realm, in what may be arguably the most significant event of the last few decades, at its 2006 general convention the AIA selected Marshall Purnell of the Washington, D.C., architectural firm Devrouax & Purnell as its president-elect. In an organization that expressly barred membership to African-American practitioners until 1923, Mr. Purnell will become the first African-American member to lead that organization in its 150 years of existence.

If the above shows anything, it is that caution must be exercised against confusing invisibility with an absence of presence; they are not the same thing. Despite conditions that have worked to obscure and in some cases erase all traces of their existence and achievements, African-American architects have been present for centuries, and in many cases they have thrived. As illustrated above, they've had a rich, if hidden, history in the study and practice of architecture and that history continues within the offices of Devrouax & Purnell, Stull and Lee, and the Freelon Group; as well as with sole practitioners Darryl Crosby & Melinda Palmore, Michael Willis, Jack Travis, and Walter Williams; in addition with practitioner/educators Nathaniel Belcher, Coleman A. Jordan, David Brown, Mabel O. Wilson,

Mohammed Lawal, and Darrell Fields—not to mention Walter Hood and J. Yolande Daniels, both recent recipients of the Rome Prize in design from the American Academy in Rome. Thus, in light of this briefest of accounts— believe me, I could go on—it should be clear to most reasonable people that the question "Are there any African-American architects? We can't find them" is empty of any credibility whatsoever. Any further use of it is disingenuous and indicative of something far less innocent than the simple ignorance the speaker would have one believe. If African-American architects indeed can't be found, it isn't because they don't exist. It's because you aren't looking, which, of course, logically leads to the next obstacle.

2. *A decided lack of opportunity to excel within majority-owned firms*—a belief that African-Americans are not readily qualified for advancement to the highly visible positions of power within the office, profession, and discipline.

If, as Kant argues, the artistic genius is *required* to eschew accepted rules, cannot be defined by objective means, and is *obliged* to top the previous design or designer, then the position of designer is by far the most prominent and powerful position in traditional professional practice. It is the position that most shapes both the face of the office and the form of the environment, and designers do this—are *required* to do this according to Kant— from a very subjective, personal, experiential position. What designers think of the world—and their/our position in it—is written on the landscape, frozen in time, and presented for consideration. As Kim Dovey writes in *Framing Places,* the will to form is the will to inform; that the motivation to build something is really about the desire to say something. This statement is critical here, because, subtle though it may be, the lack of confidence in the aesthetic sensibilities of African-American architects is really rooted in a concern about what a building designed by an architect of color might say; that what they might say through their work is inherently different and thus inherently inappropriate, if not inferior to what non–African-American architects might say—especially when it comes to highly visible projects. This belief is often masked in the question, "Don't you want the best for the project?" This seemingly innocent question embodies two very problematic, interconnected assumptions. The first is that it presumes the speaker knows what is best, and the second is that it takes for granted that the best cannot possibly be African-American. A stretch, you say? I think not.

As I have previously outlined, there are those who lay claim to being arbitrators and guardians of the high concepts of design and thus act as gatekeepers into that specialized realm. It isn't often that the gatekeepers—who commonly determine what is considered historically and culturally significant, in short, what is "best"—have been particularly interested in artistic forms of disparate cultural producers, at least not when produced from a disparate cultural perspective. Hegemony is the de facto order of the day, a hegemony defined and enforced by the gatekeepers; both art and artist must look the particular part as construed by this cultural elite. Certainly there are always exceptions, but often in such cases, the disparate is considered "other," if not "primitive," "raw," "vernacular," and the like—all terms that tend to solidify the hegemonic boundaries, not dissolve them. And if, as Dovey writes, "forms of domination, based in cultural capital, are [often] made to appear as pure aesthetic judgments,"[18] then seemingly benign claims to what is generally positioned as "best" are often very specific claims to "what *we* think is best," and what we think is best is always what makes us most comfortable. "Control of the arts is obviously control of culture," says J. Max Bond, a fellow in the American Institute of Architects and supervising architect of the World Trade Center Memorial. Where the artistic expression afforded by significant architectural commissions is positioned as the ultimate symbol of professional success, decisions made under the auspices of purely neutral aesthetic judgments often serve to enforce what Bond deems as "the right to rule, if you will";[19] the right to know better, the right to know what's "best." If what Dovey and Bond suggest is accurate, then that appropriated right is also the right to choose who will, and more important, who will not, succeed, ultimately expanding the notion of cultural imperialism to professional imperialism as well. Does the freedom and power to inform exist for people of color within the professional realm? Certainly. But, more to the point, is it available to African-Americans on an equal basis as their non–African-American counterparts, in the offices of the majority, or even in their own practices? Apparently not. This leads us to an additional problem: the problem of recognition.

As I have mentioned above, contrary to popular belief there are numerous African-American architects and firms that design and do it well. Unfortunately, this undeniably demonstrated truth is not generally acknowledged. As a case in point, in a city that has probably the longest history of African-American practitioners and perhaps the largest number of African-American registered architects in the United States, consider the 2002 comments by Benjamin Forgey, critic and columnist for the *Washington Post*:

> There are two reasons to celebrate Pepco's new headquarters building downtown. One is the architecture. With its boldly curved main facade of sparkling glass, the building does honor to its notable setting and kindles renewed respect for something often dismissed as a lost cause—the commercial glass box. The other reason is the architecture firm, Devrouax & Purnell, a 24-year-old Washington partnership. The building is a first for the firm, and also for the city —partners Paul Devrouax and Marshall Purnell had never before designed a downtown building here, and neither had anyone else of their race. Surprisingly—astonishingly—the Pepco headquarters is the first downtown building in this majority black city ever known to be designed by African American architects. Or, after all, maybe not so surprising. As slave labor, African Americans helped to build the White House, the Capitol and other major monuments of Washington architecture. As professionals, African American architects have managed to thrive in Washington for 100 years, despite the city's rigid segregation through much of the 20th century. But as the experience of Devrouax & Purnell and other black-owned firms attests,

in the architecture profession, segregation lasted well beyond the desegregation of public schools in the 1950s and the passage of the civil rights laws in the 1960s.[20]

Brad Grant offers us yet another example of this phenomenon:

> Ironically, for African American architects, their mainstream formal work becomes anonymous and is made invisible. For example, the architecture practice of distinguished African American architect John Moutoussamy was so invisible that even his design of the North Pier Towers was ignored in the architectural and planning community of Chicago. This forty-plus-story project is the largest tower next to Mies van der Rohe's Lake Shore Towers. In an architecturally sophisticated city, this seemingly controversial project received little attention, due in part, to the lack of attention afforded African American architects.[21]

Little is done to recognize and develop the rich resource African-Americans represent within the discipline. In fact, it is often just the opposite.[22] Practitioners of color, on a comprehensive scale, must daily contend with the reluctance of majority employers, past and present, to promote African-Americans to positions of representation within and without the firm simply due to perceptions of aesthetic acumen. This leads us to the last point I want to cover: where do these perceptions come from?

3. *Institutional bias, shown in a lack of recognition of architectural excellence as individual practitioners*—African-American (graduate) architects are typically only offered, and therefore left to accept, the majority of initial positions in the profession in the area of production technology. And there they typically remain.

> You can teach a man to draw a straight line ... and to copy any number of given lines or forms with admirable speed and perfect precision ... but if you ask him to think about any of those forms ... he

stops; his execution becomes hesitating ... he makes a mistake in the first touch he gives to his work as a thinking being. But you have made a man of him for all of that. He was only a machine before, an animated tool.... And observe, you are put to stern choice in this matter. You must either make a tool of the creature, or a man of him. You cannot do both.[23]

Through its efforts to limit liability, the areas that the profession is currently divesting itself of in its headlong pursuit of the big brass design ring are the areas labeled as production technology. It should come as no surprise that these are the very areas that have traditionally held the greatest opportunity for African-American entry into the profession *(although they have always been the most difficult positions, and perceptions, to shed).*

Partly because of the type of early training received from the Tuskegee model of industrial education, and partly because of the perception of the African-American in society, African-American architects historically have been allowed to demonstrate their ability in certain positions within the offices and the profession, but not in others.[24] W.E.B. Du Bois explains the objective of this particular educational direction so readily embraced by the principal academy for the study of architecture for the majority of African-Americans—our historically Black colleges and universities (HBCU) schools of architecture—as such:

> The industrial school founded itself, and rightly, upon the actual situation of American Negroes and said: "What can be done to change the situation?" And its answer was: "A training in technique and methods such as would incorporate the disadvantaged group into the industrial organization of the country."[25]

As a result of this early primary objective at HBCUs—where as recently as 2004, almost 20 percent of all African-Americans studying architecture were enrolled in the seven schools that provide architectural education—the perception of the majority of African-American architects has been limited to that historical view of their educational foundations,[26] adding credence that something other than one's educational institution—and its perceived standard of excellence—is at work in the assessment of one's skills, quite possibly the result of an "exercise [of] control through the manufacture of illusions about race and ethnic relations."[27]

Viewed through this ideological lens by educators, employers, and clients, African-Americans traditionally have found it immensely difficult to display their versatility within the constraints of majority architectural firms; they are habitually placed in the production technology areas as draftspersons, technical coordinators, and construction supervisors/administrators. Ironically, as more African-Americans enter the profession, these are the very areas that are now being divested from the term "architect," and shipped overseas. These conditions are even more exacerbated today by the production of more technical school graduates than the profession can absorb and the volatility of the economic cycle, which translates into more competition in the now devalued areas that have traditionally been an entry into architecture. All this, while the discipline of architecture, in definition and practice, is moving to embrace as its standard position in society—design and design development—the very area from which African-Americans have been traditionally shut out.[28]

University of Melbourne professor Paolo Tombesi places this whittling process into the much larger context of globalization.[29] He argues that the same process that has led to the post-industrial demise of manufacturing production in the United States and other industrialized nations—cheap skilled labor in developing countries—has now caught up to service production as well. He states that because of the "socially complex and uncertain environment of the building process, architects are required to produce, issue, and transfer design information at a constant pace,"[30] a pace that is almost always out of the control of architects. Tombesi argues that the lack of application autonomy—the fact that architecture's production is not only determined by a certain amount of fluidity and change that demands rapid responses, but also directly determines the application procedures and timelines of allied industries—has until recently required architectural production to be a localized industry. But no more. He points out that the advance of technology—and the overt acceptance of the U.N.-sanctioned globalization of service industries in general and design services in particular—has begun to rapidly decrease the necessity of such contextual and locational proximity. Through this now increasingly possible separation of the phases of the architectural process, the Cartesian separation of mind and body appears once again. This Cartesian dynamic has been described by former U.S. Secretary of Labor and Harvard professor Robert Reich in his influential book *The Work of Nations* as symbolic analysis—the abstract thinkers—and the routine producers—the task performers.[31] Here, Tombesi places that dynamic in architectural terms by arguing that the "intellectual labor" phase, the intangible commodities of conceptualization, creating, and problem-solving—and the people who do it—becomes the service marketed to the client, with the "physical labor" phase, the tangible commodities of drawings and other technical and physical materials—and those who produce them—are rendered solely "instruments at the service of the architect."[32]

With this separation, architecture, it seems, is on the move. It is heading to where the labor is cheapest, and it is riding the information highway to get there. While the exporting of services and administration of skills from afar is not new to the architectural profession, it has been rare. Now, it is poised to become the norm.

The existence of sharp wage differences casts a broader light on the global trade of professional services, suggesting an altered future relationship between work and labor. The access to foreign professional markets gives firms not only the opportunity to export services to these markets, but also to import, if necessary, the work of cheaper labor resources.[33]

This produces the painful dichotomy of more people of color in the *making* of architecture but not in the *creating* of "architecture"—the intellectual component *(of which the apex is design)*, at least for the time being. Tombesi seems to suggest that eventually, the economies of scale will tip the balance of power to those locations that can produce world-class work *(having been educated in the universities of the United States and Europe)* but for a fraction of the cost *(labor being cheaper than that of the developed world)*, which may indeed be true, but I am forced to ask, what will the nature of practice be by the time this sea change occurs and where, if anywhere, will African-American practitioners fit in?

Granted, we could—and should—look at this as an opportunity to begin on the ground floor, already at the table, for the development of these new, or specialized fields that support the architectural profession. And I surely expect that some of the largest construction management firms, interior design firms, and the like will either be started by or employ many African-Americans in the future. But we should not ignore the larger issue that if this process continues unchecked, those people who have been trained as architects, call themselves architects, and in fact have licenses will, in fact, not be practicing what is being increasingly narrowly defined as architecture—design services. If architecture—as it is currently being narrowed down to—is defined by design only, then it is clear that for the most part, design is becoming even more, both in perception and practice, the province of white architects, not only in the United States but the world over. Despite evidence that African-American practitioners design and do it well, architect Harvey Gantt has argued, *"Everyday our competence is on the line,"*[34] when it is considered at all.

Certainly, poised as we are at the dawning of this new era, African-American architects may be able to overcome, sidestep, and otherwise maneuver around this disturbing trend, and I have listed just a few ways that they have already begun to do so. Further, some, through an integration of the practice of architecture with the various disciplines and professions significantly utilized by current society, may even be able to use this shift in position to their immediate and long-term advantage. To those people I say: Well done! for they have seen the future and have decided that they will be more than a part, but a player. But, for the next generation of African-American architects, particularly the ones being educated at the HBCUs, what does this trend mean for their career opportunities?

For the students at many HBCUs, the fact that the technically proficient attitude has persisted until quite recently at some institutions and continues at others does not bode well for preparation in the areas that may remain open in the profession in the near future. Students at majority schools face their own peculiar set of problems.[35] So what do we have? An established base of African-American practitioners who are slowly being relegated to the past, maneuvered to the nether regions of the architectural profession, and a new generation of African-American architects being trained in areas of the profession that may not even BE PART of the profession when they graduate, competing for positions that are becoming scarce with the proliferation of trade schools *(drafting, CAD)* and two-year colleges *(drafting, architectural technology)* in the United States, the emergence of both the means *(technology, educated work force)* and the opportunity *(trade agreements in and between developing countries)* to transfer architectural services abroad, a suspect, ever-changing economic base, and a less-than-accepting professional and market mentality. Overall this is not an encouraging picture for the future of African-Americans in what is narrowly being defined as the practice of architecture.

Remix

Okay, that knowledge dropped in the last chapter comes full circle here. 'Cause cash moves everything around us, it is necessary to protect everyone's access to some forms of knowledge, so that those that ain't got don't get too got by those that do got. Got that? For example, it would be some bogus shit for doctors to only work for the rich and let the poor die 'cause they low on funds. Same with lawyers. But, what is the incentive for doctors and lawyers to do that, when they can keep gettin' paid? What do the rest of society have to bring to the table? Doctors and lawyers weren't tryin' to hear what the rest of society was rappin' 'bout. They were like *"Show me the bling, bling, dig? Otherwise, step off."*

Now, society didn't have the kinda pockets to pay for every-damn-body every-damn-time, but since society makes every-damn-law, it could, if it wanted, make being a "doctor" so damn hard that it damn sure wouldn't be worth a damn to try. But that wouldn't help anyone, rich or poor. So, instead, they did this: In exchange for treating everyone equally, we will grant a special status and profitable privilege—the status of "profession(al)" upon your skills, so only you and people like you can get paid doin' this shit. Wid' this kinda street cred, you get to say *who, when, how, and why somebody shall, and shall not, become a professional,* without any interference from us. In essence, y'all can do what 'cha like—and we won't f—— wid' you. But, in exchange, y'all gotta' watch our back and *protect our common interests as a society. Na, that means all of us—regardless of gender, race, creed, ethnicity and economic or social status—can get y'alls knowledge and skills when in need.* So, in essence, being a professional is a contract between the profession and society. We get some shit, you get some shit. Dig?

Okay, so basically a profession is a gig in a special area that requires some deep knowledge, yo. So fo' example, mechanical engineering is a profession, but plumbing is not. You need a degree for one and a plunger for the other *(although both require some kind of license. Check that.).* Which means if you cop yo' knowledge from any place other than a college, university, or institute—that's yo' ass, because becoming a professional is damn near impossible. *(You dig how that eliminates some of the most informative—and accessible—universities in the world: the 'hood or street [or corner, if you are an old head]. Slick, huh?)* So college *(which ain't always an option)* is still indispensable to the process of becoming a professional, meaning that it ain't only *what* you learn, but *where* you learn it.

If you have the status of being a "professional," it means you been to school, you know some shit not everybody knows and that you won't front on the peeps who need yo' skills. Architects claim to be professionals, just like doctors and lawyers, arguin' that the primary set of skills—their off-the-hook design abilities—is what sets them apart from bogus folk. While it ain't never been all they could do, it seems to be all they want to do. In fact, they frontin', sleepin' on the peeps and not holding up their end of the contract—sellin' out to the highest bidder, yo, and then do their bidding—regardless of whether it f——ks up a part of society or not. For example, if only the privileged few *(rich people, corporations and shit)* have to access the architect's skills and other folk *(broke, poor and strugglin')* keep get played by both the bling AND those whose 'posed to have their backs, how can architects argue that they holding up their end of the agreement? Soon somebody is gonna figure that shit out and decide that this contract is whack. They gonna null and void it. I mean, if you get sick, you go to the doctor. If you get in trouble, you hire a lawyer. But if you need something built, who you gonna call? Ghostbusters?

So check it. Folk think architects are frontin' on their duty, asking, if they just gonna work for the tiny group of the richest people, why architects shouldn't just be called out and jacked. Instead of just beatin' their ass, folks just say "F—— 'em" and get 'round them as much as possible in the building process. So what does that mean to Black folk wid' these mad design skills? Where do the brothas and the sistas fit into all of this esoteric shit? I'm na break ya off some.

Gettin' high: Who the hell are you?

First of all—Black folk ain't separate from what happens to architects and architecture in general. If the public is punkin' architects, they are punkin' Black ones even more. Most people—architects included—don't know Black folk have been doin' this shit—and doin' it well—for hundreds of years. If firms are surprised to see a Black face, they may think you are a novelty—and may not be interested in taking a chance on your skills—considerable though they may be. And it makes sense that if potential clients don't know you exist, they can't flip on your mad skills either.

Gettin' hired: Where the hell you think you're goin'?

From the moment you step off in an architectural school, you are told that design is the most important thing. It ain't that big a leap to figure that designers are the shit. Architects front on folks—clients, students, and the public—like this all the time. Design is the end-all and be-all of architecture and if you ain't designin' then you ain't livin'. So, of course, this is what everybody who studies architecture wants to do. Live and live large, baby. But Black folks might find it not as simple as all that. As Black folk have no "history" in this field—no evidence of Black architects' ever designing anything of note *(which of course is the bullshit)*—they are typically given work that don't require a lot of creative thinkin', just a whole lotta supervisin'. Despite the fact that in every artistic field in the United States—from music and fashion, to product and automobile, to visual and literary—the abilities of Black folk to create some off-the-hook shit is obvious, Black architects are always under scrutiny. They are typically assigned work that can be checked "objectively." They sweat a brotha (and sista) majorly.

Gettin' higher: What 'cha got that I need?

In the past, if you wanted work in a firm, "the (draftin') boards" was where you'd slide into an office, but for brothas and sistas, it was also the hardest to slide out of. But now that the profession is movin' away from the production technology—sending out work, hiring strictly CAD operators, and shit—it is even harder to get 'cha foot in the door. Na I know you sayin' that happens to all interns, and you right. But it doesn't happen the same way and it don't last as long as it does for brothas and sistas. You can't tell me that that is just a coincidence without bustin' a gut laughin'. I know it. So now what?

So, dig, it all breaks down to this: Society got this beef wid' architecture because:

- They think architects just look after the interests of the rich
- They wonder what architects provide particularly when the building process seems to manage quite fine without 'em

Such a public perspective puts the entire profession in a difficult spot and that spot dogs Black architects and offices even more. But it don't stop there for the brothas and sistas. There is also that internal shit posed by a professional perspective that:

- Refuses to acknowledge that Black architects do this shit too—have for years—and do it well
- Resists hiring any intern, but particularly Black interns (for questionable reasons), for a design position in an office
- Is becoming less interested in being responsible for the production technology aspect of professional services and when it is, it is easier—and more economical—to hire people who do just that, which makes it harder for Black interns to get hired

For brothas and sistas, being pressed from all sides cannot be good for yo' pockets or yo' soul.

Precis

PART I IS CONCERNED WITH conditions of permanence—both real and illusionary. Over the past three chapters I have striven to illustrate several critical things. First, space is fundamental to how we see, shape, and interact with/in the world. Within it, our economic, political, social, and aesthetic values are revealed and as such space plays a critical part in how we see ourselves and construct our identities and our lives. To say I am an American or a Detroiter is to call on, answer to, and wear a particular identity that incorporates specific spatial, place-based characteristics and attributes for the individual and for those who interact with the individual. But space is not neutral. How we see, experience, replicate, and deploy it is constructed and contested. At present, space is naturalized in ways that are—in varying degrees—problematic for anyone who is not white and male. The further you are away from that standard, the worse off you are; the less space is unbiased. This rather bleak assessment is born out of the American notion of space as a right, as property, as a part of being and identity. It is a claim that is invested in and ultimately positions *whiteness* as a transparent, readily accepted requirement for spatial construction in our society.

Second, the study and practice of architecture is not separate from the world at large. It is situated in a system that creates hierarchies and it is foolish to think that architecture would be exempt from such influences. The above racialized and naturalized spatial hierarchy invariably finds its way into the educational paradigm of the discipline of architecture and it is thus taught and replicated in the studio, producing both practitioners and educators who act in the world to maintain the status quo; a status quo that is at once classist, biased, and elitist. This condition has led Ralph Wiley to conclude that, as a result of how they were educated in schools and universities, most white people cannot see African-Americans the same way they see themselves. Architects are taught to produce and perpetuate our built environment based on this normative spatial framework. Thus, this dominant spatial perspective is embedded in the built environment and as such it seeps uncritically into academia in general and architecture specifically. Such unchecked absorption serves to perpetuate the problematic spatial organization by positioning it as normal and inevitable—in the environment, in the curriculum, and also in the interpersonal dynamics between educators, colleagues, and students.

Finally, any study and practice of architecture operating in this paradigm is doomed to (re)create spaces that are colonial in their hegemony and reflective of oppressive power structures; racist in their origin and manifestation, if not necessarily in their intent. The academy is just the initial site of the formal indoctrination. This willful ignorance finds its final home in the professional arena, where it manifests itself in a myriad of ways—from the number of African-American architects to their positions within majority offices, types of work accessible to black-owned firms—all of which works to mask this exclusion under the auspices of a natural occurrence, allowing the discipline to ignore how it is complicit in its operation, an ignorance that actually perpetuates this natural occurrence. The next section, "Architecture as a Verb," is concerned with conditions of transformation and will offer alternatives to this current state.

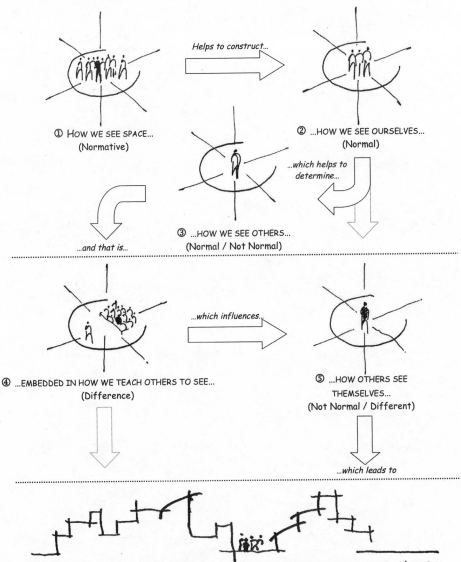

① HOW WE SEE SPACE...
(Normative)

Helps to construct...

② ...HOW WE SEE OURSELVES...
(Normal)

...which helps to determine...

...and that is...

③ ...HOW WE SEE OTHERS...
(Normal / Not Normal)

④ ...EMBEDDED IN HOW WE TEACH OTHERS TO SEE...
(Difference)

...which influences...

⑤ ...HOW OTHERS SEE THEMSELVES...
(Not Normal / Different)

...which leads to

⑥ ...HOW WE ACT AND PRACTICE IN THE WORLD, REINFORCING THE UNDERLYING PREMISE OF LOCKEAN SPACE, PLACE, AND PROPERTY -- DIFFERENCE -- WHICH ASSUMES "WHITENESS" AS THE NORMATIVE BASE

Figure 4.

Architecture as a Verb

verb (n) — a word used to show that
an action is taking place, or to indicate
the existence of a state or condition.

4 Space—Action

> The formulation of flexible strategies, the ability to move to
> and fro between positions . . . which intersect the architect's
> distanced, panoptic view of the site with the view from the
> ground, have opened up an understanding of place which is
> revelatory for both clients and planners.
> —*Hannah le Roux*

AS PREVIOUSLY OBSERVED, architect and former MIT professor
Bill Hubbard, Jr., has noted that "when social structures give the lie to what
a society says it believes, then architecture gets used as a tool in the management of the conflict."[1] Given the wealth of evidence in the built environment
that supports Hubbard's statement, one can argue that architecture as a management of conflict can, in truth, be read as a management of the conflict
of color. I am interested in how Black identity is formed in a system where
spatial and cultural dichotomies manifest themselves with a particularly cal-
lous disregard in the built environment for those considered "powerless."
It is important for my project to explore this avenue of analysis, because I
believe the development of cultural and spatial practices that might support
and strengthen the identities of marginalized people in cities—where the
spatial dichotomy starkly highlights the gulf between the ideals, representations, and realities of living in America—is key to the future development of
the architectural profession. I therefore begin this analysis by revisiting that
most fundamental building block of both architecture and identity: space.

I began this investigation by positing that the parameters of space proposed by Locke are not the only senses that can be used to determine a

relationship to spatial elements. Recalling his spatial dependence on sight and touch discussed in the notes to chapter 1, I wonder if it is not also possible to determine a position within a space—a "place"—by employing sound to touch what you may not physically touch. In fact, I argue that to recall Locke's terms, for the *"Man"* in the *"Dark,"* sound is as efficient, if not more so, than touch as a generator of an *"Idea of Space."* It follows that if Man's position within a space is not discernible by sight, it is probably much more discernible by sound than touch, particularly if the relational elements necessary to determine Lockean space are no small distance away. At the very least, in addition to sight and touch, sound is completely capable of discerning a Lockean idea of space. But the construction of sound and its place in spatial production is an issue that the concept of space as defined by Locke does not sufficiently address.

Why do I focus on sound? First, like sight and touch, this sense is of-

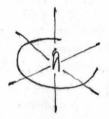

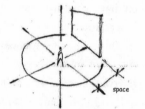

Space preexists.

Space is interrupted by objects. The location of the objects is called "place."

We employ sight and/or touch to gain knowledge of space.

Space can be perceived through the relation of a minimum of two points or places.

Sound can also be used to gain knowledge of space.

Sound can determine the location of one place relative to another.

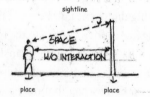

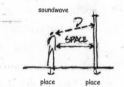

Figure 5. Lockean space with the consideration of sound added.

ten employed to locate oneself in the world. Second, like space, it is theoretically all around and thus infinitely accessible. Third—and most important—sound is not restricted to Lockean constructions of space in the same manner as sight and touch. It is capable of transcending Lockean limitations and perhaps their *whiteness* as well. The construction of sound and its place in spatial production presents us with an element that can enhance the fossilized concept of Lockean space and may help to counter the inherent *whiteness* of our current spatial understanding.

So, if Locke's formation of space is shown to be incomplete in its theoretical framework because of its, let's say ... deafness, might there be a theory or theories of space that can incorporate sound into its structure and, if so, might there be other ways not included in Lockean space to validate identity? There are several spatial theories that take issue with Locke that you can review at your leisure; I shall focus on three that, taken together, are most germane to my project.

In his book *The Production of Space,* French theorist Henri Lefebvre argues for a social, rather than Locke's abstract, construction of space. Where Locke sees space as omnipresent, Lefebvre posits that space is a social product, that "spaces are produced."[2] For Lefebvre, space is experienced by people intersecting, interacting, producing, and reproducing relationships to and with each other, a phenomenon that he refers to as social space.[3] Social space, as defined by Lefebvre, is both the interaction and what is created by the interaction, and can be understood as the social activities that occur in a particular time and place that constitute—and are *specific* to—the establishment of a particular way of life. These social activities—what Lefebvre identifies as the group's *spatial practices*—facilitate the production and reproduction of both the *place* and the *characteristics* of the spatial relationships of any particularly defined group of people. Lefebvre's space has a history, a past, and is reciprocal—it is *created by* but also helps *to create* social interaction. It is a form of performed communication, a spatial practice that can be observed, repeated, and remembered. Thus space is, in the words of de Certeau, a "practiced" place.

Lefebvre's notion of space directly calls into question the authority and ideology of a definitive, fixed use of space and the notion of an essentialized identity shorn of any liberating symbolic, linguistic, or historical dialectic with the subject—as represented by spaces that emerge from a Lockean paradigm. Lefebvre's notion of space facilitates identity construction through an ensemble of people interacting: elements engaged in the story *(who we are)* and performance *(how we represent ourselves)* of identity construction. The polar opposite of Lockean notions of space, for Lefebvre, space is where *something* occurs. Put another way, where Locke argues that space is not body, and thus interrupts space, Lefebvre sees space *as* body to a great degree, since space requires bodies to construct it. Thus for Lefebvre, both space and identity not only become specific to a time, place, and social formation (the making), but also become historical—they have a memory, a past (the making before). Lefebvre space is the space of the revolutionary, not because it comes out of a Marxist tradition nor because Lefebvre identi-

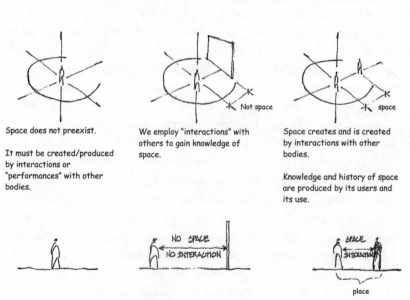

Space does not preexist.

It must be created/produced by interactions or "performances" with other bodies.

We employ "interactions" with others to gain knowledge of space.

Space creates and is created by interactions with other bodies.

Knowledge and history of space are produced by its users and its use.

Figure 6. Sketch of Lefebvre's space.

fies over three dozen types of spaces, but because at its most basic level, it is about the ability and power of the subject to recognize, create, sustain, traverse, appropriate, and control space for one's own purpose. Lefebvre provides a manner for completely different spatial thinking; thinking that is outside the boundaries of Locke's spatial paradigm.

Both expanding and complicating Lefebvre's understanding of space is Michel Foucault. He expands Lefebvre's spatial theory by positioning the social construction of space on a larger scale. He sees space as being created by relations between diverse sites, where each site is in turn defined by the social interactions that exist within it individually. As he states:

> Our epoch is one in which space takes for us the form of relations among sites.... [W]e live inside a set of relations that delineate sites which are irreducible to one another and absolutely not superimposable upon one another.[4]

However, Foucault, in expanding Lefebvre, complicates him greatly by arguing that the sites are irreducible and not superimposable upon one another, which would preclude the opportunity for any type of interaction—or performance—between sites, and brings into question just what relationships are being conducted. Foucault posits that there are sites constructed by society that are made specifically for the purpose of linking irreducible sites. These sites are spaces of performed interactive communication. In these links—which Foucault introduces as *"heterotopias"*—all of the sites of the society come together.

> There are also, in every culture, in every civilization, real places—places that do exist and that are formed in the very founding of society—which are something like counter-sites, a kind of effectively enacted utopia in which the real sites, all the other real sites that can be found within the culture, are simultaneously represented, contested, and inverted.[5]

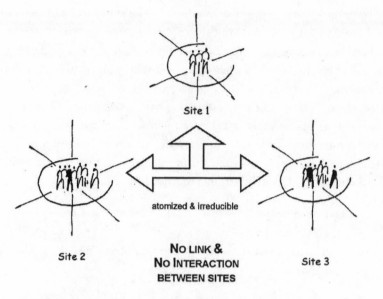

Figure 7. Foucault's heterotopian spatial framework, showing his sites of contest.

As theorized by Foucault, these heterotopias are classified as two types—crisis and deviant. The crisis heterotopias are described as "forbidden places, reserved for individuals who are, in relation to society and to the human environment in which they live, in a state of crisis: adolescents, menstruating women, pregnant women, the elderly, etc."[6] Crisis heterotopias can, then, be described as "temporary" sites, temporal in nature. Deviant heterotopias, on the other hand, are described as places in which "individuals whose behavior is deviant in relation to the required mean or norm are placed. Cases of this are rest homes, psychiatric hospitals, and of course prisons," and are more spatial in nature.[7] With this thesis, Foucault provides a useful manner in which to understand the relationships not only *within* individual sites, but *between* individual sites as well. It follows that if there is to be a link between these sites, there must be some type of interaction—some *performance*—between each site.

I will return to Foucault's heterotopias later, but for the moment it is important to understand that by their internal relations within sites, their external links to other sites, and as places where less than positive interactions take place, in addition to the spatial marginalization and assigned identities they authorize, Foucault is describing the current built environmental conditions of many sites in the United States and other countries as well.

Building on the premise that space is a social construct, hooks conceives of space from a position of marginality. She sees the margin as a homeplace, a place of radical openness. A leftover space, a neglected or secondary space, the margin is always held in relation to the center—by way of its position *(center/margin)* and its composition *(center/margin = whole)*. It is both unwanted and necessary. But, as hooks argues, it is also a space where the marginalized are free to be not the intruder, the interloper, the exotic other *(as when invited into the center)*, but the standard, the norm, the model by which all *other* things are judged.

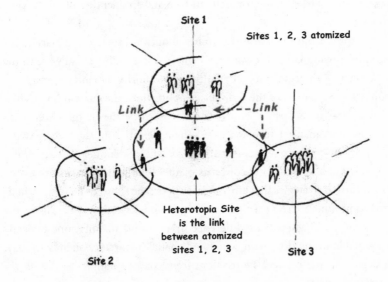

Figure 8. Foucault's crisis/deviant heterotopias link atomized and irreducible sites that are created by structural domination.

She argues that this dichotomy—A/Not A—has to be accepted, adapted, and employed because it has power. The Not A position is the space of resistance and the space of critique. For hooks, the banishment to the margin is appropriated—and altered—by the subject choosing the margins. The margin can be either a space of oppression or resistance. By choosing the margin to create a homeplace that enables and promotes ever-changing perspectives, one can begin the process of nurturing the ability to resist domination, marginalization, and erasure. As a space that allows visions both inside out and outside in, it can create a place to hold onto the "downhome" while seeking new knowledge and developing alternatives to cultural exploitation. As space that is continuously formed on the edges of spatial domination, and a space that is chosen specifically for that reason, hooks takes Foucault's notions of heterotopias and adds the possibility of agency to his spatial formation, seeing them as sites of activism and empowerment—a space where one can resist having identity thrust upon oneself and create an identity of one's own choosing.

To speak from the margins is to invite outward toward the margin, instead of moving inward toward the center, and is a direct challenge to the legitimacy of the center to act as ultimate authority. For hooks, space requires a reevaluation of the differences upon which the current hierarchies of social relationships are constructed, to provide the marginalized with the means to manufacture and assert their identities. In the face of structures of power that operate, in part, by assigning identities that legitimize the political and economic concerns of the dominant class/culture as the norm, spatial strategies that affirm and support the subjectivity of marginalized communities are a political necessity. In hooks's view, space allows the marginalized to assert their difference in a positive manner, one typically unavailable in the dominant social and spatial hierarchies already in play. Instead of being offered the freedom *from* color (*Ignore it; we are all the same under the skin—white*) at the beneficence of the dominant culture, this space provides the freedom *of* color (*Show it; my color is an essential part of who I am and cannot be used against me)* by positioning the marginalized as the determinant of the spatial and social hierarchy. We will now turn our attention to how, taken collectively, this gang of three challenge Locke's grip on space.

The active creation of space and a challenging of place

Herbert Muschamp, architectural critic of the *New York Times,* has noted that "[s]ince cultural values tend to coax up their opposites, a space dedicated to harmony and independence can easily become a battlefield."[8] This is a useful consideration when positing an alternative way to think about our understanding of, and relationship to, space. Those same boundaries theorized by Locke as marking the end of something can also, when considered from other perspectives, simultaneously mark the *initiation* of something. In this manner, bodies can be alternatively understood as not where space ends, but where space *begins.* What *begins* here is the *active creation of space* and a *challenging of place* that is fixed in time, for all time, empty or undisturbed. This challenge of space and place is fueled by the realization of both as not *preexisting*—like a condition—but as *created*—like a collage—by the interaction of people.

From a Western spatial perspective, bodies *end* space. They define boundaries as a termination of something. A particularly bleak way of perceiving bodies, this is in fact atypical of what the body actually does. The *end* that is so embedded in Locke's space is an extremely static—if not malignant—notion of the body. These *end* bodies can only be realized in the ideal where they can truly end—thus the "deadness" of Lockean space. In reality, in lieu of a body that will not cooperate, symbolic spatial substitutes become idealized. From the gridded organization of the colonial city of the past, to the signature structures of the corporate city of the present, to the delusionary nostalgia of the celebration city of the future, these are the *white ends* of space that saturate and define the majority of the physical environment. But, as Muschamp pointed out, a paradox is also at work, the *initiation* of something. This notion of space—this respect for the body—is theorized and demonstrated by the spatial practices of marginalized communities—particularly African-American communities. In a continuation and transference of the diasporic struggle to rescue the Black *subject* for the Negro *object*[9]—particularly in spaces that represent an erasure of their identity and, concomitantly, the presence of repressive white male power—what *begins* here is the *active creation of space* and a *challenging of place* that is fixed, left over, or undisturbed. This challenge of space and place is fueled by the realization of both as *actualized* by bodies that interact. This *other* space is antithetical to the anti-body, dead space that Locke theorizes, resisting its hegemony and exposing as questionable the proclamation that *"Space is not Body."* It is a space that is not fixed by dead bodies; it is alive, and it is mobile. It moves when its creators move, sways when they sway, and leaves traces on whatever it touches. It is a space in motion, a space that is transformative, transferable, woven.

For understanding the African-American condition, space as motion is an important concept to consider. Frequently noted elsewhere, African-Americans have historically been required to employ whatever means available to them to transform space in a strategy for simple survival. Understanding space as something created by social interactions is a radically different view of space—particularly urban spaces—than the one currently being employed in the built environment and affords designers an alternative framework to thinking about their work that can be employed to validate African-Americans in space. This kind of spatial paradigm—*which sees people as the primary, necessary element in the creation of space, both public and private*—allows for unfettered spatial access, rather than the current understanding and justification of spatial bifurcation, hierarchies, and ultimately segregation.

As I have previously stated, the spatially perpetuated falsehood that African-American lives are environmentally predetermined encourages behavior that reinforces these false realities, and it must be challenged. Lefebvrean spatial thinking transforms—literally gives an*other* meaning to—the symbols of Locke's space. This space reveals the environment as not immutable, and with that realization urban communities immediately become *spaces of possibilities,* not predetermined holding pens for the urban unfortunate; this space hints at the possibility of breaking free from an all too long-standing—and too limiting—battle that arises in many African-American communities over the ownership of corners, blocks, and neighborhoods.

Let us return to my earlier discussion about Foucault's heterotopias. While Foucault offers us a useful starting point, his thinking about heterotopias seems incomplete as a useful tool for spatial understanding. In fact, if we are not careful, the existence of heterotopias could be understood to undermine any liberating potential they may have for Black identity formation because, in providing only crisis and deviant categories of heterotopian spaces, Foucault does three potentially problematic things. First, he positions the possibility of social exchange as extremely limited, being created and linked only by sites that are, if not entirely undesirable, certainly extremely harsh. Second, understood as spaces where one is "assigned" by authorities, Foucault's heterotopias are as spaces of non-choice, of non-agency. And third, his theory situates the temporal and the physical aspects of these sites of linkage as separate, all of which serve to support the order of the larger society, as determined by those whom that order supports. Foucault has positioned his heterotopian links and the spaces of the urban environment—as juxtaposed against the sub-urban—as similar occurrences, essentially identical. And here lies the crux of the problem: As places of crisis and deviance, Foucault fails to see—along with most urbanists—anything other than bleak possibilities for the urban environment. They are places to clear (urban renewal), to fear (racial/spatial profiling), to manage (redlining) until they can be made desirable again (gentrification/white inflight). If we are to employ heterotopian thinking for Black identity formation, then these three things will have to be overcome.

I posit that there is another type of heterotopian link that can be theorized; one not limited to the elements fossilized by Foucault; one that combines Lefebvre's spatial production, bell hooks's notion of marginality as a space of power, the legacy of Black town spatial politics and binds them all together with the notion of sound.[10] This manner is predicated on a notion of the urban location as an ever-changing constant that is most readily visible and expertly navigated by what we have come to know in America, and increasingly around the world, as hip hop.

Why is hip hop culture, you ask, so essential to the new urbanist? Check it. Hip hop culture in general, and rap music in particular, has come to massively influence American society. From Def Jam to Bad Boy, Cross Colors to Kani, FuBu to Phat Farm, Jean-Michel Basquiat to Fab Five Freddy, hip hop is the driving force behind American music, fashion, and culture and is fast becoming a global influence as well. According to musical and cultural scholars, hip hop—an African-American and Afro-Caribbean youth culture composed of graffiti, breakdancing, and rap music—began in the mid-1970s in the South Bronx in New York City, in response to a particular postindustrial moment that saw the detrimental confluence of spatial, economic, and political urban influences. The land use practices of city planners, real estate developers, and financiers contributed to the creation of overcrowded and deteriorated housing conditions, inflated rents, landlord neglect, abandonment of buildings, and the curtailment of municipal services. This was paired with the relocation of high-paying unionized factory jobs to the suburbs and no means of transportation to get to the relocated employment. These factors, among several others, were critical in the formation of inner-city black ghettos.[11] Decay, disinterest, disinvestment, and disempowerment: these are the foundations upon which the hip hop nation has been constructed. Hip hop's central forms developed not only in relation to one another but also in relation to the larger society, and from the outset have articulated the pleasures and problems of black urban life in contemporary America.[12] The purveyors of this hip hop culture have taken something essentially powerless and made it powerful. These spaces are particularly urban, observable in the spatial practices of hip hop material culture, and, for lack of a better term, I will call them celebratory heterotopias.

Celebratory heterotopias are created by spatial practices that challenge

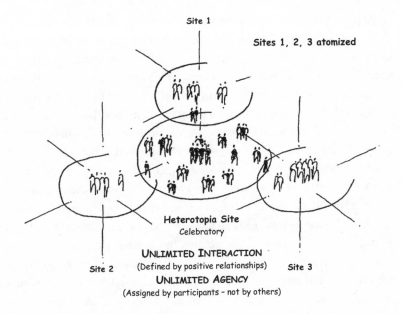

Figure 9. Celebratory heterotopias link atomized and irreducible sites and contest structural domination.

the very limitations and boundaries of crisis/deviant definitions. The relations that construct the celebratory contest constantly work and rework the very authority of these particular categorizations, in the process appropriating and palimpsestically altering dominant spatial understandings. The performed communication of the celebratory challenges the dominant spatial paradigm's essentializing ideology and questions its appropriateness as a "universal" aesthetic by demonstrating that alternate relations can be created. As such, it follows that alternate spaces—and heterotopias—can also be created. Unlike crisis/deviant heterotopias, participation in celebratory heterotopias is a decision made by the participants themselves, for themselves, echoing hooks's "choosing the space of the margin" argument. Participants consciously choose celebratory heterotopias precisely because of their marginal nature and appropriate them as part of an overall strategy of challenge, change, and spatial evolution. While this choice is partly a reaction to social marginality and the threat of being placed in the restrictive crisis/deviant heterotopias, it remains an exercise in self-determination—even if it is seen only as a mode of survival. The authority—to be assigned to another heterotopia, to be spatially marginalized, to be named—is challenged and defied, a demonstration of agency in its most basic form.

In this space, agency is a prerequisite and the relationships that construct the space are entered into freely and are influenced collectively. It is my assertion that the celebratory is a place where the challenge to cultural—and subsequent spatial—alienation produces a euphoric, empowered subject as opposed to the melancholic ones sentenced to crisis/deviant spaces. These celebratory heterotopias do more than celebrate—they cultivate, and from these spaces emerges a subject that has constructed an advantageous (counter)identity, heretofore unavailable within Foucault's spaces. Celebratory heterotopias are at once both spatial and temporal, temporary and permanent. These social activities facilitate the production and reproduction of both the place and the characteristics of the spatial relationships of any particularly defined group of people.[13]

Employing a celebratory understanding of space, the identity strategies used by African-Americans are specific to a time, place, and social formation, but are also historical—they have a memory, a past, albeit a sometimes forgotten past. As Paul Gilroy notes, "[I]dentity is fleetingly experienced in the most intensive ways and sometimes socially reproduced by means of neglected modes of signifying practices like mimesis, gestures, kinesis, and costume."[14]

In a decidedly proactive manner, this space became one of resistance. The currently employed notion of space, so hostile to the body of African-Americans, the illogical spatial and political marginalization that places them in the panoptic space of Foucault by an overdetermined exercise of power to monitor their Ellisonian existence, is transformed in the most profound sense into what Goldberg calls "a place of peace, of shelter from care, doubt

and division, a geography of relative self determination and sanctity."[15] This
place of peace calls into question the authority and ideology of a definitive,
fixed use of space[16] and the notion of an essentialized identity that is shorn
of any liberating symbolic, linguistic, or historical dialectic with the subject. Space becomes a site where differences are not fossilized, but actively
negotiated. *It tells a new story*, a story read through the dialectical spatial
practices of African-Americans, in an entirely different pedestrian speech
creating spaces other than what is presently known through proxies. It is a
performance that resists imposed definitions of the "proper" use, opening
up "spaces of possibility where the future can be imagined differently."[17]
Specifically for African-Americans, celebratory heterotopias reject any hegemonic spatial manipulations that impose historically oppressive conditions based on the systematic devaluation and erasure of Africentric subjectivity and history. The deployment of celebratory heterotopias in support of
African-American identity construction is really about *a way of being*.[18] This
"other" space has as an oppositional teleology: the reappropriation of urban
space and the liberating redistribution of bodies within it. In the dominant
spatial condition, where whiteness has become *the* signifier for desirability,
the *other* space situates the "affirmation of Black cultural differences as . . . a
starting point for self development."[19] Clearly, this space is a cause for concern because its construction and recognition is not advantageous to what
is currently offered for *(white)* identity construction. For example, white
men are understood in our nationalist culture as the natural hero, while
Black men are positioned similarly as the natural enemy. While it is obvious that both groups share common traits and even goals and aspirations,
surprise and concern is raised when Black men attempt to mobilize theirs.
Such measures seem to "underline [their] difference from . . . white [men]
by presupposing [their] natural aggression."[20]

Fanon once wrote that "[s]ince the other hesitated to recognize me,
there remained only one solution: to make myself known,"[21] and it is in that
spirit that these spatial practices are employed: to remove the peripheral

from Lockean space and make visible the transparent, requiring a different, long-forgotten manner in which to employ space; to respect and empower Black bodies; to employ Black bodies in strategies that create spaces that are transferable and transportable—spaces that affirm the identity of their users, that are in fact dependent on that identity; and to affirm that space does not have to be determined by the deconstructive symbols of power that surround many urban environments—the symbols of neglect that scream *"See ya, wouldn't wanna be ya,"* revealing the ultimate homage to Locke: leftover spaces filled with leftover (Black) bodies that stay forever in their place. The spatial practices made available by the creation of this *other* space palimpsestically transform the symbols of Locke's space. The notion that Black is no longer fossilized as a body that *ends,* but as one that *begins,* exposes the lie that their environment is unseemly, wholly without merit, contumacious, and, of course, inevitable; that they are destined to live where the physical, emotional, and intellectual remnants of this nationalist culture's civil disturbances coalesce to convince them that their lives are environmentally predetermined; and that they are required to live their lives based on false realities. The *other* space created illustrates that space and community are not immutable and, with that realization, urban communities immediately become hooks's spaces of possibilities, not predetermined holding pens for the urban unfortunate.

If we understand the *other* space to be a space created by social interactions that link sites located in the urban environment, then we take a radically different view of space—particularly urban spaces—than the one currently being employed in the built environment. We have a way to perceive urban space from a different perspective; one that considers the *other* space as the primary space, as the essential link in the urban fabric, which affords designers an alternative framework to thinking about their design. The tendency to see space as undisturbed—as Locke would have us believe—misses the point. It is a paradigm that must be jettisoned. Space must *create* the link. Michel de Certeau succinctly describes it as the process where "the street geometrically defined by urban planning is transformed into a space by walkers."[22] It is part of our responsibility, as design professionals and stewards of the built environment, to transform the empty, geometrically disconnected "street" into an inhabited, communally connected "space"; to develop alternatives to the current image within the discipline, the profession, and society that views space through these "colored" lenses.

Remix

So dig. There is another way of looking at space, eh? Who knew? Actually, there is a shit load of ways, but first, let's look at ol' Lockey boy again. He really believes that the only way we can know space is to touch or see it. That's an interesting point—but is that really true? Let's take on Locke's stance in his own 'hood. Let's say that his "man in the dark" is in a big-ass space with no light, taking away the only two ways Locke says you can know space: sight and touch. Can homeboy know—or at least recognize—space by any other way? Can he taste it? Nah. Smell it? Maybe, but that tells him more about what is *in* the space than what *is* the space, yo. Can he hear it? Ahhh … now that's some interesting shit. Could he not get some kind of idea of where he is by just givin' a shout? He might be able to hear an echo *(large space)*, or that shout might jump off right in his earhole *(small space)* or he might just hear a faint sound *(huge space)*. In any case, he could—especially in the dark *(where he can't see)* where the walls are out of reach *(where he can't touch)*—still have some sense of space, right? Oops … Busted! So … if Locke ain't got his shit together, can we really believe in this Locked out spatial theory? If not, we should look for a lil' sumpin' sumpin' that might cover what ol' boy didn't. So, let's sum up what he does cover.

After all the drama-for-yo'-mama, basically Locke says that space is what it is because we define it that way. Kinda like, it is so, because we *say* so. If we say it is between two points, we start looking between the two points for something to label space. *A classroom is a classroom because by the label on the blueprint, the sign on the door, and the arrangement of the seats and desks* WE HAVE *ABSTRACTLY* DEFINED AND LIMITED IT AS SPACE.

Now here comes Lefebvre sayin' that space is what it is because we use it as so. So check this out, he say space is so, because we *do* so. He alters Locke like this: *A classroom is a classroom because by teaching there,* WE HAVE ACTIVELY MADE IT SPACE.

Then Foucault piles some shit on top of that, arguing "Yeah, ya'll right, but hol' up a sec—everybody ain't equal, all spaces ain't for everybody." In other words, it is so, because we *do* so, but some of us *do so here,* and some of us *do so there* because *we are forced to do so.* So, yet another change: *A classroom is a classroom because by teaching there,* WE HAVE ACTIVELY MADE IT SPACE, BUT EVERY CLASSROOM IN THE WORLD AIN'T FOR EVERYBODY, DIG?

But hold up ... wait a minute. Then hooks flips the script on Foucault by sayin' that some of us *do so here,* and some of us *do so there* not because we are forced to, but because we *want to.* So, yo, here we go: *A classroom is a classroom because by teaching there,* WE HAVE ACTIVELY MADE IT SPACE, BUT JUST BECAUSE EVERY CLASSROOM IN THE WORLD AIN'T FOR EVERYBODY, DON'T MEAN IT AIN'T ALL GOOD.

Why is any of this important? Check it. Black folks have a loooooong-ass history of makin' do on the fly, dating all the way back to Africa—that is still in use today. Now ... add to that the Foucault power dynamic *(those that got, get to choose who gets)* and it is easy to see that here in the United States, Black folk have been feelin' Lefebvre and hooks more than anything else, cause they have been forced into leftover spaces and had to make that shit do. Black folk have always had to flip the script just to live. So, son, the kitchen becomes the living room when your Ma's peeps come by; it's the bank when the bills are due; the social space when the family comes over; the living room is a bedroom when your broke-ass uncle stays three months; the closet is your little brother's bedroom until you move to a betta' crib, knowwhatImean? In fact, this make-do shit is so much a part of everyday life for Black folk, that it is how Black folk define who they are. I'm a hustla (cause I gotta pay my rent), I'm a playa (cause I need a place to stay), I'm a balla (cause I gotta make my peeps proud), I'm a lawyer (cause I hate the way Five-O be doin' us up in this piece), etc.—all that comes from makin'-do in space, son.

Now ... if this is the case, which way of seein' space works better for Black folk: Locke or the host of folks that argue something else? And, if we agree that it is the "something else," then my point is that hip hop is the latest manifestation of this tradition of makin' space, or what I call Celebratory Heterotopias (CH), the center of some new flava'. A CH—for whatever reason—is a space made by the peeps themselves, for themselves, in a kinda "kiss-my-ass, we-don't-want-'cha-space" challenge. It is a way to kinda define space how they damn well please to make it livable—and to hell wid' what other folks say. Its what the eggheads call a demonstration of "agency" (the ability to decide for yourself) in its most basic form.

So dig, in these "spatial-making-do" joints, agency is a necessity. You—and everybody else like you—choose to make "somethin'" from "nothin'" and by choosin', you are recognizing that you—and everybody else like you—have got some power of your own. And if you want the same thing—like a space that makes you feel like you—you gonna work together to make that shit happen. That's what a CH is all about—it challenges mainstream ideas about space, celebrates like-minded peeps and cultivates a spatial attitude that works for—not against—them. In essence, you define yourself—like the clothing company—it's a FUBU-S (*For Us, By Us—Space*)—completely opposite of ol' boy Locke. Na, tell me that ain't exactly what hip hop does. Ghetto ain't nuttin' but a word. The existence of a Black urban space—one that can be defined as positive on the inside (*not negative from the outside*)—is alive and well in hip hop and is ready to follow in the footsteps of music and fashion to become place and architecture.

And that's got folks runnin' scared.

Discipline—State

5

The dominant view held by architectural educators that graduates will pursue a career in the architectural office generates a homogeneous treatment of the student. . . . The reality is that not all architecture graduates intend to pursue careers in architectural offices. In 1993, The American Institute of Architecture Students found there to be 107 alternative career paths for those studying architecture. . . . Traditional practice in architecture firms accounted for only five of the possible options listed. [Yet] [i]t is this minority of career options that architectural education and especially the design studio is modeled after, preparing students to work in architectural firms and to produce buildings.

—*Karen Bermann*

IT SHOULD BE APPARENT to anyone with the vaguest understanding of what constitutes disciplinary legitimacy that, as a discipline, architecture has failed to adequately acknowledge—much less address—its relationship to the economic and political forces that have shaped and supported it since its inception. Its stock response to any public attempt to engage this failure is based on an uncritical acceptance of its own dependency on economic factors as the unavoidable and unproblematic foundation of architecture. This willful ignorance compromises the validity of the architect's professional claim of objectivity. No less a keen observer of culture than Cornel West has concluded that until the discipline finds a way to address the reality of this political/economic relationship in a critical, nondeterministic manner, architectural discourse will fail to have any political legitimacy outside its own boundaries.[1]

James Mayo provides some insight into how the political avoidance that West identifies operates within the discipline by employing the basics of Jürgen Habermas's crisis of motivation theory.[2] Simply put, Habermas theorizes that to avoid a collapse in public confidence in their civic institutions—particularly in times of crisis—government enters into the areas of social and cultural concerns, placating the public by making decisions for them, ostensibly in their best interest. The results of this paternalistic intervention are that

- It anesthetizes the public (to real conditions).
- The public avoids politics (because government is taking care of the hard problems).
- Individuals are freed up to become more interested in selfish pursuits.

In essence, it encourages people to be apolitical, to believe the assurances of authorities to "Trust us" and "Don't worry. Be happy."

Mayo is arguing that a similar process occurs within the discipline of architecture. He observes that on the one hand the architectural discipline is able to encourage self-indulgence and aesthetic freedom to divert attention from the problematic political/economic relationship—a tactic that fosters loyalty to the system from its members and thus avoids a collapse. On the other hand, the architectural discipline encourages those outside it to focus on the functional and quantifiable aspects of architecture as the tangible criteria for the actions of its members—maintaining its legitimacy in the public realm.[3] The "crisis of motivation" within the discipline encourages the apolitical and, similar to the example above,

- It anesthetizes the architect (to real conditions).
- The profession avoids politics (using technical reasoning to justify its existence to the public and aesthetic reasoning to justify its existence to its members).
- Architects are freed up to become more interested in selfish pursuits.

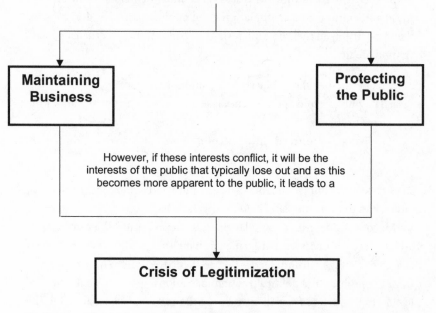

Economic Crisis

Necessitates an entry by government into the free market
system, with the *dual responsibilities* and interests of:

**Maintaining
Business**

**Protecting
the Public**

However, if these interests conflict, it will be the
interests of the public that typically lose out and as this
becomes more apparent to the public, it leads to a

Crisis of Legitimization

for the governing body, which, if not addressed immediately and/or satisfactorily,
can lead to a

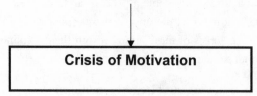

Crisis of Motivation

by the public, leading to a potential collapse in the public's
belief that the system is actually worth supporting and results
in a loss of loyalty to the system.

Figure 10. Diagram of Habermas's crisis of motivation theory.

In essence, the architectural discipline tells both its members and the public that "We will take care of it." The result of this process is that the "disciplined architect" is so anesthetized and depoliticized that s/he is unable—if not unwilling—to address the allegiance to the political and economic concerns of the ruling class.

Linda Groat provides a potential disciplinary alternative by questioning the acceptance of the Cartesian split that authorizes such bifurcated rationalizations, ultimately positing that the mind/material split is untenable—the mind being too much a "slave to self" and irrelevant to the public, and the material being too much a "slave to science" and a servant to empirical data. She argues that they cannot exist as parallel concepts and proposes that these parallel paths be integrated at the intersections of both mental and material practices, removing the arbitrary and limiting dichotomy.[4] However, such an approach implies engaging in the politics of what architects do.

Taken collectively, what these critiques provide is a fresh conceptualization of the architectural discipline as the collective site of social, political, economic, historical, and physical concerns. The discipline must reconstruct its object of study more along the lines of a cultural artifact created in the practice of everyday life. While this is without a doubt no easy task, such a shift in thinking provides a strategy that would allow for a fuller, integrated, simultaneous consideration of several aspects of architecture as an alternative to the present tyranny of the "design only" regime. A broader consideration of "what architects do" would include, but is not limited to:

- Careful critiques of the political and economic influences on physical development from commercial, nonprofit, and residential concerns; critiques of how policy decisions are affected by interpretations of these influences; how they become institutionalized and employed in particular ways that help shape social and economic behavior within the built environment; and how this implementation has often not accounted for detrimental effects on particular communities. Thus a primary focus of this approach will critique the forms of political,

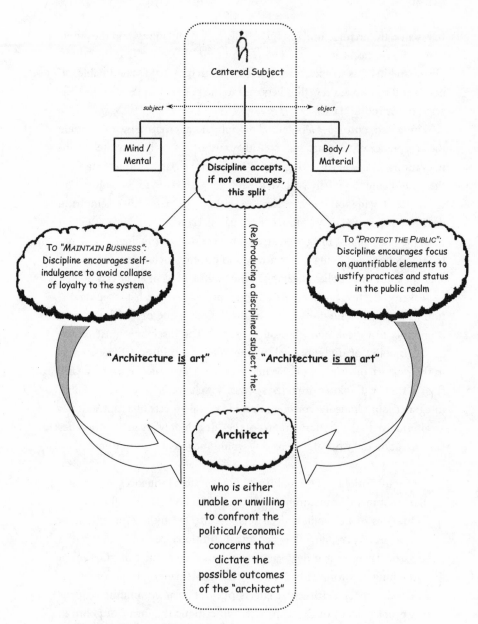

Figure 11. Diagram of Mayo's argument.

economic, and cultural power and influence and their impact on the condition of architecture.[5]

- Meticulous investigations of the diverse methods in which people conceptualize, understand, fashion, and use public and private spaces, which becomes particularly apparent when examined throughout histories and cultures. This approach encourages examining the extent and variety of socially constructed public and private spaces in terms of their architectural ramifications; sorting out relations and differences among the various positions of spatial usages; and inquiring into the interests that these positions both serve and resist.[6]

- An in-depth synthesis of the economic, political, and social issues that create the currently irreducible public/private spatial battlefield that architects are required to mold into the comprehensive urban space of the city.[7]

If this fuller consideration can be realized at the structural level, then it will also provide avenues for addressing *specific* difference with the discipline. For example, the difference in academia.

A kind of cultural imperialism

As the world becomes smaller and more multicultural through rapid developments in transportation, information, and media technologies, the profession of architecture must ask itself, What kind of architect will be required for the future global society? What kind of education will be required to develop the architect who can compete in the twenty-first century and beyond? At present, the proper framing of this debate is being held hostage by the myopic views of many instructors who reinforce what Claus Seligmann describes as a kind of knowledge-based cultural imperialism.[8] Current architectural paradigms and pedagogy are products of the same marginalization process at work in society at large and thus it is necessary that "architectural educators critically question those who label and identify the stars or geniuses [of architecture] and the process by which they do so to unveil the political and gendered practices in [those choices]."[9]

It is not my intent here to imply that the views of the dominant culture are not legitimate underpinnings for an architectural education. Far from it. I am myself a beneficiary of such an education. But given the persistence of the subjective nature of said underpinnings, I must question the universal applicability of such centrism, particularly for the design student. In this historical moment where relatively easy access to both direct and indirect cultural information is so readily at hand, what exactly is the color and culture of architecture?

Honestly addressing the political nature of architecture is a daunting task. How well we can identify and reconcile the questions raised by this investigation is a critical test for our discipline. Are we willing to candidly address and attempt to correct this and its related issues? Can architecture be used as an instrument of change? As a site for contest? It is incumbent upon us as educators in a discipline with such strong humanistic origins to expand our working definitions and the boundaries of society to consider such questions. Educators need to learn as much as possible about cultures that differ from their own if they are to understand and develop an educational program that will suit *(respond to)* the specific needs as well as the general education of students. Educators need a willingness to accept, even encourage, cultural investigation *(and the possibility of its rejection)* by students. Historically, owing to a whole host of factors, this has not been the mode of operation for most instructors when dealing with cultures other than their own, particularly with cultures on the margin. But perhaps there is a way to change that.

Where current pedagogy is perhaps faulty or unclear, a theory set forth by the philosopher Nelson Goodman to analyze the built environment can be useful in identifying areas of existing or potential bias in architectural education. Goodman's theory is based on the premise that we "must consider the question of how a particular work of architecture conveys [design culture/attitudes/theory] before we are able to address the issue of what the building may mean."[10] By understanding how and what spaces *connote* to particular communities, one is better equipped to *comprehend* what is being communicated in the resulting design. Goodman identifies four ways that buildings (or architecture) mean (convey meaning), which is documented by Lawrence Vale and adroitly applied to his own analysis of the architecture of national buildings. These ways, or sites of investigation, are labeled as *denotation, exemplification, metaphorical expression,* and *mediated reference,* which, for the purposes of clarity, I will refer to in a simpler terminology as *conceptualization, identification, creation,* and *interpretation.* It is my belief that each of these categories also has a particular significance in the educational process. By examining these four ways of meaning, I will illustrate how the process and product of architecture is adversely affected by cultural constraints and misunderstandings. To illustrate these effects, I will apply Nelson's method of analysis for architectural meaning (product) to architectural education meaning (process) by using the studio / design process / project as a site of inquiry. The African-American architectural student's experience as it relates to design will be my model, but what will be uncovered from this specific investigation is generally applicable to all under-represented cultures within this discipline. Later, I will define specific strategies to eliminate such misunderstandings.

Conceptualization: Conceptualization (Goodman's denotation) can be described as an interpretive signal or symbol of the architect's intent, most commonly known as the conceptual direction or, simply, the concept. Because interpretations and valuations by instructors in this phase of design process abound with very little framework by which to judge their objectivity, conceptualization is fraught with biases of all sorts. While bias often occurs throughout the studio experience, it is omnipresent in the initial year in design. It can be observed in its most insidious state when students are vigorously encouraged to proceed along the design path of a particularly authoritative instructor, but is present in various forms in all studios and at all levels. Its application can sometimes be problematic for students of color when "teachers, operating under professional values, elect to deal with the issues they consider most important."[11] In this scenario, students—particularly African-American students—are discouraged from pursuing culturally specific theories, ideas, or possibilities, since these issues are not considered important by many instructors. Even in studios with progressive instructors, certain directions are given more validity and credence simply by virtue of the fact that the instructor can empathize with the influences driving the concept, and can speak more confidently with the student about its possibilities. Instructors can imagine the solution in their personal/professional frame of reference, prompting an earnest attempt to support the potential that such an exploration can have for both the student and the class. Furthering the instructor's interest may also be the fact that often, students of the dominant culture who pursue sociocultural lines of inquiry at various educational levels typically operate from an abstract theoretical perspective, primarily because the empowerment of its users is not a practical consideration; the empowerment of its designer is. Thus the entire design process is less threatening for the instructor.[12]

Ultimately, the products of such culturally specific inquiries are given standing and viewed with respect by academics and practitioners; they are held to represent something of potential, substance, and value, however raw. As a possible reality built on disciplinary foundations, no matter how questionable those foundations may be, such abstract investigations are taken as a demonstration of intellectual prowess; they are the kind of work that gets noticed, acknowledged, and published, the first step down the road to "star" status. Conversely, support for African-American students in a similarly earnest attempt at abstract cultural exploration rarely draws the same kind of interest from academics and practitioners. This is truly unfortunate because often—but certainly not always—African-American students pursue lines of sociocultural inquiry not from a position of indulgence but from the recognition that as members of a historically marginalized culture they need to change something. The necessity that influences their investigation should lend an additional level of ethical, moral, and social substance to such inquiries and therefore grant the "power" Sutton mentioned (see chapter 2). Unfortunately, in this case, their power flows from a knowledge base unacknowledged by most architectural instructors—typically members of the dominant culture—and as such, is not so eagerly supported. To quote Shelby Steele, "when [the marginalized student] challenges, he may draw the dark projections of [the dominant culture] and become a source of irritation."[13] This insight must be seriously considered when African-American design exploration, derived not only from an abstract intellectual perspective but also from intimate cultural experience, is given little credibility or standing.

The road to acquiring power *that can effect change* must be counter to the status quo, for the status quo is the object of the change effort. If difference is not allowed an opportunity to gain standing on its own terms, particularly in studio explorations, a long-term, useful understanding of its existence will have difficulty in smoothly reaching fruition and most probably fail, thereby reinforcing the status quo.

In conclusion, because instructors don't empathize with cultural influences that drive certain concepts, instructors often encourage a student to pursue a different path of inquiry. In short, *architectural educators are hesitant to give culturally influenced conceptual development "standing," for fear of ascribing power to this line of inquiry.*

Identification: Identification (Goodman's exemplification) is the process of direct interaction between the instructor and student and is most clearly apparent in the dominant/subordinate roles. While this is a common occurrence in all architectural programs, identification is a particularly telling dynamic to observe when the student is black and the teacher is white. For members of the dominant culture, particularly men and to a lesser extent women, the dominant (instructor)/subordinate (student) arrangement is viewed as temporary. It is their belief—deeply rooted in the *cultural obliga-*

tion underpinning of the educational system—that the more knowledge the student gains, the more the barrier creating this relationship dynamic is dissolved. In this scenario, knowledge brings power—which is tantamount to equality—and instructor and student eventually, inevitably, become peers. For African-American students, the obtainment of equality through knowledge *alone* is a much less likely occurrence—though certainly not impossible, it is historically a much more difficult path to travel. In their scenario, knowledge does not automatically equal power, which can lead to African-American students viewing this dominant/subordinate arrangement as a more permanent professional prospect—if not in their perception *of* themselves, at least in the perception of others *about* themselves—as indeed it has generally been to this point. Instructors, historically used to viewing the educational/professional experience in this master/apprentice manner, do not help to alleviate these feelings. Equally telling is the fact that many of the design instructors in the architectural schools are the designers and principals of architectural offices, where they continue to foster the master/apprentice dynamic and its subsequent mentality. Beginning design students are less likely to question the judgment of a critic when they are less than confident that their knowledge base will be recognized as credible. In addition, while white students can expect to find themselves offered positions of authority and status within the majority firms that may eventually lead to partnerships—further erasing the inequities of power in professional relationships—this path is less likely to be offered to students of color. Thus the power inequities introduced in the educational experience can become fossilized.

In sum, architectural education is a reflection of society. The obstacle to the power for effecting change highlighted by identification is demonstrated by this phenomenon in the society at large:

Not only are blacks' complaints discounted, but black victims of [marginalization] are less effective witnesses than are whites, who are members of the oppressor class. This phenomenon reflects a widespread assumption that blacks, unlike whites, cannot be objective on racial [or any other] issues [that position black opposite white].[14]

In short, these attitudes in studio are succinctly summarized by the statement that often, particularly in architecture, *"it takes whiteness to give even Blackness validity."*[15]

Interpretation: Interpretation (Goodman's metaphorical expression) is the use of cultural symbols to reflect or invoke an expected, recognizable response based on what is believed to be a common understanding of the symbol(s). But whose culture and common understanding? For example, for many Christians, the symbol of the cross has divine implications; it can mean goodness, light, and righteousness. This same symbol has less significance to the Jewish faith, and in some circles of the Islamic faith, the cross is a sign of oppression.[16] These are three distinctly different, but widely held views of the same symbol. Which is the "common" understanding? Granted, this is an oversimplification to illustrate the potential for bias—or, at the very least, misunderstanding; other issues of symbols and culture are much subtler and need more consideration, guidance, and acceptance of difference. In the studio, when culture and symbol clash, usually the instructor is the judge and jury as to what is to become the more "common" of the understandings, and such decisions are justified by a claim to aesthetic expertise or professional experience. We previously learned that such claims are often about power, and in that context this is an example of the subjective and selective ascribing of power so very infrequently bestowed upon cultures on the margin. As legal scholar Derrick Bell explains when discussing the writings of the critical legal theorist movement and their difficulties in gaining legitimacy for the presentation format of their opinions:

[T]he difficulty many teachers have in evaluating nontraditional scholarship is rather like the resistance composers of modern music encounter with audiences committed to the standard repertoire of

Brahms, Beethoven, Haydn and Mozart. . . . I came to realize that the initial introduction to an art form, as to one's native language, creates a strong preference for that mode. Other styles can seem dissonant and unmusical—inaccessible without considerable effort.[17]

The discipline of architecture is imbued with heavy doses of history and tradition, which translate into educational paradigms of long-standing credibility. The initial introduction to this art form that Bell mentions is even more influential in architecture, not only because one learns a certain way, but also because one typically practices the same way, reinforcing the tenets of such an education daily. The obstacle to obtaining power for change indicated by interpretation is that many instructors have been educated in certain established historical paradigms and feel most comfortable educating others in the same convention. It may be quite difficult to accept the possibility that what was an acceptable paradigm for these instructors in the past may not be advantageous for (some) students today. In short, *educators may be unwilling or unable to make that "considerable effort."*

Creation: Creation (Goodman's mediated reference) is the logical extension and conclusion of Identification. It is the coupling of real-world events to the newly created symbol(s)—architecture. For the most part, architectural students are attempting to produce designs that are in some measure a reflection of themselves, balanced with the various design parameters set by the project. They are producing a personal architectural statement that will theoretically become part of our cultural collective. When understood in this light, African-American students are participating in the process of producing architecture that is a cultural statement. That statement may often be at odds with established cultural artifacts; when this occurs, it may cause untold problems for many instructors. As bell hooks explains:

> We produce cultural criticism in the context of white supremacy. At times, even the most progressive and well-meaning white folks, who are friends and allies, may not understand why a[n] [African-

American] writer has to say something a certain way, or why we may not want to explain what has been said as though the first people we must always be addressing are privileged white readers.[18]

This literary reference illustrates a particular architectural point. African-American students are often viewed, especially when pursuing a specific ethnic concept, as "ghettoizing" their work by white instructors because such an approach may address only one segment of the population, as if the work of non–African-American students, or even the instructor, is group neutral. Their design approach is viewed as architecturally less valid and is typically marginalized when done outside prescribed dominant cultural boundaries. White instructors do not, cannot, or will not understand why the first person addressed is not the dominant culture. And this is true not only of white educators. Tellingly, AIA Fellow Melvin Mitchell discusses his experience with both black and white instructors at Howard University as a student:

> The notion of a Black Architecture as a conceptual and theoretical construct was not well received. The socioeconomic, cultural, and political sense that was actually meant by those of us who were pushing the issue was lost. Black Architecture was received by the faculty and professional practice leadership as an obscenity. The notion was viewed as unprofessional trashing of the glorious, "politically innocent, and culturally neutral" western architecture. Architecture, it was felt, was a medium best suited for demonstrating the parity of black technical competence. We were socialized to believe that architecture was not an appropriate medium for the expression of black culture.[19]

The remnants of such thought can still be found today. It is difficult to imagine similar instructions being given to students of European, Asian, or Latin descent, but, as concluded by Du Bois, Negroes are from no place and therefore have no culture to express—even, it seems, to themselves.[20] Can it be any wonder that a 1993 study found that African-American students were given less presentation time and fewer substantive critiques by their instructors during studio jury?[21] Can it also be a surprise that this is the most recent information on this topic available? Having gone through this process for several years as a student, educator, and juror at predominantly majority schools, I have noticed and experienced this inequity on enough occasions to confirm its validity. That this phenomenon has been initially confirmed by empirical, rather than experiential, means is at once reassuring and unsettling. Marginalization in this situation is characterized in many ways, most often by the juror's paternalistic and condescending verbal or nonverbal manner toward the student's work that says, *"This will never become real architecture, so an extensive discussion of its merits is unwarranted."* Of course, none of the projects presented are likely to become "real" architecture, but in the mind of the juror, that is beside the point. This lack of feedback, from students, instructors, and jurors alike, can mean a few things, all of which are unflattering to the educational process and are particularly damaging to those whose input is so summarily dismissed.

The obstacle to finding power for effecting change in this discussion is indicated by the fact that when culturally influenced concepts are developed and manifest themselves in a product for debate, African-American students are given the impression that such work is not worthy of in-depth discussion. They are left to conclude that such exploration is meaningless when based in a cultural knowledge that is particularly, but not exclusively, theirs and that it is not a viable path to educational and professional success. In short, particularly in the case of students historically placed on the margin, *educators are not facilitating the belief of students in their own ability, only their belief in our ability to determine theirs,* or, as law professor Lani Guinier states, "I was defined entirely by [the dominant culture] ... who took control of my image."[22]

I have focused on the African-American student because as always, African-Americans and the dominant culture "represent the deepest lines of division" in social inequities that are reflected in the architectural discipline.[23]

While these inequities are the easiest to identify, it must be understood that what we discuss can be attributed to all marginalized cultures within the architectural discipline—and in society—in varying degrees. There is no way of knowing how many of these causes are actually at work, nor to what degree, at any given time. Suffice it to say that they are all instruments that exist to break down the communication between instructor and student, and therefore need to be combated. If not, the validity of our architectural educational value system comes into question. As I have written elsewhere, "The acceptance of the existence and legitimacy of culturally dictated influences is essential to the self-development of the beginning design student and therefore imperative for educators to accept as well."[24]

An examination of the present architectural educational process has highlighted a few, but critical, chinks in the curricular armor. Anyone wearing this armor will be less than fully equipped for the task ahead. The question we face as educators is how to forge a more complete suit. How can we instill a sense of cultural obligation or connection, so key to the development of this educational system, in students who have been subjected to the process of marginalization? How can we, as educators and practitioners, facilitate the realization of their architectural expression? I suggest that architectural educators attempt to instill a cultural connection between the marginalized student and the discipline of architecture beginning in the first year of design education and continuing throughout the educational process.

First, where architectural educators are hesitant to give culturally influenced conceptual development "standing," for fear of ascribing power to this line of inquiry, they must be made to understand the importance of initiating and sustaining serious efforts with their students to bring information concerning marginalized cultures into the curriculum. In creating the cultural connection, educators must begin to infuse design exercises and projects with cultural aspects that speak to a wide variety of communities, if not concurrently, then consecutively. The key here is to design studio investigations in such a way that allows for examination of many perspectives, free from paternalism or cultural hierarchy. This will begin the initial educational process of building a cultural connection between students and architecture, setting the stage for future student development on a more inclusive path. To this end, educators must acknowledge and overcome the difficulty of recognizing (and consequently ascribing power to) a knowledge base that may be different from their own. Often instructors will rationalize their indifference to this approach by saying, *"I can't help this student achieve his/her goal. I'm not familiar (or don't understand) enough about the approach (influences) that they are taking."* There may be approaches, experiences called into play, and results that instructors just do not expect or appreciate, and resistance may occur. This is counterproductive to the cultural connection objective. That the student may find irrefutable power in an informal knowledge base resistant to cultural marginalization is the real issue. Such knowledge—and informal education in general—tends to be suppressed, invalidated, and discounted. The instructor, by subjectively setting the standards by which to judge and the boundaries in which exploration can take place, establishes his or her knowledge base as exclusively primary. While both instructor and student feel threatened by a knowledge base that they have little access to and are unwilling to attempt to incorporate into their own, instructors are in the position of imposing their knowledge base on the student, with the explicit paternal authority of their position as studio instructor or professional design expert. It is imperative that educators avoid such crutches at all costs. In light of the general direction of society, such action is detrimental to the complete development of architects and can no longer be tolerated, if only because it doesn't empower students to compete effectively in a multicultural society. To resist such temptation, educators must remember that experience and influence *must* be considered a legitimate knowledge base, even when it resides outside prescribed boundaries outlined by the dominant culture. Educators must learn to ingenuously question, push, bend, even mutilate these arbitrary boundaries and establish a much more inclusive arena in which to discuss, debate, and ultimately, design.

Second, where studio participants harbor attitudes in studio that can be succinctly summarized by the statement that "it takes whiteness to give even Blackness validity," we must reconsider our educational emphasis to ensure a substantial, sustainable, and inclusive cultural connection.

History, particularly in the interpretation of the importance of architectural artifacts, is customarily written by the prevailing powers of the moment, and we typically accept this perspective not as *a* truth but as *the* truth. Still ... what of the powers that have yielded, displaced, or been removed to make way for the prevailing culture? Assimilation may cover some of this territory, but certainly not all. Indisputably, if we are to instill a cultural connection in traditionally marginalized students, the dialogue must include truly different, displaced perspectives. By discussing and debating a currently displaced perspective in the same context with the established perspective, we create new paths of study in the architectural discipline, imbued with the ability for change. This is fertile ground, lightly plowed but ready to bear fruit. Educators must learn to cultivate it; to realize and seize upon their students', as well as their own, potential to effect change within the discipline and in society.

Third, instructors who have been educated in historical architectural paradigms and feel most comfortable educating others in the same convention must be made to comprehend and embrace the value of the "considerable effort." In this case, the considerable effort is synonymous with an effort to become comfortable with difference. As mentioned above, African-Americans have a long and storied history within the profession. Are their names not known to the architectural discipline? I must ask why this is so, but, more important, non–African-American educators must ask why this is so. Are instructors making the effort? I think not. How can instructors properly educate African-American students, or any marginalized culture for that matter, without being able to refer them to work that will make the critical cultural connection? Would this be acceptable if the roles were reversed—if the instructors were African-American, the students were not, and all the images, case histories, and architects that were shown and discussed were exclusively African-American or Asian? Equally important, how can educators expect other students to respect the work of the marginalized if they do not refer them to those same practitioners, just as easily as they are referred to practitioners that embody their own cultural connection? There can be little argument in this regard.

> The role of architectural education and the larger system of practice needs reevaluation. The challenges of designing in a multicultural society, especially African American culture, should become a part of any school's curriculum. The practice of architecture that makes hidden and anonymous the works of African American architects reduces the obvious positive influence to African American architectural students, but it is detrimental to all students.[25]

The fact that African-American educators and practitioners survive is surprising and the fact that they, for the most part, thrive is quite remarkable—certainly a story worthy of inclusion in architecture's canonical historical narrative. As such, their efforts and work are as worthy of scholarly discussion and dissemination as the plethora of books, articles, and exhibits concerning heretofore little-known *(and oftentimes deservedly so)* European architects and the bevy of monographs of the "up-and-coming" young American architects. An important piece of architectural education is missing from the curricula. It is not only another key to creating a cultural connection between students and architecture, but also an opportunity to begin developing the cultural connection between student and student.

If you believe that this self-image issue is not important, particularly beginning with design students still trying to establish their identity in society and this discipline, the text below should provide some insight as to its importance, an importance that the dominant culture takes for granted:

> I cannot impress upon you what it has been like to go to museums . . . learning to be impressed by all the art there, and learning to accept

those depictions as being what is, grand but unlike you at all; and when like you, like you in a way you might not wish to be but must accept as the only way you can be represented in art. I can't tell you what it feels like to go to a museum where the images resemble you, or the people you've known, or could have known. I cannot express to you the peace and reassurance of these waves of feeling. But if you are White, I don't have to express it. You simply accept it. It never occurs that others require the feeling of accomplishment, of foundation, of pricelessness, of knowing their history, of being essential to the panoply of civilization.[26]

It is an inescapable fact that when people do not feel connected to something, especially something as prevalent as culture or society, then they will seek to redefine it in their own image.[27] Through little fault of the members of marginalized cultures, they have been placed in a potentially difficult, if not culturally hostile situation. If educators are not establishing a positive atmosphere for marginalized students in design studios, then they are truly doing students an injustice today that the profession, and society, will pay for tomorrow.

Designers are taught to rely on formal and informal education, empirical and intuitional knowledge, common and aesthetic sense to reach appropriate design decisions. These elements constitute the basis of their ability to create architecture. In short, they have been taught to rely on what they think and feel is aesthetically correct, within the context of the problem presented, and they commonly draw on history—their history—to assist them in this task. But histories are not always similar and are certainly not interchangeable. As products of this society, we are constantly besieged with unsubstantiated and superfluous information about one another. It is inevitable, but correctable. As it is the responsibility of educators to instill a cultural connection in design students, they must wrestle with some tough questions about their own understanding of culture and its effect on their design pedagogy. They must work to create an architectural framework that is more reliable, malleable, and durable than presently exists by separating societal and cultural myth from reality. As the studio is a place for experimentation, exchange, discovery, and hopefully enlightenment, what better opportunity to put these myths to the test, and then address them or put them to rest as the case may be? Educators must begin, at the first-year level, to question the context they establish for architectural exploration within our studios, and carefully examine the objectives set for the education of the beginning design student. It is more productive and profoundly more educational to help students understand why *they* do something than to teach them to understand why *I* want them to do something. This distinction should be a primary component of the objectives set for the education of the beginning design student. At present, educators commonly set boundaries that reinforce certain cultural icons with which they feel comfortable, to the exclusion of encouraging true individual development, exploration, and difference. The key is to examine *why* the boundaries have been placed where they are, what type of work can be expected to emerge from within these constraints, and what that will mean for the students who must operate within these boundaries, particularly the marginalized students at the initial level of design. Are these boundaries reasonably set in light of the obvious marginalization of students by society and the discipline of architecture? Are educators making the considerable effort for themselves, their students, discipline, or society?

To address these and other issues, I argue for an approach that would necessarily incorporate a broader cultural obligation into the educational objective—one that would include, rather than exclude, African-American and other marginalized educators and students.[28] A lack of cultural sensitivity is in large part a result of a dearth of African-Americans in proportional numbers on the faculty of architectural schools, in addition to several other factors detailed elsewhere. As students historically placed on the margin, many African-American students are still being measured, to paraphrase W.E.B. Du Bois, by the tape of others. Having been on two occasions, in two separate decades, in two regions of the country, one of only three African-

Americans in a graduating architectural class of more than forty students, it didn't take me long to recognize this fact. But, in my over two decades as a student, intern, practitioner, and educator in this discipline, I have often found myself attempting to correct misconceptions about the "naturalness" of history and precedent in architectural education to the majority of my colleagues. As Symes stated so eloquently, "Architectural education, like most other professional education, is based upon a kind of *universality of cultural expression* representing mainly that of the predominant white American culture."[29] What these debates with colleagues on the nature and existence of a universality of cultural expression has revealed is an abhorrent lack of cultural cognizance by many instructors, practitioners, and students that I've found alarming and quite unacceptable in any discipline —particularly one with such humanistic origins as architecture.[30] The disciplinary framework we employ must be more malleable than it is at present to separate myth from reality, and the responsibility for initiating and engaging in this project should be significantly influenced by African-American practitioners, faculty, and students.[31] As the ambivalence —if not hostility—toward marginalized communities within the discipline of architecture marches inexorably into this next millennium substantially unchanged, African-American practitioners and educators cannot allow this trek to continue in its present direction. As African-Americans—against the odds and despite the obstacles—progress through the discipline, reaching intermittent but well-deserved individual positions of influence, what is the nature of that vision that Du Bois calls for, and what will be the knowledge needed to secure it?

Expanding the current definition of architect

In the spring of 1997, an international symposium on architectural design education entitled "Negotiating Architectural Education: Intersecting Perspectives, Identities and Approaches" was held at the University of Minnesota College of Architecture and Landscape Architecture. During the two-day symposium, which brought together educators, practitioners, and students to discuss the evolution of architectural education, architect and Aga Khan award recipient Jimmy Lim put forth an interesting notion. In an effort to address what he saw as the lack of cooperation between the academic and professional wings of the discipline, Lim proposed a reorganization of the architectural discipline's knowledge boundaries that would expand the current definition of "architect" to include not one, but several interconnected areas of praxis.[32] Theoretically, Lim's proposal would accomplish three very critical things:

- Allow for more diversity, as there would be more areas of influence in the public realm and therefore more areas for entry and advancement
- Increase the cross-disciplinary interaction of architecture by presumably loosening the boundaries that have been constructed around the discipline

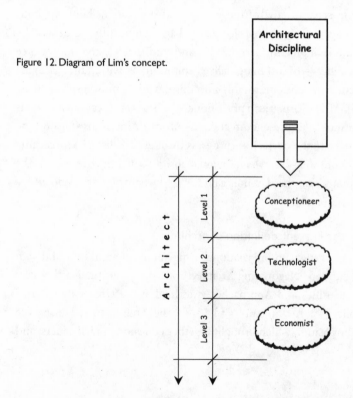

Figure 12. Diagram of Lim's concept.

- Allow space for both the professional and academic objectives to be realized and integrated

Lim describes his vision for this professional—and subsequently educational—reorganization:

The first tier [of architectural education will] concentrate on all theoretical and academic aspects of architecture. The second tier streams students into specialization groupings, consisting of the following:

- Architectural conceptioneer;
- Architectural technologist; and
- Architectural economist.

All students will graduate with an Architectural Degree, which will allow them to call themselves architects. This ought to produce a comprehensive profession that is able to co-operate among itself, self reliant, self confident, and able to meet with the challenges of the profession in the new Millennium.[33]

I agree with the basic principles that inform Lim's educational hypothesis; however, I think what he ultimately proposes—three areas of specialization within the discipline that would in practice create what he refers to as the "global architectural team" modeled after the legal and medical professions—is a valid, but ultimately flawed, solution.[34] Valid, because it recognizes the necessity of allowing for the broadening of the definition—and with it, the domains of influence, responsibility, and economic potential—of the discipline. Flawed, because while it recognizes the need to allow for and legitimize several fields of research and practice for the architect, it replicates the hierarchical value system within the discipline that is already in existence. To question and challenge the very premise on which we make our value judgments about space and architecture, to make visible the biases embedded in the discipline's foundation, and to lessen the influence of the market mentality within the discipline, it is necessary to define a framework that will assist architects in strategies of engagement that focus on the synthesis of economic, social, and political influence in the physical environment. In the end, this will broaden and redefine the professional responsibilities of the architect in society. In response to the three-level model hypothesized by Lim, I propose a horizontal—rather than vertical—alternative educational/professional model of the architectural discipline.[35] I see an alternative architectural educational paradigm at the interdisciplinary axis of the architectural, planning, academic, political, and cultural arenas. It would draw selectively on the resources of—among others—geography, history, political science, and sociology, building on architecture's ability to synthesize seemingly disparate areas of information, respecting both

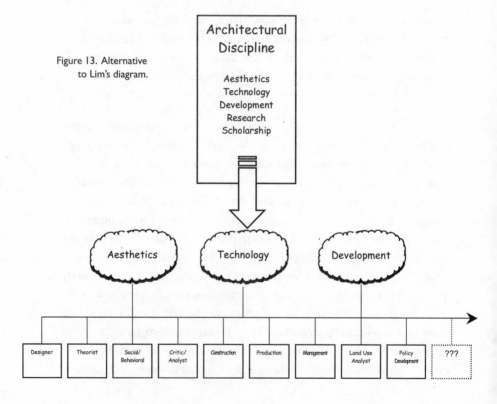

Figure 13. Alternative to Lim's diagram.

the physical and the critique that inform each other and benefiting from a shared knowledge of academic theory, criticism, research, and professional practice. Implied in this approach is rethinking the boundaries established by the educational institutions for what constitutes the study of architecture and by the profession about what constitutes the practice of architecture. This proposed shift in the focus of the discipline leads to its long-term strategic objectives:

- the development of multiple, legitimate points of entry into the discipline of architecture, *which will lead to*
- more areas of influence in the built environment industry, *leading to*
- more opportunities for professional compensation, *which will facilitate*
- more opportunity to participate and, *this is important,*
- more diverse, validated, and relevant areas of entry and long-term skill and career development for those marginalized by the current disciplinary structure.

In objection to this perspective, it is consistently argued that the architect "can't do it all, can't know it all." My response to this statement is always the same: That it is an uninteresting, self-defeating, and not very intellectually grounded criticism—a response primarily informed by the question of liability and the perpetuation of design as the defining characteristic and exclusionary ability of the architect. Other professions have figured out a way to do it—why can't we?

Doctors, dentists, psychologists, lawyers, and journalists identify themselves, either through their educational specialization or their professional experience, as practicing a subcategory of their profession. However, architecture has traditionally not acknowledged subspecialties in education or practice.[36]

While the legal profession encourages and markets practice in such diverse areas as family law, corporate law, tax law, criminal law, at the very base of what they do is the term *lawyer*. Similarly, the areas of obstetrics, surgery, pediatrics, and so on, are all unquestionably under the well-recognized and respected moniker of *doctor*. Why is it, then, that to practice construction management, specification systems, write and critique architectural work, develop public land use policy, and so on, one must relinquish the privilege of calling oneself—and more important—being recognized by colleges and the public alike, as an *architect*? The continuous adherence to and defense of increasingly obsolete disciplinary boundaries is foolish at best. A truly sustainable professional model will cultivate careers that integrate architec-

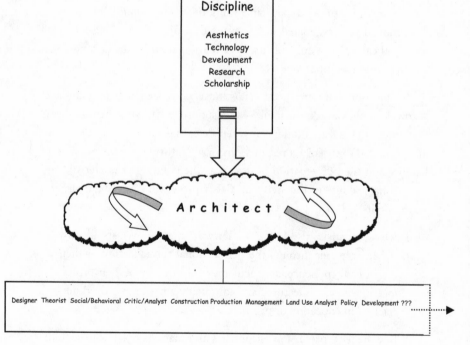

Figure 14. Teleology of a horizontal pedagogical framework.

ture, urban design, public policy, planning, private, public, and community development, architectural performance analysis, aesthetic criticism, and academia for its members. It will also serve as a catalyst and constant influence in the development of the profession—and even make lifelong learning necessary, the purpose of which would be to create a seamless environment for continuous individual, professional, and disciplinary growth in a global society and to create broad thinkers who are capable of taking on leadership roles creating, as Lim suggests, a complete, if not indispensable, architect. This objective must put the establishment of a broader definition of the practice of architecture *and* the establishment of a cross-disciplinary mode of study and criticism—focusing on issues of economics, sociology, psychology, law, urban/local politics, business, and real estate—as the centerpiece of any discussion of the future of architecture as a viable cultural entity.

Architecture must be seen as having "juice"

The failure to raise the status of architecture in the African-American community is especially short-sighted. In years to come, notes Wright, America's population, and hence the potential client base for architects, will include many more persons of color. If schools and the profession have been unmoved by their better angles to make diversity a top priority, perhaps they'll awaken to the profits to be made, as new markets to be tapped, in bringing more minority youngsters into the architectural field.[37]

From Benjamin Banneker, the self-trained inventor and surveyor who completed the plan for Washington, D.C., from memory after Pierre Charles L'Enfant, in a dispute with Congress, took his plans and returned to Paris, to Julian Abele, who designed much of the original Duke University and the Widener Library at Harvard University, to J. Max Bond, the Harvard-trained architect of the Schomburg Center for Research in Black Culture in New York and the Martin Luther King Center for Nonviolence in Atlanta, to the partnership of Sims-Varner, whose design for the Museum of African-

American History in Detroit was inspired by the African diaspora, African-Americans have had a rich history in the study and practice of architecture. Unfortunately, this participation has not been without its problems—deep systemic problems—that have kept even more African-Americans from fully participating in this discipline. Seen in the light of the structural obstacles outlined in this chapter, it is a wonder that as many as 2 percent of the profession are African-Americans, and it makes the accomplishments of architects of color even more notable. But even as we celebrate a long and stellar history of participation in the built environment by African-Americans, we must lament the fact that many of those who have desired a career shaping space have been denied the opportunity or have been slowly but steadily discouraged and marginalized by the discipline such that they have traded that dream for another that seemed more attainable. In honor of all those who have gone before to learn full well the answer to Langston Hughes's question concerning a dream deferred, this chapter was written in an effort to prevent the ranks of the permanently discouraged from swelling.[38] Architecture must be seen as having "juice"—the power to change economic, political, and social status, be it in the creation of, the placement of, the environment of, or the criticism of the process and the object. As Rodner Wright, dean of the architectural school at Florida Agriculture and Mechanical University, explains:

> The nature of the profession promotes the idea that it's mainly about signature architecture by signature architects, as opposed to urban planning and development of the total community. . . . So if you are a young kid thinking about being in a profession in your community, you don't necessarily see where architects might fit in.[39]

I have highlighted what I see, at present, as some of the obstacles to full participation for African-Americans in this discipline. I recognize full well that what I have presented here is a work in progress and will undoubtedly meet with detractors. Fair enough. I don't claim to have all—or even a majority—of the answers. However, what I do hope to accomplish with this chapter is to create a framework around which architects of all types can begin to address the issues outlined above, in a collective, integrated effort to remove them. It is important to recognize that these systemic problems exist, and, in truth, the discipline has intermittently admitted that. I am encouraged by the recent selection of Marshall Purnell to lead the AIA and the activity of its National Diversity Committee (its Web site and annual conferences on diversity are particularly worthy of note), and its local member organizations in Baltimore, Columbus, New York, Seattle, and Boston, who are obviously dedicated to the process of professional inclusion. In addition, journals like *Blacklines, Appendx* (unfortunately both have ceased publication) and *National Organization of Minority Architects Magazine* (formally the *African American Architect*), books like *Designing for Diversity* (2001) and *African-American Architects: A Biographical Dictionary, 1865–1945*, and organizations like the National Organization of Minority Architects (NOMA), Society of Spanish Engineers, Planners, and Architects (SSEPA), Asian American Architects and Engineers (AAAE), Filipino American Society of Architects and Engineers (FASAE), and the Organization of Black Designers (OBD) are also encouraging development in and around the profession. They hold much promise for making headway into the seeming intractability of diversifying the profession in the future—if there is cross-organizational dialogue and cooperation. Otherwise, the fragmentation of the profession will continue exponentially. But there does seem to be some initial attempt at collaboration among several of the organizations mentioned. We can only hope that it continues and expands.

However laudable the above interventions are—and they are worth both praise and support—problems remain, primarily because there has been little effort to identify what the problems might be and even less effort to examine their origins. In this chapter, I have done just that, since it is only after identifying the constitution of any problem that strategies can be devised to ameliorate it. What these strategies may be are also hinted at in this piece, but again, they are by no means comprehensive or complete. What they represent are possibilities, initial forays into the problem at hand. To be sure, there are other possibilities and how—or whether—any are to be implemented is still an open question. But one thing is quite clear from this work: *There are systemic and specific barriers inherent in the discipline of architecture that are hostile to African-American participation at both the academic and professional sites and no amount of denial will make that fact disappear.* Only the recognition that they are not permanent and a concerted, sustained, collective, inclusive effort by not one but all interested parties will bring about change. This means the task falls to the instructors within the academy to vigorously pursue this end. It is imperative that the first-year instructors be leaders in establishing the groundwork for these goals and African-American instructors—the few we have—must be in the forefront of this effort. As law professor Lani Guinier eloquently states, "The purpose of leadership is to speak until the people gain a voice.... Through the constant process of dialogue and the struggle to communicate, we can build coalitions."[40]

I firmly believe that within the studio context, educators can establish this coalition by developing a cultural connection to succeed with formerly marginalized students, and take a major step toward leading the development of more complete architects for the global community. As the navigators of this inclusive paradigm, it is important that we lead:

> knowing that multiple perspectives can be a source of creative innovation. Let us lead knowing that multiple perspectives strengthen and enrich our democracy.... Let us lead knowing that problems must be identified and solved collectively. And if we persist, eventually we will be heard over the thunderous silence.... We will speak until all the people have a voice.[41]

And we must continue to speak until that voice is fully recognized.

Remix

So ... the architectural discipline has a hard time dealing with its cozy relationship to the bling and how it has been pimped throughout history. Who wouldn't? Admittedly, that's some tough shit to swallow—that you been somebody's ho' for longer than you can remember. It ain't hard to figure that architecture might wanna keep that on the down-low, but you can't squash that kinda news forever. A few folk are startin' to peep some of the discipline's late-night creeps.

The first creepa peepa, Cornel West, drops a lil' knowledge, sayin' that until it confronts and resolves its problematic stance on the politics of class and cash, it will continue to have little juice in the world. A slave to the chedda can get played at any time, ya know?

The second creepa peepa, James Mayo, outlines how the discipline continues to play both architects and society close so it doesn't have to deal wid' the political/economic relationship to the folks wid' the cash. This is how they run their game: first, the discipline plays to the architects' ego, shoutin': "Yo, my brothas. Ya'll artists, right? So folks should pay you to create wonderful things. That is your contribution and folks betta recognize, son." Of course, that kinda dick-holdin' will encourage a kinda self-indulgent "I'm-da'-shit" artistic freedom. In this scenario, architects are pimped by the discipline through their own desire for fame and bling, so much so that they don't even know or care 'bout anything else—especially that pesky little bullshit contract with society. Like a crack-fiend, architects don't ask how the design jones is fed—they just want it, and if that means turning a blind eye to being used by the ruling class to feed their habit, then shit, so be it. F—— it. Pay me, bitch.

Na ... out the other side of its mouth, Mayo says the discipline whispers to society, "Yo, check this shit out. We are scientists. We know how and why things go together. We make sure the building works as it should. We keep you safe, warm, and dry. You need us. Without us, your life is in danger—that shit might fall down. We watch out for your best interests."

Smart move, scare the shit outta them, and then get the law ta get 'cha back. In this scenario, the discipline keeps society focused on the consequences if it wasn't there to protect 'em. By doing that Bush-Soprano shit, it keeps society from seeing that really it's cash—not concerns—that moves everything around the discipline.

Then here comes Linda Groat sayin' that the above argument is just forked-tongue bullshit. She says that you can't have people—particularly architects—believing, and therefore teaching, this double-speak 'cause on the one hand, you encourage selfishness and, on the other, selflessness and after a while, somebody's gonna call you on the shit in between. Like them creepa peepas. They have looked at this relationship with cash, went back and checked the contract and said, "Wait a f——in' minute. I ain't gettin' what I paid for, yo." Problem is . . . ain't nobody tryin' to hear that shit. So, what that got to do wid' you? Well, until architects decide to address this shit, the prospects for black folks is gonna be tight. This blindness and double-talk finds its way into academia as a way not to deal with the real—like the appalling lack of black folk walkin' the halls not carrying a broom or a mop. Don't believe me? Okay. Let's check the design studio as an example of how you get played in architecture's historical state of denial.

One of the most important—and effective—locations for this forced conformity is in the design studio. We talked about how a kind of *cultural imperialism* is deployed in the studio in the previous chapter 2. Okay . . . so, dig, how is it that we are learning to make architecture? This cat Nelson Goodman raps about ways in which we can peep that understanding through sumpin' I call *conceptualization, identification, creation,* and *interpretation.* While his rap is meant to help us understand buildings in particular, I'm gonna use it to help us understand how the education process is a direct attack on the ability of Black folks to keep it real and become an architect at the same time.

First, let's deal with *conceptualization,* which is your design idea—how you see and solve the problem. Think of it as the *why* and the *way* you wanna design. Now, often—but not always—the prof will sweat a student that isn't thinkin'/doin' the work the way the prof wants. In other words, what the prof thinks is always proper—which means their *values* are always right and correct. It is easier to *think* like the prof if you *look* like the prof, but if you can't, don't expect the prof to get inside your dome/home. They ain't interested. So ... the sharing of values is important—but *whose* values? The prof's, of course—which ain't necessarily the same as the students that don't look like the prof. So dig. For example, if you throw some culture into the mix—particularly some culture the prof ain't got—you stand a snowball's chance in hell of them to come strong behind yo' shit, if they come at all. So ... in the end, they expect you to do the work to get wid' *their* program, but not the other way around. Their way becomes your way—and their way is aligned and defined by their relationship to the bling, baby, and those who have it. It's like the pipe. Can't get away from it. And you know those wid' the ice and chedda ain't tryin' to feel marginalized folk in general *(hence their marginalization)* and Black folk in particular. So dig ... ask yourself: Are these really the values you wanna be workin' wid'?

Okay, what's next. Oh, yeah, *Identification,* or how legit your experiences are in the field of architecture. Knowledge brings power; what you know comes from your experiences, right? So why would that be a problem? Here's why. At the beginning, you don't know shit about architecture, so the prof has a certain level of authority/power in any interaction, but you would expect that at the end of the process you'd be on an equal footing with colleagues and even former profs, 'cause you now know what they know. Now you may not know everything that someone else knows, but that ain't the point, 'cause in turn, they don't know everything you know either. But we all have to have a certain amount of base knowledge, dig? We all pass the same classes, IDPs and registration exams, ya know? But for Black students, this "level of knowledge" that makes them "legit" is always in question. Black folk can never know enough. Where white students can see themselves as colleagues and partners with their former profs and fellow classmates, for Black folk that picture is less clear, which helps to destabilize their knowledge base and legitimacy. Black students know that for them, what they know *alone* ain't never *automatically* be enough, so they may never get their props. In the end, no matter how much Black students know, they need white folk—sometimes those who don't know as much as they do—to basically say, "Yeah, you got game."

Next we got this thang I call *interpretation*, 'cause it can be defined as using cultural symbols to get people to dig a certain thing and respond a certain way. You see where this is headed, right? Who gets to choose what culture or common understanding? For Black students in studio, it is the prof, who often got no access, don't want no access, or at the very least, makes no attempt to check out yo story. So all they know is their own professional and cultural shit, which, of course, is tied to the values of the bling that's got it all f——ed up in the first place. Should Black students trust that judgment without question?

Holla at a brotha.

The last Goodman piece is *creation*, or makin' new cultural symbols that grow out of your meanings in the world. It is a cultural statement—often one that reflects the designer—who, why, where they are. For Black students, that statement may often be in opposition to—or at the very least inaccessible to—the power structure, which can—and does—piss 'em off. The argument made in this scenario is that Black students are not stretching, that their work is only for one particular group—Black people. And profs say this shit wid' a straight face, not realizing the hypocrisy in such a crazy-ass statement. They assume that work for the ruling class is neutral and not for one group also. And in the end, if you say "F—— it. I'm gonna do this design anyway 'cause it's sweet," your prof might just start actin' funny, givin' you bogus looks or comments or maybe just ignore your ass altogether. What can you conclude from that? It's not worth it to do something culturally specific to you. This ain't gonna get built. There ain't no clients for this. I ain't gonna get hired doing this kind of stuff. This ain't architecture. Tell me yo, just who, exactly, does that type of feedback serve? That's easy. The more difficult question is, what cha' gonna do about it?

In the matter of *conceptualization*, profs must be made to get off their ass and do some work. They gotta expand they mind as much as they are asking the students to do—particularly when it comes to the Black students. Just because profs feels threatened by shit they don't understand don't give 'em the right to front. This needs to be clearly stated and out in the open so that both students and profs know what's at stake. Individual personal experience ain't universal, but personal experience is. Everybody has it and if the Black student is to accept the experience of the prof, the prof gotta do the same, yo.

As for the issue of *identification,* we need to rethink this legitimate knowledge bullshit. It ain't just what the bling boy decides—there's a whole shitload of other ways of knowing, ya dig? You can learn as much being on the outside as you can on the inside. Clearly it ain't the same knowledge, but who's to say it ain't just as valuable? Black students—who often deal wid' both Black and white sets—may be better equipped with knowledge than their white counterparts. You betta recognize.

Now … for the *interpretation* issue, again, profs gotta put in some work—they gotta be made to make the effort to "hook a brotha up." Find and understand that cultural shit is important to every student, even if that student isn't able to articulate the need or desire. If it can be done unconsciously for the white students, it can be done consciously for the Black students.

Finally, back to *Creation.* Dig, if designers are supposed to infuse their worldview, their value system and personal experience into their work, then how you gonna play the Black students when they do just that? Yo, I don't care if it is "a Black thang, you wouldn't understand," it's the prof's job to try. If you don't get it, damn it, try again. And again—hell, that's what you make the students do. Expand yo' mind. It is easier to just step off and say, "I don't know what that shit is" but that is just an intellectual sell out. Represent!

Yo … I know this shit ain't easy—never said it was—but the alternative is the status quo and we can't go out like that. We got to declare war on an educational system that (a) assumes that Black folk gonna continue to accept their own oppression, (b) expects Black folk to accept and employ the images and symbols that have historically been hostile to them, and (c) requires Black folk to teach and reproduce both Black and white architects who will simply continue this bogus shit. Foolishness!! It "nation time." Gotta drag folks kickin' and screamin' into a new day.

So dig, what would that new day look like, eh?

This cat from Indonesia, Jimmy Lim, takes a run at what a new day in academia might look like, but he runs right into a door. See, he also is a marginalized architect, and sees with both eyes, so to speak. He argues that the definition of architect should be expanded, ya dig, so more folks that look like he and I can get a lil' sumpin' sumpin'. So dig, he says to expand, we should reorganize education and practice into two tiers. Tier 1 (academic) = theory, technology, and practice, and Tier 2 (practice) = conceptioneer, technologist, and economist.

Nice try, but it ain't happenin'. Know why? By proposing a top-down model, he keeps the power hierarchy and exclusion in place, even though he expands the definition of the architect and offers more opportunity for people to participate. Here's what I think. I'd rather see a side-to-side model: it expands the definition and opportunities and status for all, but without all the "I'm-betta-than-you" shit. In this way, architecture can get some juice for change and be able to not only attract—but retain and expand—Black students whose cultural background ain't necessarily tied to the values system of the ruling class.

Dig?

6 Architecture—Motion

For most architects this [will be] the first encounter with
previously disenfranchised clients as citizens: the first
admission of black demands in a white space. As the power
of architects to speak for or plan for their subjects is
suspended, the placing of material to make space becomes
an act of negotiation between parties. The relationships
between the architect and the subject of the design become
more complex, redefining the binary roles played before:
maker/user, planner/subject, controller/controlled.
Now architecture could be said to emerge from a negotiable space,
one defined in flexible processes and materials, as a preliminary stage
to the fixed spaces of built work.
—*Hannah le Roux*

FRANTZ FANON SAID in his seminal work *The Wretched of the Earth* that
"[e]ach generation must, out of relative obscurity, discover its mission, fulfill it, or betray it."[1] Our mission has been identified, but there has been
little indication of which path educators and practitioners of architecture
will follow. Not being the most patient of people, typically adhering to "it's-
better-to-ask-forgiveness-than-permission" theory of engagement, I will be
so presumptuous as to make a choice. Bring the noise!

It has been argued that "architecture, as a voluntary captive blinded by
its own narcissism, [has] isolated itself from socially and ethically relevant
issues."[2] Given what we have discussed to this point, there is clearly support
for this position. I would put it this way: at present in architecture there is a
decided lack of something or someone to believe in outside of the pursuit of

Kantian genius—the greatness of one's self. For the sake of argument (there will be plenty of material for that later), let's call this a crisis of faith—where faith is defined primarily as a largely, but not entirely, selfless loyalty or allegiance to a cause or idea. Lately, it seems that even the capacity for faith has been replaced with something quite the opposite, the propagation of myth—an a priori story accepted as the truth, which obfuscates what is in essence a particularly self-centered worldview. In this case, that worldview is the myth that architecture is primarily an exercise in personal aesthetic expression. Faith in architecture is currently a distant and aggressively ignored memory. And while faith has had only brief moments on the architectural stage—with each time, the acting uneven, the reviews mixed—it has provided glimpses into what, with some effort, might be the core of an imaginative new play. For brevity's sake, below I will speak of two of these moments and in doing so will concentrate on what we might glean from them about our current and future condition.

The first moment is constructivism, which emerged alongside the newly formed Soviet state. The constructivist movement seemed perfectly aligned with the Marxist project in that each was concerned with similar principles. The Soviets wanted to create a "new species of man" for a modern nation without borders, discarding "all forms of backwardness: economic, technological, social and cultural"[3] while parallel to that effort, the constructivist spatial paradigm attempted to "prescribe a domain in which individuals were organized into a proper proletariat."[4] Constructivists employed architecture to bring that social order into being and, like the Soviet state itself, they relied on the machine, using new, mass-produced materials and technology to obtain their goals. The essential task for constructivist architecture was the "creation of 'social condensers': buildings, complexes or even whole cities that could not only perform their immediate functions but also motivate users (or, if necessary, constrain them) to new actions, new habits and thereby, new ways of living"—in short, a faith.[5] A faith based on the belief in a new Soviet culture displayed in a new Soviet city that would eliminate the division between labor and wealth inherent in the capitalist social and spatial organization. In recognition of shared objectives, constructivism won official sanction from the Soviet authority and, by way of state architectural and planning projects, became an important tool in Stalin's first five-year plan, from 1927 to 1932. Although seemingly ideally suited for the Marxist revolutionary project, by 1935—as the tenor of the Soviet culture moved from progressive to oppressive—constructivism fell from grace, its practitioners engaged in their last state projects, and a once-promising movement died an ignoble, premature death.

The second, most recent, and arguably most visible moment I'd like to briefly touch upon roughly follows the constructivist period and even boasted a few of the same proponents for a time—modernism. A development of immense importance in architecture begun in earnest in the 1930s, the modernist movement can be blamed for many things: a semi-successful social agenda, a melding of technology and aesthetics,[6] and an influence on some very strong responses to its ideals, but it cannot be legitimately argued that it did not have a clear, if often debated and derided, passionate vision. Matthew Smith writes that despite "its inherent shortcomings, modernism in architectural design was initially rooted in a socio-political consciousness that spoke to the needs of the masses of working people," again, in short, a faith.[7] It was a faith based on the belief in the power of architecture to engage and change social conditions and inequities; a faith that initially elevated work above individual avarice to social importance; a faith that was publicly accessible and whose merits were often debated by that same public. Unfortunately, as some have argued, the principles of the movement became corrupted shortly after World War II and were finally usurped as modernism became frequently associated with the financial elite. As a result, the modernist philosophy, applied in doses small *(Philip Johnson's original Caan home, Mies's Barcelona Pavilion and Farnsworth House)*, large *(Brasilia and Chandigarh)*, and everything in-between suddenly met with opposition, mutilation, and derision *(Paul Rudolph's Yale Art and Architecture Building, Le Corbusier's Pessac)*. As a result of this attack, architecture lost its faith in modernism completely and was content to become more stylistically inclined, regulating the movement's broader agenda to a minor role. This shift marked the (re)coronation of the myth of design that continues to this day.[8] This injection of myth—masquerading as "professional" or more accurately "design" expertise—has effectively moved the debate away from public participation and back to the province of architects and even then, only to an enlightened few.[9]

As I've mentioned previously, Cornel West has written about the product and the consequences of such mythical posturing by the discipline. I'd like to return to that critique for a moment. West argues that architectural criticism in its present form—and by implication, architecture and architects—adds nothing to the cultural debate, primarily because architectural critics fail to fully acknowledge external factors outside of site (nature) as affecting their decisions. As a result, the discipline fails to analyze the relationship between architecture and the state, commercial, and cultural interests—which each have their own agendas. He concludes that critics are afraid to discuss or even acknowledge the political aspect of architectural practice: *how authority sanctions the way buildings are made.* Instead, served up for consumption are the notions of "universality of design" or "individual creativity" of architecture, disguising the essentialism at work. Afraid such discussions will reduce architecture to what West calls the grub of pecuniary avidity, the discipline's critics, practitioners, and educators do not discuss the critical underpinnings of what authorizes architecture to be/do what it is/does. They instead attempt to explain away, mask, or in this case ignore their real material actions and their consequences in the world, which, of course, is the essence of myth: an unsupported story constructed to explain events not understood. West concludes that the reason for the critic's silence on the issues of what is not being said—the "who benefits and why" question—is because it not only means analyzing the establishment of the discipline's boundaries, responsibilities, and alliances, but also rethinking the critic's role in perpetuating the inequities inherent within the current system, as well as interrogating the results of practices based on the system. This disciplinary silence has called its political legitimacy into question, resulting in the current crisis of faith both within and without its ranks.

At present, there is little effort within the discipline to address what I am calling a lack of faith, partly because it does not want to admit that there is a problem—dismissing this crisis of faith as one in a long line of epochal upheavals that have risen and fallen in the course of architectural history— and partly because those who do recognize this moment as a potentially fundamental shift are so utterly unequipped to address it. In other words, somewhere, deep down, some members of the discipline realize that they are socially—if not politically—bankrupt, but they don't know how, who, or what to believe in to alleviate that bankruptcy. Still, one thing is becoming increasingly clear: "Architects can no longer afford to create structures in isolation, which are meant to be autonomous pieces of artwork. The old fashioned myth of architect as romantic genius, who draws all inspiration from within, has passed."[10]

So, where to look in this moment of falling cultural capital and the volatility of social markets to restructure the discipline's debt to faith and emerge from bankruptcy court? Further, if, and when, the discipline emerges from the debilitating crush of this debt's interest, how will it pay the principal? What will it have faith in and how will that faith be converted into cultural capital?

Let's focus on getting out of debt first. West argues that one potential model to follow lies in French theory and criticism. Jacques Derrida, Roland Barthes, Julia Kristeva, Michel de Certeau, Michel Foucault, Jacques Lacan—to mention just a few—have in various ways all taken an oppositional stance against traditional intellectual categories and have left behind as useless any unifying concept of meaning based on a structurally identifiable origin, binary opposition, and/or a unified subject. In short, they shun the idea of universality for more nuanced, critical critiques that recover and allow for difference. The insistence on and search for a unifying aesthetic, as evidenced by Peter Eisenman's claim that "architecture will always look like architecture"[11] has throughout the discourse of architecture erased specific histories—particularly histories of the marginalized *(as well as its own role in creating that marginalization and erasure)*—to achieve its "universal" end, much to its own detriment. As to the value of this intellectual tender to the study and practice of architecture, Robin Burkhardt-Pennell posits that:

> [I]f the notions that buildings must be classical, or modern, or simply functional are cast aside temporarily so that the outcast ideas can surface to the top, the design of a building can be a deconstruction of the building and user function. The notion in deconstructing architecture is not to completely displace beauty or function in a building, but to let other marginalized ideas surface.[12]

With this critical model throwing a universalizing discourse into serious question, architectural critics, educators, and practitioners are now presented with an interesting choice by outside critics: Incorporate these new, seemingly decentered currencies of thinking and their areas of concern into the analysis, scholarship, criticism, and production of your stubbornly unified humanist object, or lose authority over it. For the most part, the discipline has responded to this honest intellectual challenge in the mature, rational, and disciplined manner that scholars and practitioners are accustomed to—alternating between sticking their fingers in their ears and humming, refusing to even acknowledge the discipline's precarious situation, or stating in unequivocal terms that such "new" concerns are not important to the making of architecture. And there you have it—the perpetuation of bad credit in the larger social markets. How can architecture restore its good rating among the public and its allied professional peers? I think that one *(but not the only)* way is a return to faith: to complete the modernist project's social justice agenda and make good on its fiduciary responsibilities to the public.

> [I]t might be useful to begin architectural theorizing by acknowledging its primary (if usually unspoken) premise, namely, that those

who most desperately need the services of architects—or rather, the services that architects would be expected, in a better ordered, more just society, to perform—can afford them the least.[13]

Tom Fisher, author, editor, and educator, has commented that "[e]very profession is a public trust, charged with addressing public problems."[14] Other professions have faced a similar crisis and have made clear their belief in the practice of their trade as a privilege, not a right. As such, they have developed institutional systems that both fulfill their social *(as they define "social")* contractual obligations to the public and instill in their members a sense of importance and dedication to that obligation. For example, as opposed to the abundance of trades, according to Wasserman, professions are "particular types of occupations" that are differentiated from other commercial enterprises by a minimum of three principles:

- Specialized expertise exercised with judgment in unique situations
- Autonomy of the professional group
- Commitment to public service and trust—a public duty[15]

Architecture, medicine, and law were initially considered the first established professions and have responded to their professional obligations each according to its nature:

Professional Positions Concerning Social Responsibility

Legal

Ethical Claim: "Better one hundred guilty men go free than one innocent man be convicted."

Infrastructure: Pro bono / public defenders / programs to work off (student) loans

Medical

Ethical Claim: "First, do no harm . . ."

Infrastructure: Doctors Without Borders / community clinics / programs to work off (student) loans

Architectural
Ethical Claim: ???
Infrastructure: Rose Fellowship / Community Design Centers

Architecture's position on its social responsibility has not always been so equivocal. As Thomas Fisher observes, "[Historically], what architects created was linked, in the public mind, to broad social, political, and moral goals ... [but now] other than giving the owner of a building a slight marketing edge, architectural aesthetics—which we still view as central to our profession—has little value in people's perception."[16]

But it has a great deal of value to architects. Today, architecture has mostly become a self-referential, isolated, almost proprietary act.[17] In this scenario, anything outside of the "art of architecture" is a waste, viewed as marginal, radical—an act of rebellion. This brings me to Le Corbusier and his (in)famous cry, "Architecture or revolution." In a passage that could easily have been penned yesterday, he states that:

> Society is filled with a violent desire for something which it may obtain or may not. Everything lies in that: everything depends on the effort made and the attention paid to these alarming symptoms. Architecture or Revolution. Revolution can be avoided.[18]

The think tank Architects/Designers/Planners for Social Responsibility (ADPSR) has engaged and furthered the theme of Fisher's observation, perhaps with an eye to redefining that revolution. They have developed a number of aims and objectives that address the (perceived) social (ir)responsibility of the discipline, hoping to encourage architects and engineers to establish a more substantive dialogue interrogating the issue of social responsibility. These principles are: promote social responsibility; develop a humane professional ethic in the use of technology; and, campaign on specific environmental issues. Margaret Crawford is even more explicit in this area, making a more expansionist, market-based argument:

Focusing on social concerns can establish a professional base from which architects can claim more control over building and challenge professional rivals who occupy even narrower areas of competence. ... By creating compelling stories about social needs, the architectural profession can envision a new set of ideal clients, not the generic masses of modernism, but the specific groups whose needs are not being served by the architectural marketplace.[19]

Building a critical architectural practice that intentionally opens up and takes on questions of social responsibility is a revolutionary act in itself—especially so in the study and practice of architecture. The recent hurricanes in Texas and Louisiana offer the profession a window of opportunity to act as Crawford suggests—and to their credit, architects are doing so; the work of Architecture for Humanity is particularly notable—but still, it shouldn't take the catastrophic to see the value of Crawford's claim. Further, waiting on such events is no way to build a practice. So, again, how to build such a practice? More important, how does one even conceive of such a practice in our current educational and professional paradigm? What impact can such a practice have? What questions can it engage to make anyone listen? In keeping with the radical/revolutionary theme set by Le Corbusier, I suggest that one question that architecture can ask that would garner immediate attention centers on the one thing that we are infinitely familiar with and that literally supports our engagement with the world—*property*. In fact, it is an area that Le Corbusier and the Congrès International d'Architecture Moderne (CIAM), whose urban views established in the 1920s came to dominate the form of the urban environment all over the world for decades after, spent not a few hours considering:

CIAM's ideals also included social justice concerns, notably the distribution of urban resources (housing, education and health) on an egalitarian basis ... Like [Ebenezer] Howard, CIAM saw private land ownership as a major obstacle to social justice and proposed means to eliminate it. CIAM advocated public ownership, controlled by an assumedly benign state ... while Howard (1902) proposed co-operative community ownership.[20]

Now, before I begin to put this theoretical thread in a decidedly American context, I want to acknowledge that while I am acutely aware of and appreciate the fact that there are more fundamental differences embedded in the concept of property than I will be addressing next (see chapter 1) and that those differences may make this portion of my argument moot in the future, the resolution of this most axiomatic dialogue may still be some ways off. Therefore what I hope to accomplish here is to perhaps confuse the issue even more, possibly hastening that moment of resolution just a tiny bit. To do so, I would like to approach this notion of property not so much by taking issue with what Locke hasn't accounted for in his construction of property *(which is much)*, but by addressing what he has explicitly laid out as its fundamental characteristics. To bring Locke into this century's debate, I will look at the context of how his theory of property is described today by those who most vigorously appropriate, espouse, and defend it: the Property Rights Movement (PRM).[21]

The PRM argues that America—if not all of present-day Western civilization—is firmly rooted in the idea of private property, and the protection of property is the proper—if not the only—function of government. The PRM argues that property is "essential to the individual liberty and [therefore] is the birthright of every American ... [it is] the natural right of free persons ... [which] enables people to satisfy life's material needs."[22] The PRM further posits that access to private property is an inalienable right that predates the establishment of America, a right established by natural law. It also finds that the "protection of property rights is a preeminent function of government ... that it may protect the aggregate rights of the numerous victims who otherwise might be stymied by the difficulty and expense of bringing individual lawsuits."[23] As such, the PRM concludes that it "is crucial that the property rights movement be grounded in moral and legal principle, for without such a foundation, resulting legislation could be ineffective and even subversive."[24] Putting aside for the moment the more fundamental differences between Locke and his detractors and the internal contradiction in Locke's own philosophical construction of property mentioned briefly in chapter 1 and fully discussed *ad nauseam* in texts elsewhere, the PRM accepts as self-evident Locke's construction of property as summarized again here:

1. The natural world has been provided in perpetuity to be shared in common for the sustenance of individuals.

2. Individuals have rights to and ownership of their own natural abilities and, as a result, have rights to and ownership of what they can produce from the world with the labor of their own natural abilities.

3. The right of individuals to what they can produce from the world with the labor of their own natural abilities extends to their right to the material employed to produce something from the world, including the right to the world itself.[25]

4. This right to the material employed to produce something from the world removes that material from the shared, in-common state where it was originally situated and places the material in a private, non-common state—hereafter understood as private property or, simply, property.

5. Property that is unused or unsecured by labor is considered in an unjustified "non-common" state, or a "wasted" state. Wasted property returns to its original "in-common" state and is therefore subject to appropriation and reuse by other individuals.[26]

The PRM furthers fortifies this construction by making explicit these additional points:

1. Property is the essential requirement for the satisfaction of material needs and expressing individual freedom.
2. The primary function of government is to protect individual rights to/ of property—particularly for those who cannot do so on their own.
3. Property rights—both application and protection—are grounded in both legal and moral principles.

A fairly logical and straightforward set of suppositions and conclusions to be sure, but as the legal scholar Joseph Singer suggests, the concept of property is imbued and fraught with tensions and contradictions that require deep contemplation about the concept of justice. Even as we accept the notion of property as presently constituted, we cannot escape the fact that "property is not just an individual entitlement but a social institution."[27] This social institution includes an acceptance of the ideals of fairness and justice as much as the concepts of autonomy and liberty. The Lockean scholar Richard Ashcraft has concluded that even Locke believed that a civil society "could never be understood merely as the protective outgrowth of the interests of property owners."[28] Take for example the oft-uttered claim "This is my property and I can do what I want with it." Ashcraft suggests that Locke would never have held to such a declaration, for it is clear that such a person fails to understand the internal tensions and the myriad laws, rules, regulations, restrictions, ethical and moral considerations, and—perhaps the most important—obligations of the *practice* of property needed to keep the *concept* of property in place. Property requires choices and judgments and defies simplistic attempts to equate or adjudicate it by reference to a single scale. Again, Singer notes:

> Property is defined not by reference to a fixed conception but by reference to human values.... It requires a judgment of some kind. Either we balance the interests of the parties, or we consider the overriding interests of the community, or we make a moral judgment about which uses to favor. In any case, this solution to land use conflicts requires the exercise of judgment.[29]

So, as we accept the notion of property as presently constituted, that the right to property is an inalienable one, essential for the pursuit of life and liberty *and* inasmuch as property is the means by which life and liberty come into being, *and* considering that property was originally given "in common" to everyone for their pursuit of life and liberty *and* in view of the fact that the proper function of government is to protect the rights of all its citizenry, *would it not follow that it is the duty of government to ensure that all of its people have equal access to property so that they can pursue life and liberty?* To do less would be to condemn the propertyless to something less than life and liberty—and ultimately doom the concept of property itself, for in the process, "[t]he propertyless are not only themselves deprived of property. Their inability to recognize freely the property rights of others undermines the rights of those who have property."[30] It would be a system bound to collapse under the weight of its own hypocrisy. To pursue this line of reasoning further, would it not follow then that if property is necessary for human identity and happiness, the role of government—described by both Locke and the PRM as protecting the rights to, and concomitantly the concept of, property—*must favor one individual's need for sustenance over another individual's desire for abundance?* To do less would be to protect those who hoard the materials of life and liberty, abusing the benevolence of the common—by whose trust in the belief that there will be sufficient material for all they are allowed to appropriate property in the first place. As Singer explains, "property right[s] involves not merely the owner and the land but also a decision, in the words of Laura Underkuffler-Freund, to 'reward the claims of some people to finite and critical goods, and to deny the claims to the same goods by others.' "[31] For Locke, it was only logical that land be removed from the common because it was understood that the land would be used for the "owner's" sustenance—the proof of which was the visible occupation and improvement of that land by the owner's labor. Here again, the moral component of property arises—the belief in the fairness of an individual act sanctioned by the common; a trust that such benevolence is indeed in everyone's best interest, and that said goodwill would not be abused. It is in this assumption—this trust—that the moral authority to remove land from its in-common state lies, establishing trust as the hidden underpinning of the entire property foundation:

> Indeed, ... the entire institution of property would fall if most people did not believe that it is right to respect the property of others. Property cannot exist without trust ... "No trust, no property."[32]

If this trust in that moral authority is to remain, remedies such as redistribution of property and an individual's right to occupy unimproved land must be reaffirmed and widely employed, particularly when the land, in the Lockean sense, is wasted, lying dormant, unimproved by labor, and causing harm to its neighbors and community. Even theories in classical economics, where the notions of property as a capital commodity are argued most passionately, still argue strongly that property as defined, even in its exchange value commodification, cannot be defended without some obligation—moral, legal, or otherwise—to preserve and improve the land. To do any less is to threaten the existence of the system as we know it and the level of distrust in both the rural and urban areas concerning property has been dangerously increasing.[33] As this phenomenon becomes more and more transparent, private property moves perilously closer and closer to losing its moral component; since the concept itself is untenable, it is certainly not unreasonable that some display of reciprocal benefit to the common be shown. The vacant lot, abandoned building, or foreclosed farm only work to reduce the utility of surrounding property. To be fair, we do have mechanisms in place that address the issue of reciprocal benefit—tax foreclosures, eminent domain, public easements, homesteading—however, few of these provisions categorically requires the visible, physical improvement that should be explicit in all, no matter how casually such improvement is defined. No moral component, no trust. No trust, no property. No property, no piece. No piece ... no peace.

By now, my support for Locke might strike readers as odd. On the one hand, to problematize as I did in chapter 1 Locke's construction of space and then, on the other hand, to argue for a more substantive adherence to Locke's construction of property as a means for environmental justice might at first glance seem at least incompatible, if not hypocritical. After all, Locke's view of space and property is heavily supported by, but not completely dependent on, elitist, exclusionary, and static dimensions that make their presence felt in the built environment through phenomena like redlining, spatial and racial profiling, white flight, and environmental racism. However, my position is not as contradictory as it may appear on the surface, as the idea of property can be supported by other notions of space as well. I am thinking particularly of the type of space discussed in chapter 4, which for clarity I will refer to here as UnLocke space, whose fundamental characteristics of inclusion and engagement are actively created by material actions, and which supports an understanding of property that is the foundation for innovative interventions such as land banks, CDCs, inclusionary zoning, participatory design, and equity planning.

To demonstrate what this examination of property fueled by an Un-Locke view of space might provide for the urbanist, let us take, as a simple example, an undeveloped, abandoned piece of land in a disenfranchised urban area or an abandoned structure—conditions that can be found in every major industrialized city in America and beyond. Let us further describe this land as unoccupied by any person and refer to it by its common name—a vacant lot.[34] Finally, let us observe that this vacant lot is laden with unchecked and unwanted debris and has been for some time. Now, it is obvious that such land is neither occupied nor improved, the two instances by which land can be removed from its original shared, in-common state identified in Locke's construction of property. Further, it is perhaps less obvious, but nonetheless accurate to say that these conditions "contribute nothing to city tax rolls and are a drain on already stressed municipal finances ... [as well as] impacts beyond neighborhood aesthetics, economic vitality and fiscal health."[35] By the standards set by Locke and the PRM, shouldn't this land therefore be considered forfeit and subject to redistribution, with the subsequent appropriation and reuse of that land seen as the deployment of a legitimate right to property, regardless of who holds its "title"? Certainly some will retort *"when an individual owns a piece of property—it is theirs to do with as they wish. It cannot be taken away from them simply because it is not improved or occupied."* If this is so—then what is the basis of said ownership in the first place? The only legitimate reasons for the shared, in-common materials of life and liberty to become private, non-common materials or, in other words, appropriated as property as originally defined by Locke is through labor and/or occupation—neither of which are currently being deployed in this scenario. Consequently, by the condition it was first deemed private, non-common land should revert to its original shared, in-common state, available for occupation and improvement. To argue that it is not proper to appropriate property in the last instance is to negate the appropriation of property in the first instance.[36]

Think for a moment what just the threat of losing unimproved property would do for the built environment—in particular, the inner city. In fact, it isn't necessary to imagine, only to observe an embryonic example occurring in Brazil. Unlike the United States, where the individual right to property is sacrosanct, the constitution of Brazil defines the standard by which one is granted use and title to property and that standard recognizes that "wasted, unused" conditions make property ripe for redistribution, thus explicitly confirming the principle that the right to private property should not supersede the dictates of social justice. Argentinean architect Jorge Jáuregui, in conjunction with the Brazilian Institute of Architects (Instituto de Arquitetos do Brasil, or IAB), national and local Brazilian governments, the European Union, and other concerned organizations, has taken this principle and engaged it architecturally, creating an intervention called "Favela-Bairro."[37] This multidisciplinary program was conceived as a way to weave informal settlements into the fabric of the formal city. Differing from past strategies where city authorities tried to eradicate the favelas based on a traditional slum clearance model, Favela-Bairro engages designers, planners, social, economic, and health service providers equally and concurrently to transform the favelas into integrated neighborhoods. This has meant replacing muddy dirt paths with paved walkways, creating streets capable of sustaining vehicular traffic, building sewer systems and cleaning up polluted streams and rivers, and providing communities with social centers, clinics, daycare centers, athletic complexes, and homes. These changes have allowed the disenfranchised inhabitants of the favelas to participate in the life of the city. By the standards established by the interested parties this project can only be declared successful if the original inhabitants continue living in the area after the intervention plan is over and they consider the new houses as really theirs. In addition, understanding that architecture can be an essential element in creating environmental equality for the marginalized of Brazil, the program includes the Center for Urban and Social Assessment, where architects and social workers, acting on behalf of the local government, assist the residents in creating both their private and communal spaces. Jáuregui has received Harvard University's Veronica Rudge Green Prize for his work and the program has been recognized by the United Nations with the prestigious Habitat Award in addition to receiving several other international awards. As of this publication, the program has reached more than 450,000 people in 105 shantytowns and is being implemented in other countries as well.

Now clearly, the United States is not Brazil; however, to dismiss this intervention as foreign and unworkable in this country is to completely miss a potential faith-building perspective worth engaging, because even a slightly similar shift in our general understanding of the built environment would be a positive boon. In many cases, for entrepreneurial communities, CDCs, and NGOs, it would provide real economic and political opportunities to shape the built environment. In this scenario, there is—as there should be— reciprocal benefits in the taking of common land; for architects, it would provide extensive opportunities to redress their recalcitrant dealing with the urban environment. As a simple example, imagine if every vacant lot was under an explicit time frame for improvements to be provided to the property as a way to secure ownership. Based on Lockean foundations, PRM additions, and current property definitions, such a requirement would be neither an onerous or new requirement to property ownership *(initial support for property ownership lies in improvement)* nor would it be an overextension of government police powers *(zoning and eminent domain are just two examples of generally accepted powers of the state over property uses)*. Perhaps through the creation of special districts, new categories of zoning, and flexible-use designations, frameworks might be put in place to facilitate the enforcement of a very old requirement. To speculate, what if an alternative zoning framework included designations such as "improvement phases"— for example, 0–1 year: *visible*, 2–4 years: *temporary/transitional*, 5 or more years: *permanent*—that managed and enforced the improvement element of property. In this scenario, perhaps the minimum 0–1 year improvement might simply be to require a well-manicured and accessible lawn, grass field, or play area. The effect this basic requirement would have on the inner city—notorious for its dearth of open spaces and amenities, particularly for children—would be immediate. Some neighborhoods—previously viewed as less than pleasant places to be—might be instantly transformed into some of the greenest places in the city. In a more complex example, such a legal position would spur housing and commercial development on these lots, forcing long-term private and public planning and development strategies to be created and implemented in and with communities that up till now have suffered from a massive lack of comprehensive attention from both. With the development of land banks in Atlanta and Cleveland, in addition to the intermittent efforts by HUD and cities like New Richland, Minnesota, and Marquette, Kansas, at urban and rural homesteading, some cities are already experimenting with elements of a similar overall strategy.[38] This simple requirement, or others that seek to revive the responsibilities to the common of property ownership, could provide much in the way of community empowerment and transformative urban and architectural design. Lest anyone get the wrong idea, what I have speculated here is not a taking of property, but an enforcing of moral and civil behavior that authorizes the reception of property in the first instance. In case you've missed it, it is the same promise of moral behavior under which professions themselves are authorized as well. As architects, we should be inextricably involved with supporting and developing such strategies.

There really should no longer be any question of whether this is an issue for the architectural profession. Property is the lifeblood that sustains what architects do—both physically and financially. On the one hand, it is the very appropriation of property that keeps us working. On the other hand, the excessive appropriation of property seems to violate not only the justification by which it exists, but by our tacit support of the system, also violates the notion of the impartial, nonpartisan professional as champion of society, threatening our very existence or, at the very least, our public authority. It is not surprising that in choosing to ignore one moral obligation, we have failed to recognize the other. Hopefully, the reverse is also true; that by embracing the civic component of our obligation—in this case, a discussion concerning property, but there are undoubtedly others—the practice of architecture will become engaged on a much broader and deeper level in its dealings with all the various groups of citizens for whom it serves as champion. For African-American architects, an engagement with the notion of property is even more critical. As architect Brad Grant, former president of the Association of Collegiate Schools of Architecture, explains, the "character of the landowner seeking design, starting with the plantation master, moving to segregated Black institutions and, presently, to the government, has conspired to make the African American architect professionally invisible," precisely by not hiring them to do work.[39] However, don't get it twisted—this is not just a concern for Black architects. That would be asking them to shoulder an extremely difficult burden for a profession that has given them little reason to do so. If the profession itself is hell-bent on ignoring its side of the social contract, then indeed Black architects have the right to choose to be as selfish as anyone else. In no way is this a call to arms in which underrepresented practitioners must bear the brunt of change alone. As long as the profession places the idea/image of the lone aesthetic genius architect at the zenith of professional aspirations, then African-American architects have as much right to pursue that professional fulfillment as their non–African-American colleagues. In fact, I suspect that it is their collective cultural creative and aesthetic legacy in every possible branch of artistic endeavor that infuses their belief not only in their ability to design, but also in their belief of the attainability of design genius, despite evidence put forth by the profession to the contrary. Oh, no. By no means is this a job for the underrepresented alone—far from it. Practitioners of color should be allowed to be as narrow-minded and unconcerned as the next architect. However, running the risk of sounding essentialist, I will speculate here that African-American practitioners are particularly suited to this project, due to their diasporic foundation, their experience in overcoming specific professional, disciplinary, and environmental conditions, and their particular vulnerability to the consequences of maintaining the status quo. Still, it is no more or less their job than anyone else's who claims the title of architect. As Jacqueline C. Vischer succinctly and correctly states:

> Just as there will always be persons for whom the pursuit of architecture as a profession is an opportunity to "practice" art ... there will always be those for ... whom the practice of architecture is an acceptance of social responsibility.[40]

Having said that, for those who, for whatever reason, accept the professional challenge, the most critical question becomes, how can a balance be struck in a system that is full of unresolved and continuously shifting contradictions? Where are these architects to locate themselves in this political, economic, social, and aesthetic debate, especially when:

> the profession's adherence to the belief that architecture's greatest aspiration is to be inspired by an artistic vision, [implies] that anything that is not is, by definition, lesser. As a result, although another person might produce architecture that is socially responsible, cost effective, technically innovative, or meets some other criterion of excellence, it can never be quite as excellent as "art." ... [In fact], for

some contemporary architectural theorists, architecture that is inspired by an artistic vision cannot solve social problems and cannot
even play a role in social change if it is to be "pure" as an art form.[41]

Perhaps a place to begin is to recognize that the legitimate practice of
architecture as a profession demands that the practitioner balance the needs
and desires of the client and/or the user, the public, and the designer—all
of which may be at times quite different, if not oppositional, to say nothing
of mutually exclusive. Like the concept of property, the concept of professional also depends on a level of trust from the public for its status, and that
trust is also based in a moral component.[42] As such, Sharon Sutton suggests
that property is an issue that architects must grapple with:

> For architects to launch a debate against the very social institution
> that sustains them would be dangerous—dangerous but necessary.
> As the rate of humanizing of the Earth intensifies, it will become in-
> creasingly fraudulent for architects to claim that they are protecting
> the public's health, welfare, and safety while cities decay, farmland
> is paved over and energy resources are depleted.... In this time of
> global economics, multinational corporations do not possess but
> rather appropriate property, determining from afar and on a mas-
> sive scale the fate of persons whom their wealthy chief executive offi-
> cers do not even know.... This situation is unacceptable if individu-
> als and communities are to be empowered to determine their own
> sustainable futures. To advocate the fight for self- and community-
> determination, an enriched mission of architecture would necessar-
> ily tackle the dishonorability of appropriating property.[43]

Sutton removes the Corbusian dichotomy. Architects no longer need to
choose between one end and the other. In this manner, architecture *is* revolution and the ethical/ideological foundation for what I will call an activist
architecture: a way of perceiving, teaching, and practicing architecture that
derives from, is relevant to, and vigorously engages the community in which

the architecture is placed. It is a *process* of design and development in which communal sustainability and environmental equity influence the physical growth and economic direction of the built environment.

The philosophical foundation of an activist architecture lies in its refusal to believe that local communities, working closely with activist architects and urbanists, are without power over their built environment. It is this legacy of an activist architecture, born out of the Black power movement of the mid to late 1960s, that I will now engage and attempt to extend in the remainder of this document. As I mentioned in chapter 2, Sharon Sutton observed that those on the outside of traditional power structures are motivated to find roles that will bring about change. I have pondered long and hard about not what, but *how,* that statement means, as her observations highlight a plethora of realities and possibilities that are relevant to me both as an architect and as an African-American. They are, in no order of importance: Where is the power for permanent change in architecture that can be obtained and welded by/for the powerless? If there is no real power in architecture, why would Sutton's outsiders be drawn to it? And what does that say about those traditional outsiders who are drawn, in spite of its apparent powerlessness? Where, then, does their motivation lie? Having been historically placed in the community of outsiders, Sutton's observations suggest for me a motivation—a way into the property debate that Hannah le Roux makes explicit:

> Emergent practices which flout the proper disciplinary modes can serve to renew architecture through being aberrant.... [T]hey interrogate the habitual modes of making architecture by following, intermittently, paths set out by new users of space. At these moments of departure from the disciplinary norm, the possibility of other forms of practice emerges.[44]

To answer these questions, the study of hip hop culture in general and rap music in particular is essential to the new generation of urbanists. Hip hop has appropriated the dispensable and made it indispensable and the concepts and information from/about the site of environmental conflict constructed by hip hop culture in today's society are infinitely applicable for design, particularly architectural and spatial theory. As hip hop's most visible export and primary spokesperson, rap music has come to massively influence society. It is the driving force behind music, fashion, and culture and is logically and inevitably developing its own ideology. Currently a rapidly shrinking site of authentic marginalized African-American resistance, rap music has become the voice of the disempowered inner city. It is authentic because it has rejected being defined by economic or political concerns other than its own. Eschewing a host of other authorities, rap has defined itself in its own terms—as only a pure art form can—by creating a space in which it can reach its fullest potential.

> While popular music often provides effectively empowering experiences for its audiences, its effects may be more concretely described in terms of a popular kind of temporal-spatial creation. In a variety of ways, it provides or can be used to create dimensions of "free space."[45]

It is most difficult to limit the resulting free space of this community, since it "is by its very nature full of power and symbolism, a complex web of domination and subordination."[46] Historically available architectural approaches are not transferable to this project. A new architectural design perspective is necessary to practice in this community and design for the object of this free space.

I must take a moment here to acknowledge that my enthusiasm for the liberating potential of hip hop is not universally shared, even within the hip hop community itself, to say nothing of the African-American community and American community at large. In fact, a growing number of critics are arguing that hip hop's most influential element, rap music—with its growing predilections toward homophobia, crime, misogyny, and violence—are undermining the very tenets that initially made it a force—well, a liberating force, anyway.

One of the most common arguments against the culture of hip hop is that it has failed in its mission of empowering the disenfranchised community from which it was born by becoming too concerned with material, rather than political and social, gain. As pointed out in a National Public Radio interview, Ray Roker, publisher of *URB* magazine, makes the comment that:

> if you want to talk about political struggle or what we need to do to, to save the world around us, that stuff's boring. It doesn't get on TV. It doesn't get on the radio. And hip hop music, and I think people who really consider themselves real fans of hip hop music in the old school and everything wish that it had taken that place that it made for itself, that platform and used [it] to really say something.[47]

Ken Gibbs concurs with Roker's assessment, and offers a condemnation of the squandering of the political and social potential of hip hop:

> Rap began as the most democratic of art forms, an expression of innovation and skill that was open to all. You didn't need formal musical training to write a rhyme, and no instruments were required— you didn't even need to make your own music, since you could use segments of songs that were already recorded. As the genre became commercially successful, however, rap became less about creativity and all-inclusive self-expression and more about getting signed, releasing hits and making money.[48]

Some argue that hip hop does promote a social agenda, just one that has less to do with political and social empowerment and more to do with embracing and glorifying a lack of political and social relevance as a means to justify disenfranchising patterns that sell records. Ernest Allen comments that "the messages of gangsta rap are content to describe in a fatalistic way the world 'as it is,' disclaiming any responsibility for the negativism to which gangsters themselves contribute."[49] Those who mine the music for messages that are broader than the dominant gangsta milieu still find much to be concerned about. Consider the observations about the more educational/ political genre of hip hop, "message" or "conscious" rap:

> So what is conscious rap? ... Essentially, it's a noxious brew of racist delusions skimmed from the diverse streams of black separatist rhetoric, Afrocentric propagandizing, Nation of Islam theology and a kind of Cliff Notes Marxism.[50]

Even those who find that message rap has merit are still disturbed by its constitution:

> Message rap tends to carry with it considerable antisocial baggage characteristic of, but hardly limited to, the rap phenomenon in general: misogyny, homophobia, vainglorious trippings, interethnic malevolence, and—if these were not sufficient—a moral relativism that repudiates any responsibility of one's own actions, including all of the above.[51]

Allen is the kindest in his denouncement of these tendencies in the music. Others are less so:

> Critics of rap have fiercely argued that one of its most detrimental aspects is that it loudly, crudely, and constantly promotes violence against women and other forms of misogyny. Even politically oriented rap, it is argued, supports the patriarchal view of a subservient role of women in the struggle for black liberation espoused by many nationalists. Frequent references to "ho," "bitches," "punks," and "faggots" do give a consistent misogynist and homophobic cast to rap that is not just confined to gangsta rap.... [G]iven the constant attacks against black gays and lesbians found within rap lyrics, both the exposure to rap and the belief that rap provides a legitimate source of information within the black community contribute to negative attitudes toward gays and lesbians. Rap music contributes to black homophobia.[52]

Still others have never seen hip hop as having any political or social agenda at all. They argue that hip hop is nothing more than a commercial fad that will soon become anesthetized and assimilated, much the way rock, grunge, punk, and other "rebellious" and "counterculture critiquing" art forms were.

> Adolph Reed starkly represents the point of view of the detractors of this artistic project when he bleakly argues that even the so-called political wing of hip hop culture "spew garbled compounds of half-truth, distortion, Afrocentric drivel, and crackerbarrel wisdom, as often as not shot through with reactionary prejudices" (Reed 1992, 228) ... The current black artistic consumerist fad, according to Reed, is neither critiqued nor influenced by a dynamic mass movement.[53]

More generous critiques of its supposed lack of political involvement acknowledge that:

> Market forces will play a decisive role in shaping and propagating the message itself. In an era characterized by the collapse of significant political life and by the relative success of media forces in defining symbolic meaning for large numbers of African Americans, message rap remains decapitated from any mass political movement for social change, and overwhelmingly dependent on the market for dissemination—a significant political weakness.[54]

All are valid arguments to be sure, and there is some evidence that at least some of the above conditions are not lost on the hip hop community. Rappers face the tension of balancing the "demands that record companies ... make about content, and a desire to remain true to their own artistic and political vision.... [with] the corrosive effect that 'getting paid' has on the content of many rap songs,"[55] which influences the proliferation of gangsta rap by record companies who refuse to market or distribute positively politically oriented rap—a condition that worries many rappers.

Yet there are many who still see the enormous potential in the music and find it well worth trolling for gold. For example, Michael Dawson argues:

[The views above are] not exactly compatible with that of Michael Dyson and other defenders of the more particularly political veins of rap.... For these scholars, the new black culture represents the cutting edge of a rejuvenated critical black public sphere—a space that would provide black Americans not only the ability to critique the racist ills of American society, but also a social space that facilitates the process of consciousness raising necessary for rebuilding the black movement.[56]

Houston Baker, Jr., adds:

It would be salutary ... if the "grim neighborhoods" of public housing were to reap the benefits of the type of hearing provided by the Central Park moment.... [W]e might also find in our new public concern both exacting and effective ways to channel the transnational capital of everyday rap into a spirited refiguration of African-American urban territories.[57]

In spite of the above issues within and without the hip hop community, there is too much evidence of its power and influence to ignore it as a viable tool to employ in any strategy for urban interventions, particularly in African-American urban communities. As Dawson's study shows,

[both] exposure to and opinion of rap shape black public opinion. Even with the crude measures, definite connections between rap on the one hand and homophobia and black nationalism on the other were established. A direct relationship was found between rap and two of the four domains that were tested (ideology, sexism, homophobia and general political attitudes) ... on the other hand, there was no general connection between exposure to rap music and a more critical view of American society and its institutions.[58]

In this vein, and in the hope of retrieving some of the liberating potential that hip hop embodies, I engage hip hop as a model for this project.

This hip hop spatial paradigm

Elvis Costello once remarked that writing about music is like dancing about architecture and, while his notoriously prickly constitution devised that derisive response to a journalist's query, below I will endorse its validity (sans contempt) by identifying and analyzing the space produced by the hip hop revolution; a specific spatial understanding of hip hop culture as it reverberates from rap music into the built environment in response to spaces that represent the power of oppression. This hip hop spatial paradigm at once recalls, creates, and deploys new spaces that speak to the Africentric diasporian project of identity embedded in rap music.

Ready for a little sumpin' sumpin' special? I'm 'bout to break you off some.

Music both *creates* and is *created by* a distinct social context essential to the development of identity and subjectivity. This reciprocal relationship anchors my view of sonic foundations of hip hop and is reinforced by several theoretical claims that form the basis of the music/space relationship.

> Dancing is one way of speaking through the body both to others and oneself, and as such when people dance they usually like to be saying the right things, or at least [be] in control of what they are saying.... [W]e come to believe that we are momentarily seeing into someone's personality when we see someone dance.[59]

Simon Frith and Angela McRobbie in their essay "Rock and Sexuality" position rock and pop music as the place where "boys and girls learn their repertoire of public sexual behavior."[60] By drawing on theories that posit sexual subjectivity as a primary element of defining an individual's or a group's identity, and focusing on music's capacity to construct male and female identities among teenagers through socially sanctioned public sexual expression, they reject the notion of rock music as liberating a long repressed sexuality and instead posit that "the most important ideological work done by rock is the construction of sexuality."[61] They further argue that this construction is controlled by the " 'gatekeepers' of the industry, who determine how people listen to [music]."[62] This suggests that those who control the choices and forms of music that become available to listeners have an overdetermined influence on the construction of sexuality and identity of those listeners.

George Lipsitz, in his book *Time Passages,* directly links the (sexual) identity produced by music to the notion of time and applies the concept of dialogical criticism—defined as a conversation with history and critically dependent upon memory—to the study of music.[63] It is his position that "one reason for popular music's powerful affect is its ability to conflate music and lived experience, to make both the past and present zones of choice serve distinct social and political interests."[64]

In his analysis, Lipsitz posits that the socially defined public arena—that place where the everyday interactions of society takes place—"is the matrix of production and reception of popular music" and memory is central to the construction of that public arena.[65] In his analysis, not only is memory necessary for the construction of music, it is also central to the construction of social context and thus necessary for the construction of identity.

Finally, in the essay "The Sound of Music in the Era of Its Electronic Reproducibility," John Mowitt takes Lipsitz's position a step further and argues that current technology has separated the production and reception of music, and has "privileged the moment of reception in cultural experience," further illustrating the social context of music's construction and its influence on subjectivity and identity.[66] Key to this argument is Mowitt's assertion that subjectivity is heavily influenced by the fact that experience "takes place within a cultural context organized by institutions and practices," which in this case is the *institution and practices* of the music studio. He argues that the experience of hearing—and its concomitant effects on memory—is less influenced by initial *production* than by technical *reproduction* done in the studio, and this phenomenon positions memory as both "fundamental to music and profoundly social."[67] Mowitt posits that a primary, if not *the* primary, reason for music's social importance is precisely this organization of sound *(noise)* around socially sanctioned public structures of listening that define normal, or "proper" ways of making sense of what we hear; a "standard of normalcy" that helps to define a social order, or, to use a better word, community. What is critical to understand from Mowitt's argument is the idea that music can *create* and *be created by* a community.[68]

The central themes for my project are the demonstration that music creates, and is created by, a distinct social context through experience *(interaction with others)* and memory *(of that interaction and past interactions)*, and also, that musical experience and memory play an important role in constructing specific identities and communities. *Sound* in *space* creates *identity*. These sonically constructed communities are linked to time through an interactive, reciprocal conversation with history that shapes the socially defined public arena in which music is produced, reproduced, and received. *Music, then, becomes integral to a way of life.* We live in sound-defined spaces. Albert Murray says as much when, writing on the painting influences of Romare Bearden, he states:

> [N]ot only was impeccable musical taste an absolute requirement for growing up hip, urbane, or streetwise, but so was the ability to stylize your actions—indeed, your whole being—in terms of the most sophisticated extensions and refinements of jazz music and dance.[69]

Understanding sound in this fashion is useful in positing the notion of music as an element of individual and collective identity that is:

1. A phenomenon of sonic organization and use created in a distinct social context
2. Dependent on experience and memory, linked to time—past, present, and future
3. Defined and communicated by people through patterns of use

We will see similar themes emerge as foundational elements of not only a notion of music, but also a particular notion of space. Space, for them, is a "performed communication."[70] We will return to this concept below.

As detailed previously in chapter 4, Henri Lefebvre posits that space is a social product. He argues against the dominant Western notion of space as preexisting and instead proposes that spaces are produced. Lefebvre's space is reciprocal; it at once recognizes, shapes, and affirms the identity and subjectivity of the people that shape, produce, and reproduce it. According to Lefebvre, because social space is dependent upon people for its (re)production and people are ever-present in the socially defined public arena, he concludes that "[n]o space disappears in the course of growth and development: the worldwide does not abolish the local."[71] For Lefebvre, there exists, at any given moment, a multiplicity of distinctive social contexts, all of which produce spaces that, as opposed to Foucault's heterotopias, "interpenetrate one another and/or superimpose themselves upon one another."[72]

Furthering this spatial theory, Michel de Certeau, in his book *The Practice of Everyday Life*, theorizes the communication and navigation of these multiple, simultaneously socially constructed spaces and demonstrates how Lefebvre's social space becomes legible through the language of movements, "pedestrian speech acts," that in fact "secretly structure the determining conditions of social life" by implying interaction between a speaker and observer that communicates meaning.[73] Within a framework of communication that reciprocally is transformed and transforms, the elements of language *(musical, verbal, and pedestrian)* are consistently chosen, appropriated, adapted, and employed by people to communicate meaning that is unique to that particular group, space, and time.[74] In other words, sometimes "bad" is bad, sometimes "bad" is good. De Certeau describes what this analysis means to the understanding of space:

> Thus space is composed of intersections of mobile elements. It is in a sense actuated by the ensemble of movements deployed within it.

Space occurs as the effect produced by the operations that orient it, situate it, temporalize it, and make it function. . . . In short, space is a practiced place.[75]

In sum, what is vital to understand from Lefebvre's spatial theory is the notion that space is produced by *bodies (people) interacting.* This interaction is specific to a time, place, and social formation, but is also historical —it has a memory, a past. Space—like music—cannot be static; it is dynamic, adapted by its user for the communication of specific meanings. For Lefebvre and de Certeau, the formation of space is dependent on the interaction, the understanding of the interaction in a dialogically critical way, and the memory of interaction communicated through the language of the pedestrian speech act. At its very essence, space, for them, is a "performed communication." Lefebvre, de Certeau, and others have allowed me to posit the notion of space as reciprocal and as:

1. A phenomenon of spatial organization and use, realized in a distinct social context *(people interacting)*
2. Dependent on experience and memory, linked to time—past, present, and future
3. Defined and communicated by people through patterns of use

This hypothesis is almost identical to the previously outlined notion of music and, as such, uncovers a heretofore hidden opportunity for further critical spatial inquiry. If space is derived from experience and memory, *whose communication is performed,* AND music is derived from experience and memory, *whose form of communication is performance,* then might we not look at sound and space as similar occurrences, constitutive of each other? If so, then space might be defined more specifically as:

1. A socially constructed phenomenon of sonic organization and use
2. Dependent on experience and memory, linked to time—past, present and future
3. Defined and communicated by people through their patterns of use

So, sound mediated/performed space becomes the key to understanding hip hop's cultural creation—rap music—as the principal foundational element of hip hop architecture.[76] I examine these propositions below.

Space is *a socially constructed phenomenon of sonic organization and use . . .*

Rap music is unquestionably music born of technology and is, as Mowitt has concluded, socially constructed. The ability of the musical production *(DJ, producer, engineer)* to manipulate particular sounds, breaks, ruptures in continuity and flow—recalling their existence by their absence—and mix several disparate sources of sonic pleasure into the listening experience is the core of rap music. With the use of what is termed "sampling"—the digitally enhanced process of transferring a sound, or series of sounds *(the sample)* from one source to another source—"[r]ap technicians employ digital technology as instruments, revising black musical styles and priorities through the manipulation of technology."[77] The primacy of studio/tech production has been key to the development of the rap genre and the epitome of a musical phenomenon created in a distinct social context—the studio.[78]

Space is *dependent on experience and memory, linked to time— past, present, and future*

"Music is nothing but organized noise. You can take anything—street sounds, us talking, whatever you want—and make it music by organizing it."[79] As Mowitt has previously noted, music's social importance is precisely this organization of noise around socially defined structures of listening. It is our shared understanding of the "correct" way to listen that is embedded in our memory and creates *community*. What becomes important to discern is, "Which community is forming in the musical technologies of the collective memory, and what is its relation to those technologies that facilitate the exact reproduction of the musician's actions for listeners?"[80]

Black music in general, but rap music's historical connection with the collective memory of the African diasporic community in particular, is complex and varied, and the hierarchy of its components is not at all universally agreed upon.[81] What is generally acknowledged as important, essential, and historical about black music is: its nature *(rhythm, repetition, layering, flow, rupture)*, which recalls the link to its African origin;[82] its orality *(toast, call-and-response, storytelling griot)*, which descends from specific African, Caribbean, and American influences;[83] and its content *(oppression, segregation, self-determination, self-naming)*, which is constituted in part by the postmodern condition of fragmentation and the project of reclaiming the Black *subject* from the Negro *object*.[84] These elements help to link the African diaspora over distance and time to a collective memory that is Africentric in origin and nature, but is—and this is key—*specific to its current locale* and defines a particular type of spatial practice, a principal tenet of Lefebvre's social space.

Space is *defined and communicated by people through their patterns of use*

The identity created by sound is best illustrated and understood by studying the use and influence of music on the lifestyles of the diaspora. As alluded to earlier in this essay by Albert Murray's discussion of Romare Bearden, Black music is really an integral part of the way Blacks live and communicate.[85] At its most basic level, music is for the diaspora an unconscious way of being that informs both the physical and mental response to its call and is acted out in a variety of ways, subtle and not. At its most heightened, it is a recognition and celebration of an Africentric life force. But at all levels, it is important, even essential, to the *performance* of life—Gilroy's enhanced mode of communication—for diasporic members.[86] This *performance of life* manifests itself in a variety of ways in the diaspora, but all are inexorably linked by the project of reclaiming the Black subjectivity.[87]

Rap music is clearly a tool to use in the process of redefining self. Whereas Dick Hebdige's analysis of punk culture/music reveals as a central theme punk's desire for an escape from the principle of identity, in hip hop culture/music, identity is paramount. To produce a style that nobody can deal with, one that is *"bigger and deffer,"* is primary to rap music's significance.[88] With and within the music, producers express their individual and collective identity—*the "who" we are*—and, in a confluence of structuralist and Africentric discourses, the music calls upon the listeners to express their identity—*are you "who" too?* Thus an Africentric spatial practice, and a corresponding community, is at once recalled, produced, and enhanced in the music of the hip hop culture.

> Every subordinate group fashions a "hidden transcript" out of its ordeal—an embodied and spatialised critique of power that is almost always spoken behind the back of the powerful. Thus, much more likely than open resistance is an opposition to domination or the powerful that is spatialised, occurring within specific places, and clandestine.[89]

So, what does all this have to do with space, or, for that matter, architecture? This next section will specifically address a spatial understanding of hip hop culture that employs this confluence of space and music as a paradigm that recalls, creates, and deploys new spaces that speak to the Africentric diasporic project of identity in the built environment. Hip hop architecture creates spaces that are constructed by the intersections of mobile elements—people (bodies)—but often includes objects of material culture (debris, monster speakers, and cars) as well. Hip hop space is made readable by the ensemble and interaction of people and elements engaged in the performance of everyday life. These particular performances are a function of diasporic spatial practices that have survived the Middle Passage and are specifically recalled and enhanced by the music of rap.[90] Hip hop architecture is the recognition of, and participation in, specific pedestrian speech acts or performances of communication that make the space function and communicate. As such, hip hop architecture is the latest manifestation of both the need and desire to create a stage for an emergence of Africentric identity that includes the *bembe,* the plantation praise houses, the church, and most recently, the jook joint in America and its counterpart, the *shebeen* in South Africa.[91] The space of hip hop invites us to ask whether it is logical to expect a culture that has been placed on the margin of society's concerns to employ the same language *(pedestrian speech patterns/performances)* used by those responsible for such marginalization, thereby reinforcing the very practice that is repressing them? Is it logical to expect the response of this community to spaces that represent the power of their oppression to be the same as of those who developed such spaces? The answer that the paradigm of hip hop space provides to these two critical questions, so central to the validity of the discipline and profession of architecture, is a resounding, emphatic, and unequivocal—NO. Below I will outline four primary principles necessary for the physical manifestations of hip hop space. I posit that strategies can be adapted from this *transnational capital* of hip hop space and manifested in built form.[92]

Hip hop architecture: palimpsestic

The architecture of hip hop is linked to the urban context in which it was born.[93] This is where the call-and-response for the physical manifestation of this space is strongest. Part of the social context of the inner city—particularly in predominantly poorer African-American communities—is one of disarray and decay.[94] Every day, intentionally unclaimed, naturally deconstructivist structures are allowed to fall away, piece by piece, in untended lots that are typically appropriated by the local residents as places for sundry nefarious activities. These are the available—and appropriate—sites for the construction of hip hop spaces. The charge here is to remake/reclaim Black subjectivity, and this calls for a remaking of these places; the erasure of the dominant "proper" and the repositioning of these urban spaces as empowering. Thus, the first, most basic principle of the physical manifestations of hip hop architecture is that it be *palimpsestic* in nature and intent.[95] It is an *erasure of both dominant spatial understandings of "proper" and their hegemonic physical manifestations,* while simultaneously—in the same location—the construction of a hip hop spatial consciousness and its physical manifestations.[96] Hip hop architecture is palimpsestic in the fact that it is engaged in reclaiming the subject from the object. Consistent with the foundations of hip hop's flow, layering, and rupture, the palimpsestic nature of hip hop architecture reorganizes and rewrites the "[v]isible boundaries [of architecture], such as walls or enclosures in general, [that] give rise for their part to an appearance of separation between spaces where in fact what exists is an ambiguous continuity"[97] in the *same location* of the dominant culture's hegemonic definition of "proper" spatial use. The primary objective of this reorganization is to recapture the Black subject from the "Negro" object and affirm the body's identity in spaces that have historically done just the opposite.

Hip hop architecture: anthropomorphic

A principal purpose of hip hop architecture is to create a "homeplace" *(as bell hooks has referred to it)* or, for the purposes of this book, a space that engages and employs similar identity (re)construction strategies that take place at various sites within the diaspora. Therefore, another primary principle of hip hop architecture, as it concerns reconstructing a positive Black identity, is that it be *anthropomorphic,* which is "in many respects, one of architecture's universals . . . [and] is also a frequently expressed feature of architectural traditions in Africa."[98] The anthropomorphism in hip hop space is not concerned with typical Western understandings of the concept that focuses centrally on the physical attributes or appendages of the body. It is instead concerned with a holistic understanding of the place the body inhabits. It is similar to the DJ/Producers' call of "who we are" and as such is intimately connected with the identity of the body within space. Unlike in the West, where "architectural anthropomorphism had its primary basis in the valuation of the human body as an expression of God's creative perfection, African architects more characteristically see in the human a model of life and vitality and an expression of social relationships and values."[99]

Hip hop architecture: performative

To paraphrase Shakespeare, if "all the world's a stage, and we are merely actors" then the physical manifestation of a hip hop spatial understanding is this phrase's most recent—and important—connotation. The notion of "simultaneity"—the intersection of body and stage around the construction of identity—communicated through performance is a primary element of the diaspora and must be a part of hip hop space.[100] The organization of hip hop spatial understanding can be found in the deep call of the diaspora in rhythm and repetition. Hip hop architecture is the emergence—*in form*—of the base and the beat, the flow and the rupture, the call-and-response. Consequently, an additional primary principle of hip hop architecture is that it is *performative*. It is about both providing the stage *(backdrop)* and privileging *(inviting)* the performance where space is produced through the conjunction of people within it. The importance of performance—both the everyday and the ceremonial—in the creation of space in the diaspora, "underscores the centrality of architecture itself both as a setting for everyday life and ceremonial action and as a theater for the presentation of dramas for the community as a whole. Through these performances, key aspects of architectural meaning are given expression."[101]

Hip hop architecture: adaptive

Finally, hip hop architecture is *adaptive*. It has to be. The sites that are available for the emergence of hip hop forms necessitate it; the people for whom the structures will be built will demand it; the availability of materials for this *(these)* project(s) requires it; the assemblage of these structures compels it. Hip hop architecture's diasporic dialectic is inescapable. From its vegetal and mud/clay site-specific African origins, to the design of "shotgun homes" of the late eighteenth-century Caribbean and early nineteenth-century America, to the late nineteenth-century Tuskegee Institute/University project, to the thatched roofs of the early twentieth-century "critter houses" of South Carolina, hip hop architecture is also committed to using and re-using materials transformatively and creatively, removing the hegemonic "proper" not only from spatial communication but from symbol and material communication also.[102] The architecture of hip hop embodies the spirit that architectural professor Laverne Wells-Bowie describes as "architecture as a cultural practice . . . that sense of architecture acknowledg[ing] diversity of location, that wherever folks are dwelling in space, they can think creatively about the transformation and reinvention of that space."[103]

In exploring a particular relationship between rap music, space, and architecture, I am rejecting previous investigative essays that also have as their focus music, space, and architecture as being inadequately probative. I have found it more useful to employ a counter-quest for an aesthetic paradigm of architectural and sonic production, one that approaches the question of music and architecture from the "inside-out," and from such an investigation, I have positioned rap music as the womb from which hip hop space and architecture are born. Unfortunately, theory in architecture is all too often discussed in terms of form only. The ideology in architecture—which permeates the profession and discipline—is rarely analyzed, at least from the perspective of communities of color. My primary purpose in engaging in this examination of music, space, and architecture is to begin to explore new paradigms of architectural spatial theory and manifestation that are initiated from the marginalized citizenry—specifically, the African-American community. This search is for a spatial paradigm that resists the power of dominant hegemonic understandings of space embedded and accepted in architecture and creates power for the marginalized from their built environment, primarily by identifying ways they can and do express their spatial practice in physical form to affirm their validity and their property. The revolutionary production of hip hop space has clearly been identified as a prototype demonstrative of an African-American spatial practice that is available for physical expression.[104] As such, the production of hip hop architecture is an attempt to "recover a sense of community outside the state-regulated and commodified universe" dependent on "a systematic reorganization of space to enlarge the realm of public discourse and physical freedom . . . a new code of space" and build upon the foundations of "expressive rather than instrumental (institutional) social relations."[105] Urban design strategies to date primarily have been developed outside the affected community under the current understanding of Locke's construction of property. Strategies developed by "experts"—who look at the architecture of survival, of identity, of erasure and determine that it is nothing more than vandalism—have emerged out of both a failure to understand what that architecture is really saying about the community that produced it and a willingness to impose narrowly defined spatial theories—which masquerade as "universal" aesthetics—upon an "other." Historically, design in these marginalized communities from a universal spatial understanding has not been universally successful, only highlighting the flaws in a homogenizing discourse of the universal.

This exploration has led me to concur with Guy Debord when he states that, "Architecture must advance by taking emotionally moving situations, rather than emotionally moving forms, as the material it works with."[106] As such, hip hop architecture is one model for addressing questions of property, halting the destruction and deterioration of African-American urban communities and its best hope to restore their viability as sustainable communities. The architectural entities that evolve from a hip hop spatial paradigm draw on the best of the past and the present. Employed in communities where there is a need and cry for an environment that does not repress but relieves, hip hop architecture replaces the constrictive with the supportive. It defines a particular African-American identity. Like rap music, hip hop architecture reuses and renames space and in the process "render[s] visible 'black' meanings, precisely because of, and not in spite of, its industrial forms of production, distribution and consumption."[107] It nurtures a place where African-Americans can see a positive portrait of themselves in their environment.

In the process of writing and discussing this work with fellow colleagues, students, and various segments of the public, I have often been asked—sometimes politely, sometimes critically, many times dismissively and always skeptically—"Yeah, yeah, whatever. So, tell me, what exactly does hip hop architecture look like?" I suspect that many of those reading this book have had—and still have—similar thoughts as well. If you have reached this portion of the book and have yet to divine that this is a question I do not feel compelled to answer, both you and I will be disappointed. And so you won't think that in refusing to do so that I am just being recalcitrant, I will provide some insight into why I have chosen to take such a position. Still, I leave it to the reader to determine whether my position is consistent or a cop-out.

The first glimpse should be easy enough to catch. By now you may have noticed that in this book I am, with very deliberate intent, critiquing the image-driven paradigm of the profession. While I am as interested in what architecture looks like as others in this profession, I am extremely troubled by the predominance of—in fact, the obsession with—the image as the be-all and end-all of architecture's value to both practitioner and society. It is as important to me to understand and explicate other aspects of this discipline that too often get short shrift, namely what architecture does, how it does it, and what its effects are on people and places. So, to have based this particular portion of my overall argument on an image or images seems to me to undermine the very spirit of my investigative foundation. There are more image-driven tomes about architecture—from the built to the unbuilt, the functional to the experimental—to satisfy that particular disciplinary craving to the point of addiction. One more would not make that much difference. My intention here is to fan another type of architectural flame in the reader, one that is interested in what lies beneath the veil of the image.

In addition, it has been my experience that too often when dealing with difficult issues—particularly from a decidedly marginalized perspective within a dominant cultural arena—the governing attitude taken by those in power—who may or may not be predisposed to the idea presented—will be "Show me and then I'll determine its validity."[108] This position too often lets power off the hook, relieving it from having to do the difficult and messy job of thinking through a concept or hypothesis. Such is the privilege of power, which I have also been critiquing, and as such I do not wish to place myself—or the reader—in either position. Granted, since I have admitted upfront that the hip hop portion of this work is ongoing and speculative and since I have written in the opening of this book that theory without practice has no value, I recognize that ultimately some sort of manifestation must prove or disprove the hypothesis. I have speculated as to what the nature of this work might be on both levels and continue to do so, but as to what that manifestation of proof might ultimately look like, and what its success as a mode of architectural and social intervention might be, only time and work will tell. As with most practices—particularly those that led to the birth and growth of hip hop—the application of methodologies cannot (and perhaps should not) accurately be predicted and has found sanctuary and substance in the most surprising and strangest of places. To negate that process by unilaterally defining the parameters of its eventual emergence is to betray one of the basic principles of hip hop itself. Now why would I want to do that, just for you?

Finally, I must point out that what I have done here is a common method of practice in the architectural discipline. The CIAM conferences concerning international architecture spurred the dissemination of both the image and the practitioners of that style across the globe; postmodern thought gave birth to postmodern architecture; and the materialization of deconstructivist forms flows from the philosophical and theoretical underpinnings of that school. In that same vein, this work is in part attempting to build a hip hop theoretical foundation from which an architectural intervention can follow. It is speculative, but not arbitrary, and the fact that perhaps it has yet to emerge certainly does not mean that it can't or won't. To immediately dismiss its value would be, in my view, extremely premature, if not extremely prejudicial.

Remix

So, yo, B. Word is, architecture is all about the "me," ya dig? True that, but what ain't? All that represents is a definite lack of belief in anything beyond the now, but ain't that always been the way? No, son. See, these old school cats in the 1960s tried to do both—image and impact. Back in the day, they believed in the power of architecture to engage and change f——ked-up social conditions and didn't punk out when it came to the tough questions about their role in creating the conditions. It is this roughneck style that made the public think architects were about something. Of course, this kinda architecture back in the day had some successes, and some spectacular f——k-ups, but it was the f——k-ups that helped move it away from impact to image. And that is where we be at today, shuttin' out anything that doesn't have to do with the architectural style. After folks got in their asses 'bout some of the bogus blocks of bullshit and other "modernist" works done in the 1960s and 1970s in the name of the people—think Pruitt-Igoe, Cabrini-Green—the profession just bugged and said "F—— 'em. We tried it their way. Now, we gonna do it our way. If it ain't about us, it ain't about shit."

So now, bro, folks like Cornel West ain't tryin' to hear that. He says that 'cause architects are basically "it's all 'bout us," we can't believe anything these suckas got to say. They are just spewin' the bullshit myth to cover their ass—'cause they fail to acknowledge the real—which is how architects and architecture is partly responsible for the shitty urban condition today. He implies that until architects acknowledge the real—the actual impact—they ain't legit. They are just the bitches of style, without a clue of how to change the shit.

So who does? Here's where it gets deep.

He says that these French cats can help us find a way through image to impact, primarily because they don't believe the one-size-fits-all "universal" shit—universal meaning, universal understanding, universal style, whatever. Focusin' on the style ignores the impact and the insistence of a universal style erases history, especially the history of everybody who ain't considered "universal"—wealthy, white, and male, the very folk that define just what "the good, the true and the beautiful" is, dig? So, these French cats say "F—— that. Not buyin' it, son. I got somethin' to say 'bout this universality of beauty shit, and it ain't you. Na, you can either come correct or step." West thinks that by comin' correct, architects can find a way to deal with both the image and the impact—the beauty and the political. But architects are not havin' it. They still argue that image is everything, impact don't matter, and we get to decide what style is beautiful and what ain't.

Except now, they keep gettin' called out by folks who think the French make some sense. So they have been gettin' punked again and again by other disciplines. "Architecture can and will be critiqued," they say, "You can either get real or get played." "But your critique ain't legit," architects shout back, " 'cause you don't know jack 'bout what architecture is." "Bullshit" the critics respond, "It's *you* don't know jack 'bout what it is or does, fool!" Punked again with no comeback, architects label these crazy-ass folks illegit—unauthorized to make claims 'bout their shit. But no one really believes 'em anymore; fools are only foolin' themselves. The emperor has no dashiki, the rapper no bling. So what, yo? How do we fix this shit? How can architecture get some street cred? Where can the discipline find some rep? Yo, by being professionals in the true sense of the term and placing (political, financial, and cultural) impact on the same level as image. "Architecture or revolution, bitch. Who you wid'?"

Okay, let's say you choose to keep it real and side wid' the revolution. How you gonna make that shit work? Just how can you do, you know, the social justice, critical practice thang? How do you begin to think about that kind of work? Well ... we could start with where the last revolution left off—the social justice of property. Yeah, I know, that's more of that abstract bullshit that don't go nowhere, but slow yo' roll son, let me holla at 'cha for a sec.

Okay, pick up you Locke handbook and dig his shit about property again:

1. Earth, and all that comes from it, is for everyone, for all eternity.
2. Everybody owns his or her own body and mind, and if you make something with either, you own that shit, too.
3. Now if you make something with your mind and body through the earth, you can keep that shit.
4. That part of the earth that you are using is no longer for everyone. It is yours for as long as you keep using it. It is now part of your property.

5. If you ever stop using it, it is no longer yours to keep. It becomes free again for anyone else to use it.

Now, let's let the PRM finish this shit:

6. Property is essential to life and freedom.
7. The main role of government is to protect people's access to life and freedom.
8. Property is a moral imperative, based on fairness and justice.

Okay, yo, got all that? Good. Ok, so property requires judgment about fairness and justice. Now, with that in mind, riddle me this, Batman:

1. *If the right to property is necessary for people's life and liberty and it's the government's role to protect the people, then shouldn't the government make sure that everyone has property?*
2. *If number 1 is true, shouldn't the government ensure that nobody has more than their share for life and liberty, so that everyone can have what is guaranteed to all?*
3. *If number 1 is not true, then under what moral authority does such a government determine who is fit to have life and liberty and who is not?*

That's what they mean by no trust, no property. No property, no piece. No piece ... no peace. Folks have to believe that this shit is fair if they are gonna buy into it. And dig ... the legitimate professional practice of architecture requires a similar kinda trust. People gotta believe that for architecture to hold the position of a profession based on a moral and ethical basis. That it's gonna do right by them. No moral component, no trust. No trust, no property. No property, no work. No work, no peace. Think about that while I show you how this shit comes together.

From Sharon Sutton to droves of disgruntled pre- and post-professionals, it has been argued that architecture has little juice to empower change in general, and no juice for change in particular for Black folk. So ... why the hell are da brothas and sistas still being drawn to this shit and what can we do to provide them some juice before they go searching elsewhere for it? In other words ... how do we make the study and practice of this exclusionary, depoliticized, elitist profession relevant to the African-American community, many of whom are marginalized precisely by the same exclusionary practices that they are required to study and implement?

Two words: hip hop.

Why? Yo ... son. Where ya been? Hip hop has taken all the shit tossed away by folks and has given them a new life and, in the process, made them indispensable—a model for our urban core *(not to mention to scores and scores of marginalized residents in those urban cores)* that is begging to be expanded to property—those vacant lots we been talkin' 'bout, B. Not even the modernist had such a slick-ass example to play with. They guessed at what was being said in the urban, dig, and they f——ked up 'cause they made assumptions about, instead of listening to, the folks in da 'hood. Hip hop ain't got that kinda problem. Hip hop is—although less today than yesterday—the voice from the 'hood, a voice that has made itself heard from the 'hood and made that a force. The very existence—not to mention the longevity and influence—of hip hop breaks down many of those sorry, tired-ass clichés 'bout the (inner) city. But how to make this "voice" into architecture? The tools we have right now can't even understand it—much less address it. We need something more to adapt the flow of hip hop into a spatial—and architectural—manifestation. We need an activist kinda architecture.

Okay, so how does this hip hop shit translate into an activist architecture—and, more to the point, how can it be used to address the spatial and architectural ills of the inner city? How does hip hop take on the question of property? How can it provide some much-needed juice to the brothas and sistas doin' this thang here? How, how, how, yo?

As Snoop says, "Come on, follow me, follow me, follow me, follow me ..."

First things first, I Poppa, let's connect some music and space. A couple of old theory-heads—Frith and McRobbie—say rock and pop music is where boys and girls learn certain ways of moving, dancing, and shakin' that ass on the dance floor that identify you as a "B-boy" or "fly girl." Check it. If a guy who claims to be straight does something he ain't supposed to—like pop and make that ass drop—yo' boys gonna let you know that shit was whack, for the honeys only. So, how you act on the flo' lets folk know who you lookin' fo'. Ain't nobody born knowing what to and not to do to look like a "man" or a "woman" on the dance floor, dig—these shits are learned. Furthermore, the music that helps shape your definition of a "man" and "woman" is played by somebody else, controlling what you hear, when you hear it, how and how many times you hear it, what videos you will see with it, etc. This suggests that somebody you don't know got a whole lotta say in what kind of "boy" or "girl" you can choose to be. For example, if all you see is gangsta rap—which depicts a particular type of "man" or "woman"— then, in many cases, that's what you think a man or woman is. Check all the suburban kids dressin' all gangsta down, like they live on MLK and you'll see what I'm sayin'. Music—and videos—are doin' that. Ghetto fab ain't nuttin' but a section at the Gap to them.

Next ... another theory-head, Lipsitz. Funny name, big brain—he say that music is a product of the social and political context of the time—that the meaning of music comes from the when and where it's played and heard. In other words, when JB sang "Say it loud—I'm Black and I'm proud" that shit meant more in the 1960s than it does in the 1990s, son. That's 'cause it came out of a particular time—the Black Power movement. For us, JB is slick and shit, but Tupac and Jay-Z talk about today. Lipsitz says memory is the power of music—so memory is critical for meaning. Why? Check it —you are not born knowing how to act in public. There ain't no rules stuck to the bars of your crib. You know, 'cause you watch other folk, you learn and you *remember*. Same with music. It has a history—I remember where I was when I heard that song. I remember what I was doing or who I was doing when I hear it now. It means sumpin' to me. So, Lipsitz figures that not only is memory necessary to make music, it is also necessary for the social context in which the music is made. Both are needed to be a "man" or a "woman." JB was tellin' you to be a particular kind of Black person—a proud Black cat—and the memory of that stays with you.

Finally, Mowitt picks up Lipsitz's flow and rolls a step further by sayin' that current technology has separated the production and reception of music, so that hearing is most important. This shows and proves even more that music is created socially. He argues that both hearing and remembering music is less influenced by the playa than the producer. For example, when performing, playas may find reading music unnecessary 'cause they already memorized their shit. So, for them music ain't on the page, it's in the head. It is a group memory that they "remember" having *heard* each other playing. The sound is memorized by the group until a "correct" memory is understood by everybody. So dig, a correct memory defines the "normal" way to listen and a community of people who recognize it as "correct" is born. In this case that community is the group—but it could be anybody. Mowitt says that a primary, if not *the* primary, reason for music's social importance is precisely because this organization defines "normal" ways of listening that define a "right" way of making sense of what you hear. For example, you know a hook from a break—even if you don't know it's called a break or hook. Again, music shapes us, this time as a group. We know what to expect in types of music. It's hard to listen to music that doesn't stick to these expectations, 'cause we don't know what to do when we hear it—how to make sense of it, ya know? That's why rap is hard for old folks to get wid'. It ain't what they learned as music—they don't know how to listen to it 'cause they don't know what to expect. Music is important because it helps to create a communal identity by setting this standard of "normal." And who is creating that standard—the playa or the producer? What you hear, ain't necessarily what you heard, yo. So Mowitt is sayin' that music can *make* and *be made by* a community and, if the producers can make the music, then they can make the community—and do it in any way they choose. See how Dre changed how we listen to and respond to music? A gangsta is born, B.

Okay, freeze. This is what you need to remember: music makes, and is made by, our interactions with others, times and places we remember, and gives us choices about types of people and groups we wanna be. In short, *sound* in *space* creates *us*. So, *music is life*. We live in sound-defined spaces, dig?

Good.

Remember back in chapter 1 we rapped about Lefebvre? Okay, so you peeped that he says space is a social thang defined by what we do. Na here come de Certeau sayin' this social thang is a way of talkin' 'bout space, tellin' us things about it. I know you all can get to that. How you move says shit about both you and the space around you without you even having to say a word. How you move through a room, how you step to a sista, it all communicates. He calls this *"pedestrian speech acts."* Both these Lefebvre and de Certeau describe a kinda "performed communication" similar to the production of music. Space and music are made in a similar kinda way. Deep. If you can get with this, you can keep goin'—if not, go back and try again. Don't go further until you do—you'll only get lost.

Na, if space is made of experience and memory, WHOSE COMMUNICATION IS PERFORMED, AND *music is made of experience and memory,* WHOSE FORM OF COMMUNICATION IS PERFORMANCE, *then might we not look at sound and space as similar shits?* If that is true—and it is—we can now talk about the rap formations of space and the very real possibility of a hip hop architecture. How so? Peep this, it's the money shot.

Rap music is unquestionably a music of technology and it must be, as Mowitt said, socially made. The proof is that the core of rap music lies in the skills of the DJ, producer, and engineer to manipulate particular sounds, breaks, ruptures in the flow, and mix several disparate sources of sounds into the listening experience with the use of sampling. The music is made in the studio, on the boards. No denyin' that.

As far as the "correct" way to listen based on memory, history, and community, in the case of rap/hip hop, the correct is based in a community with very deep Black roots. Rap music's historical connection with the collective memory of the Black folk all over is complex but that shit is nonetheless clear. Rap and its roots—its strategy—is undeniably Black and that essential connection can be seen in the form, which comes from its African origin; its vocal style, which descends from African, Caribbean, and American influences; and its content, which comes from its urban experiences. These elements link Black folk all over the world to a collective memory that is Africentric in origin and form, but is still *specific to spots*—think East Coast/West Coast/Dirty South, etc.

As to being able to communicate and construct identity through a pattern of use, if Black music is really an integral part of the way African-Americans live, rap music is clearly a tool to use in the process of redefining self. In hip hop culture/music, identity is the ultimate objective. Bigga and deffa, B-brush the dirt off my shoulders. An Africentric spatial community is embedded in hip hop music.

So, what does all this have to do with space, or for that matter architecture? Just this: Hip hop space is made by the collection and interaction of a large portion of Black people engaged in doin' everyday shit; specific pedestrian speech acts that make the space function and communicate. Okay, so what are the primary principles of hip hop space?

1st Part: The rewrite

The inner city is fallin' and callin'—so it's the spot to start. Thus, the first, and most basic principle of hip hop architecture is that it be *palimpsestic* in nature and intent. It will rewind and rewrite some new shit on the same spot, a desirable identity in a place where there was once only the bullshit. Using hip hop's flow, layering, and rupture, hip hop architecture—like making the turntable the instrument—redefines what is "correct" in the same space that was previously seen as "incorrect." What was once "power*less*" now becomes "power*ful*."

2nd Part: Body style

Hip hop architecture creates spaces that link the different successes and struggles Black folk go through on their body—it becomes part of the space and the link. So, another primary principle of hip hop architecture is that it represent the body of black folk.

3rd Part: Work it

The organization of hip hop space is in the deep call of rhythm and repetition so recognizable to Black folk. Hip hop architecture is the base and the beat, the flow and the rupture, the call-and-response. So, it must be a place that makes you move, a place respectful of how you move, a place that celebrates that funky beat.

4th Part: Mixin' it

Finally, hip hop architecture is always adaptin' and changin', B. It has to be 'cause the shit for these projects will be found tossed out and must be reused. Hip hop architecture's roots in the struggle for survival of Black life is inescapable—both are, for better or worse, required to creatively reuse materials. So, dawg, check it. Hip hop shows and proves at least one way in which we can combine all the elements mentioned previously—property, responsibility, legitimacy, and social justice—all within an activist architecture. Yo, B . . . how can there not be the possibility of a practice—some serious and seriously creative shit—happenin' here? The types of conditions that call for an activist architecture are ubiquitous across the country. There ain't a city in the world that couldn't use this kinda design work, knowwhatI'msayin'? Practicing in this area addresses an ever-growing and seeming intractable condition in the 'hood—environmental and cultural deterioration. Hip hop architecture is only one model for halting the destruction and deterioration of African-American urban communities, but it is possibly the best one we got. So just do it, yo.

Precis

> One might hope that these undisciplined practices will
> bring about a liberating architecture, in which unforeseen
> intersubjectivities continue to undermine the historical
> power relationships between architect and user. It would
> be an architecture through which the given roles of race,
> gender, and cultural affiliation in the shaping of space
> would be shaken up. It would be an architecture without
> orders, without a naturalized set of values vested in a priori
> forms or procedures.
> —*Hannah le Roux*

AS I MENTIONED in the beginning of this work, to tear down a system is considered reactionary, but to tear down a system and replace it with something else is revolutionary. Typically, responses to architectural theories and philosophies are more the former than the latter. Perhaps this work will also eventually fall into the category of the former, but it is my hope that what I have done here is provide a blueprint for the latter.

In "Architecture as a Verb," I have been concerned with conditions of transformation, in opposition to the conditions of permanence I spoke to in "Architecture as a Noun." In "Verb," I wanted to theorize an alternative to the conditions and conclusions identified in the first part. Thus "Verb" is about settin' things in motion; 'bout gettin' a lil' sumpin' sumpin' started. I began by highlighting what I've come to understand as the general problems with the Lockean notions of space and place from the previous chapters: that as a critical element in the construction of identity and property, both space and place are particularly racialized and this racialization, codified and embedded in the built environment, invalidates any claim to neutrality. Lockean space creates conditions that are often egregiously iniquitous and injurious to members of non-white cultures and particularly so to African-Americans. Operating in such a paradigm, African-American identity construction is contextualized by an unnecessary and unjustified comparison to *whiteness*. Thus, I have found it necessary to argue for a different spatial appropriation and usage—one that is more in tune to and advantageous for the construction of African-American subjectivities and identities; a spatial construction that not only allows for difference but also encourages and celebrates it. Unfortunately, any spatial paradigm that clashes with the dominant Lockean view is almost immediately seen as aberrant, prompting the mobilization of all kinds of private and state-authorized preservation forces in various forms *(police, private security, restrictive covenants, neighborhood watches, red-lining, surveillance cameras, etc.)* to enforce Locke's boundaries. Alternate spatial paradigms are needed to reexamine the urban environment and theorize strategies for intervention. Truth be told, such paradigms are already in operation, and have been for some time, employed by the residents of these spaces. It would be useful to study these already existing spatial understandings at the very least for what they may reveal about the current study and practice of architecture. If the architectural discipline's understanding of the world in which it operates is racialized and naturalized, then how can the environment it produces be anything less, especially without any active attempt to ameliorate such influences? Taking that position as my starting point, I have posited a strategy to dismantle the systemic nature and the ways in which the academy operates both to support class and racial bias and specifically to impede African-American participation in the discipline. Previously, I identified how the racialized dichotomies authorized by "normative" spatial expectations are institutionalized in the academy, not only through the curriculum, but also—and perhaps more important—through relationships with students and colleagues of color. As such, the academy reproduces practitioners and educators who continue to view the racialized environment as a natural occurrence, perpetuating the status quo. What I have proposed is that if the academy adopts a different manner of seeing and being in the world—a spatial paradigm that allows for difference—we can then begin to form the foundation of new paradigms more amiable to rethinking the environmental status quo and the discipline's historical alliance to the economic, political, and social elite. Finally, I have outlined how the collective amnesia of the philosophical and moral origins of Locke's foundations for property continues to facilitate racial bias in physical manifestations of space and place and I have theorized what may emerge if the first two alternatives are adopted and implemented. While it might be easy to dismiss this position as utopian, socialist, or both, this argument is not so much about free or cheap work, divesting people of property or lowering the aesthetic bar, so much as it is about a particular disciplinary mindset that sees equal access and the commitment to social justice in the built environment as an integral element of what it does and enough of a primary objective that it is taught, institutionalized, valued, and supported. As Crawford has noted:

> After nearly a hundred years of professional existence, architects have almost completely surrendered both the tools and the ideological aspirations that might allow them to address the economic, political, and social concerns posed by modern life.... In order to maneuver successfully, the profession needs to give some serious thought to renewing and refashioning its ideological premises.[1]

What I am proposing is an ideological premise for what the architectural profession does and whom it finds worthy of its services that has at its core a recognition of a humane and socially just built environment as an important, if not a primary, objective in the process and production of its object.

> What are the real possibilities for you, the architect, in your position in society, not as a hero who is going to save society, but as a worker who is engaging in practices that have the possibility of opening up new ways of doing things here and there ... being integrated into a

general social and political process, and, unfortunately, in so doing, having to make choices as to what kind of social relations you seek to support, and what kinds of social relations you want to suppress? We inevitably repress as we seek to emancipate.[2]

What if architecture were to follow the lead of the legal and medical professions and develop a similar sensibility and call to duty beyond the immediate, personal concerns of its members? What if it were to take the position that it won't wait for problems of/in the environment to be presented for solutions but would actively identify issues and address them? What would that academic and professional infrastructure look like? It would be both traditional and nontraditional—entrepreneurial at its base and expansive in its application. In short, it would look like an activist architecture—one that not only redefines architecture and architect, but that is worthy of the discipline's enormous gifts/abilities to make lives better.

Having taken up the challenge posed by Le Corbusier's bifurcation of architecture, I find that I must reject the proposition that architecture will always look like architecture and thus I attempt to explore a philosophy and design emerging from/for hip hop's temporal-spatial community. It is becoming increasingly clear that the architectural discipline is guilty of complicity in the systematic marginalization of people and hip hop has shown that this marginalization is no longer inevitable, if it ever was.[3] It has taken dated technology and devalued material from the trash heap and made a global community out of the discarded parts of a postindustrial urban environment. It is my contention that these tactics can be invoked by architectural designers when developing the structures for/in this new community. By adapting hip hop culture's "shared approaches to sound and motion found in the Afrodiaspora ... flow, layering and ruptures in line,"[4] incorporating hip hop's ability to transform existing, if discarded, materials into new and creative uses in our design approach(es), we can reverb our way to developing that style that no one can deal with. Hip hop snatches questions of property—particularly the concepts of existence, rights, and ownership—from the abstract theoretical, philosophical, and legal musings and places them front and center in a most messy, materialist debate that architecture can no longer ignore. Through sampling, hip hop has forced the issue of intellectual property to the surface and revealed the gaping flaws and cultural and class biases in the premise of property itself.[5] At the same time, it has also clearly become comfortable and reified with, if not entrenched in, what Murray Forman describes as "a pronounced commitment to narrowly conceived capitalist ideals of wealth and power," an overaccumulation—a hoarding, if you will—of material property, sparking yet another debate.[6] A hip hop architectural paradigm—as part of an activist architecture agenda—is just the logical extension of this agitation and its development will also bring to the surface and exacerbate the tensions embedded in the notion of natural, or landed property. While the first two instances of the property question currently demand the most immediate attention, it is my opinion that the latter is the more profound and important agitation, because it goes to the heart of the justification of the first two and shapes how we will live in the future as access to all forms of property potentially becomes much more scarce and thus more sacred.[7]

> Property is something we must collectively define and construct. It is not given to us whole; it does not emerge fully formed like Athena from Zeus' head. It is closer to a piece of music that unfolds over time. Like music, property gets its sense of stability from the ongoing creation and resolution of various forms of tension. The tensions that inform property are the tensions inherent in social relations.[8]

The "tensions inherent in social relations" are the very tensions that are the be-all and end-all of rap music. Whether it is about the use and abuse of power that authorizes class, race, or gender, rap music is first, foremost, and always about delineating, demonstrating, agitating, and creating social relations. They are the genesis, the method of construction, and the message of the music. Hip hop architecture is asking the questions about the nature of property that the misapplication of Locke authorizes and it can best be illustrated in the organization of urban sites, which, if studied carefully, leads us to:

a heightened awareness of the real social structuring of the city, of the complex way in which cities are divided into distinct quarters, based in class occupation or function, self-contained yet reliant upon other components in the urban machine....

No one could deny that urban reorganization has been a stock response among modern states faced with social instability, a process usually involving slum clearance and the improvement of communications.[9]

So ... the stage is set; the revolution that Le Corbusier decried is upon us. The tools and strategies of this movement have been munificently supplied by those who would have this revolution crushed at its inception—if only we choose to take them up.

From the Past	To the Current	Leading to the Future
Constructivists	Creative New Technology/ Globalization	Creative Material Reuse/ Sustainability
Situationalists	New Urbanism	Hip Hop Urbanism
Individual/ Property Rights	Equity Planning	Property / Property Rights *Interrogation*
Squatter Collectives/ Spontaneous Settlements	Environmental Justice	Environmental Insurance
Community Design Centers	Community Development Corporations	Participatory Design Practices

Table I. Activist Architecture—Physical and Philosophical Lineage

Architecture "can and does produce positive effects when the liberating intentions of the architect coincide with the real practice of people in the exercise of their freedom."[10] With such a public palette upon which to work, by what right does architecture deny the direct benefits of what it provides to those who need them most and most likely pay the biggest price for the creation of the said environmental amenities? The answer—any answer—to this question by the discipline can make an important contribution to the property debate, and, like our fellow creative practitioners in the music and fashion arenas, property is an arena that architecture and architects should be on the forefront of exploring. "If property shapes social relations, we need to ask ourselves: 'In which world would we rather live?' "[11] Architects deal in the physical world in which we live and must be deeply concerned with its interventions. As Karsten Harries states:

> Like language, architecture is on one hand a product of human activity while on the other it helps to create the environment which gives shape to man's activities. To build is to help decide how man is to dwell on the earth or indeed whether he is to dwell on it at all, rather than drift aimlessly across it.[12]

Movements/styles/philosophies develop in history to respond to specific issues/problems of the time. When those problems have been solved, the legitimacy—if not the use—of these design styles or forms cease to exist. Even Le Corbusier recognized this when he argued "if we challenge the past, we shall learn that 'styles' no longer exist for us, that a style belonging to our own period has come about."[13] Snap! Check that. Le Corbusier is (subconsciously?) stating that the discipline of architecture *flows*, with periodic *breaks* in its *continuity*. It is, in effect, breakdancing. Architecture: hip hop(ping) through history.

In closing, I must note that as a theoretical example, this hypothesis makes a logical argument for the cultural applicability touted both implicitly and explicitly throughout this book. Admittedly, physical examples are more challenging; however, there are several instances—disparate portions of this argument manifested in both distant and local sites—that provide hope that a comprehensive strategy and application may not be as far off as one might think. We are in one of those moments in time where a "pop" or "rupture" in the dance is necessary. The old solutions (styles) no longer apply. Our problems at this time are different. Architecture should be about that, about responding to society now, all of society, for the future. When Bone Thugs-n-Harmony rap "It's the first of the month" or Luniz "I Got 5 on It," this speaks to the concerns of a broad spectrum of the populace, and suggests modes of aesthetic solutions. Where are the structures that reflect this? Where is the building that I can say "I Got 5 on It"? I see the "God Bless America" buildings every day. I live in a "Boogie-Woogie Bugle Boy" building, but I'd much rather live in a Boogie Down Productions space. Because of that, here I am—here we are—with rap as the blueprint, calling on the architectural flow to develop a space:

> that nobody can deal with—a [space] that cannot be easily understood or erased, a [space] that has the reflexivity to create counterdominant narratives against a mobile and shifting enemy.... In the post-industrial urban context of dwindling low-income housing, a trickle of meaningless jobs for young people, mounting police brutality, and increasingly draconian depictions of young inner-city residences, hip hop style is black urban renewal.[14]

So, let's get started. Do bop down and hop on in the Doo Bop Hip Hop Inn. "Don't make me wait. Come into [our] house."[15] It's gonna be a lil' sumpin' sumpin' special.

NOTES

Preface

1. Jack Travis, "African American Architecture: From Idea to Published Product," *Journal of Architectural Education* (September 1993); Richard K. Dozier, "The Black Architectural Experience in America," *AIA Journal* 65 (July 1976) and "Black Architects," *Black Enterprise* (1976); Raymond A. Dalton, "Admission, Retention and Support Service of African-American Architecture Students: A National Survey" (Ph.D. diss., Purdue University, 1990); Bradford Grant and Dennis Alan Mann, eds., *Directory of African American Architects* (Cincinnati: Center for the Study of Practice, 1995); Dell Upton, ed., *America's Architectural Roots: Ethnic Groups that Built America* (Washington, D.C.: National Trust for Historic Preservation, 1986); Lee D. Mitgang, "Saving the Soul of Architectural Education: Four Critical Challenges Face Today's Architecture Schools," *Architectural Record* (May 1997); and the National Architectural Accrediting Board Annual Statistics Report, among others. These statistics are as of 2004.

2. Gary Stevens, *The Favored Circle: The Social Foundations of Architectural Distinction* (Cambridge, Mass.: MIT Press, 1998), 110.

On the Organization of This Book

1. Bill Hubbard, Jr., *A Theory for Practice: Architecture in 3 Discourses* (Cambridge, Mass.: MIT Press, 1995), 65.

2. Tricia Rose, *Black Noise: Rap Music and Black Culture in Contemporary America* (Hanover, N.H.: Wesleyan University Press, 1999), 61.

1. Space—Place

1. William Kirby Lockard, *Design Drawing* (New York: Norton, 2001), 39.

2. Rhys Isaac is quoted by William Gleason, "Chestnutt's Piazza Tales: Archi-

tecture, Race, and Memory in the Conjure Stories," *American Quarterly* (March 1999), 35.

3. Joseph Chilton Pearce, as quoted by Lockard, *Design Drawing*, 27.

4. Murray Forman, *The 'Hood Comes First: Race, Space and Place in Rap and Hip-Hop* (Middletown, Conn.: Wesleyan University Press, 2002), 23.

5. Aspa Gospodini, "Urban Morphology and Place Identity in European Cities: Built Heritage and Innovative Design," *Journal of Urban Design* (June 2004), 232.

6. Edward T. Hall, as quoted by Lockard, *Design Drawing*, 26: "Space itself is perceived entirely differently [across cultures]. In the West, man perceives the objects but not the space between them. In Japan, the spaces are perceived, named and revered as the *ma,* or intervening interval."

7. Paul Weiss, as quoted by Karsten Harries, *The Ethical Function of Architecture* (Cambridge, Mass.: MIT Press, 1997), 214.

8. Alexander O. Boulton, "The Architecture of Slavery: Art, Language and Society in Early Virginia" (Ph.D. diss., The College of William and Mary, 1991), 139.

9. Cheryl I. Harris, "Whiteness as Property," *Harvard Law Review* (1993), 1727.

10. Barbara Flagg, "Was Blind, but Now I See: White Race Consciousness and the Requirement of Discriminatory Intent," *Michigan Law Review 1992–1993* (1993), 969–70.

11. John Hartigan, Jr., "Establishing the Fact of Whiteness," *American Anthropologist* (September 1997), 496.

12. See various texts on "white" and its (spatial) implications, which include, among others: Theodore W. Allen, *The Invention of the White Race* (London: Verso, 1994); Alastair Bonnet, "White Critical Studies: The Problems and Projects of a New Research Agenda," *Theory, Culture and Society* (1996); Richard Dyer, "White," *Screen* (Autumn 1988); Richard Delgado and Jean Stefancic, eds., *Critical White Studies: Looking Behind the Mirror* (Philadelphia: Temple University Press, 1997); Michelle Fine et al., eds., *Off White: Readings on Race, Power, and Society* (New York: Routledge, 1997); David Theo Goldberg, *Racist Culture: Philosophy and the Politics of Meaning* (Oxford: Blackwell, 1993); David Theo Goldberg, ed., *Anatomy of Racism* (Minneapolis: University of Minnesota Press, 1990); Peter Hall, *Cities of Tomorrow* (Oxford: Blackwell, 1994); Harris, "Whiteness as Property"; Hartigan, "Establishing the Fact of Whiteness"; John B. McConahay, "Modern Racism and Modern Discrimination: The Effect of Race, Racial Attitudes and Context on Simulated Hiring

Practices," *Personality and Social Psychology Bulletin,* vol. 9, no. 4 (1983); Thomas Nakayama and Robert L. Krizek, "Whiteness: A Strange Rhetoric," *Quarterly Journal of Speech* (August 1995); Steve Pile, *The Body and the City: Psychoanalysis, Space and Subjectivity* (New York: Routledge, 1996); David Roediger, *Towards the Abolition of Whiteness: Essays on Race, Politics and Working Class History* (New York: Verso, 1994); David Stowe, "Uncolored People: The Rise of Whiteness Studies," *Lingua Franca* (1996); and Margaret Talbot, "Getting Credit for Being White," *New York Times Magazine,* Nov. 30, 1997, among many others.

13. John Locke, *An Essay on Human Understanding* (New York: Dover, 1959), 219: "I shall begin with the simple idea of Space. I have shewed above, that we get the Idea of Space, both by our Sight and Touch; which, I think, is so evident, that it would be as needless, to go to prove, that Men perceive, by their Sight, a distance between Bodies of different Colours, or between the parts of the same Body; as that they see Colours themselves; Nor is it less obvious, that they can do so in the Dark by Feeling and Touch.... This Space considered barely in length between any two Beings, without considering any thing else between them."

14. Ibid., 169–71: "Another Idea coming under this Head, and belonging to this Tribe is that we call Place. As in simple Space, we consider the relation of Distance between any two Bodies, or Points; so in our Idea of Place, we consider the relation and Distance betwixt any thing, and any two or more Points, which are considered, as keeping the same distance one with another and so considered as at rest.... That our Idea of Place, is nothing else, but such a relative Position of any thing ..."

15. Edward S. Casey, *The Fate of Place: A Philosophical History* (Berkeley: University of California Press, 1998), 165: "Place as determined by measurable distance can be nothing other than a mode, and at that a particularly delimited mode, of space."

16. Ibid.: "It becomes evident that with Locke's conception of place as distance-determined, as with the phoronomic physics of Galileo and the analytical geometry of Descartes, the decisive steps have been taken toward the fateful reduction of place to 'site' that will become the pervasive destiny of place in the eighteenth and nineteenth centuries."

17. John Locke, "Second Treatise on Government—An Essay Concerning the True Original, Extent and End of Civil Government (1690)," available at: http://odur.let.rug.nl/fflusa/D/1651-1700/locke/ECCG/governo5.htm.

18. Ibid.

19. Ibid.

20. Ibid.

21. Harris, "Whiteness as Property," 1725–26, quotes Jeremy Bentham in the *Theory of Legislation,* 111–13: "Property is thus said to be a right, not a thing, characterized as metaphysical, not physical."

Harris quotes James Madison in *The Writings of James Madison,* 101: "[P]roperty 'embraces everything to which a man may attach a value and have a right.'"

22. Harris, "Whiteness as Property," 1726.

23. The notion of creating value is also central to the Lockean spatial/property theory—a principle underscored by Harris, "Whiteness as Property," 1721: "Although the Indians were the first occupants and possessors of land in the New World [and] the land had benefit in its natural state, untilled and unmarked by human hands, it was waste and therefore, the appropriate object of settlement and appropriation [by Europeans in America].

The ability to create value—as proof of usage; as an indication of a right—is central to this concept of identity; it is fully indebted to the notion of 'whiteness' and is difficult to locate as this idea of usage, or labor, of securing land to create value from the property, obscures it. This ability to create value is central to the notion of identity that Locke enables."

24. Boulton, "The Architecture of Slavery," 150.

25. Boulton, 145.

26. John Locke, *The Works of John Locke: Volume V* (London: Thomas Davidson, Whitefriars, 1823), 386–87.

27. Boulton, "The Architecture of Slavery," 154–56.

28. Harris, "Whiteness as Property," 1728.

29. Dred Scott, a slave who lived in the free state of Illinois and the free territory of Wisconsin before moving back to the slave state of Missouri, filed suit along with his wife Harriet against Irene Emerson for their freedom on April 6, 1846. The case lasted for twelve years and was appealed all the way to the United States Supreme Court. The Scotts' struggle for freedom culminated on March 6, 1857, when the Supreme Court, led by Chief Justice Roger B. Taney, ruled that all blacks—slaves and freemen—were not, and could never be, citizens of the United States and therefore were unable to bring suit in a U.S. court—a privilege constitutionally granted only to citizens.

30. Radhika Mohanram, *Black Body: Women, Colonialism and Space* (Minneapolis: University of Minnesota Press, 1999), 32–33. "This idealization of the body leads to making 'qualitative distinctions' between the different sorts of human beings and their different bodies. Cohen's assertion that Locke achieves the idealization of the body by freezing it outside of time is extremely pertinent to any analysis of racialized, sexed or sexualized bodies in that there is an ideal body implied within Locke's framework which functions as the norm. This ideal body can be achieved only by placing 'the body' outside of history, by ignoring historical events such as colonialism and slavery, and facts such as racism and sexism; in short, by ignoring the cultural and historical constructions of the body."

31. Frantz Fanon, *Black Skin, White Masks* (New York: Grove, 1967), 111–13. Fanon illustrates the continued existence of always-already residual master/slave dynamics:

> The elements that I used had been provided for me not by "residual sensations and perceptions primarily of tactile, vestibular, kinesthetic, and visual character", but by the other, the white man, who had woven me out of a thousand details, anecdotes, stories ... some identified me with ancestors of mine who had been enslaved or lynched.... I was the grandson of slaves in exactly the same way in which President Lebtum was the grandson of tax-paying, hardworking peasants.

Also see Winthrop D. Jordan, *White over Black: American Attitudes Toward the Negro, 1550–1812* (New York : Norton, 1977).

32. Sally E. Hadden, *Slave Patrols: Law and Violence in Virginia and the Carolinas* (Cambridge, Mass.: Harvard University Press, 2001).

33. Donna De La Cruz in her article "ACLU: Drug War Based on Race" (*Philadelphia Inquirer*, June 3, 1999, A22) quotes Ira Glasser, head of the American Civil Liberties Union, saying: "Skin color has become a substitute for evidence in a way that really resembles Jim Crow justice on the nation's highways."

Also see Ruben Rosario, "Race-based Assumptions by Police Are Decried," *St. Paul Pioneer Press*, June 7, 1999, 1B; Angie Cannon, "DWB: Driving While Black," *US News and World Report*, March 15, 1999, 72; Chitra Ragavan et al., "A New Flap over Racial Profiling," *US News and World Report*, March 3, 1999, 10; Brent Staples, "Why 'Racial Profiling' Will Be Tough to Fight," *The New York Times*, May 24, 1999, 26; "Racial Profiling in New Jersey," *The New York Times*, Editorial, April 22, 1999,

30; Harriet Barovick, "DWB: Driving While Black," *Time*, June 15, 1998, 35; Stuart Taylor, Jr., "Racial Profiling: The Liberals Are Right," *National Journal*, April 24, 1999, 1084–85; Kit R. Roane, "A Risky Trip Through 'White Man's Pass': In New Jersey, a Losing War on Racial Profiling," *US News and World Report*, April 16, 2001, 24; and Siobhan McDonough, "Racial Profiling Widespread, Human Rights Group Says," *Minneapolis Star Tribune*, September 13, 2004, 1, among a host of others.

Richard Carelli, "Court Strikes Down 'Street Gang' Law," *Associated Press*, June 10, 1999, looks beyond the highway for other examples of profiling and finds: "Such general anti-loitering ordinances, once common, were viewed by many as thinly veiled attempts to keep [African-Americans] out of certain towns and neighborhoods." In discussing the Chicago law, he observes: "The justices struck down as unconstitutionally vague the city's anti-loitering ordinance.... But the court has long barred communities from using anti-loitering laws to discriminate against racial minorities by, for example, trying to keep [African-Americans] out of some towns or neighborhoods. 'We are grateful ... that it is not a criminal activity simply to be a young man of color gathered with friends on the streets of Chicago,' said Harvey Grossman, the American Civil Liberties Union lawyer who successfully challenged the ordinance."

Still further, this phenomenon operates in other quotidian locations, like shopping. Recently, three black males filed a lawsuit in federal court alleging that the Ward Parkway Shopping Center in Kansas City, Missouri, its management company, and its security company had engaged in a pattern and practice of detaining and arresting blacks at the mall. According to arrest data the plaintiffs' attorney obtained from the Kansas City Police Department, 83 percent of people arrested at Ward Parkway for trespass or disorderly conduct in 1997 were black, but the percent of black shoppers at the mall rarely exceeded 35 percent. Debra Jones Ringhold in the journal *American Behavior Scientist* (February 1995), 578, has defined target marketing as "the intentional pursuit of exchange with a specific group through advertising or other marketing activities. Targeted marketing activities are designed and executed to be more appealing to the targeted market than to people in other segments" and any assertion by commercial malls that African-Americans are wanted, welcomed and valued customers should be measured against this definition. The actions of most commercial-center security personnel seem to fly in the face of this statement. Current research on the mix of stores, the percentage of sales to, and the shopping experiences of, the African-American communities do not support this kind of rhetoric in many malls. As I wrote in a commentary for the *Minneapolis Star Tribune*, July 17, 1999, A19:

> Now, standing in a shopping center waiting to talk to another person should not have been a problem for the security guards—unless some very problematic assumptions were made and justified. People stop in a mall to wait, talk, look and desire all the time. That is one of its major purposes: It is designed to facilitate looking. A mall that doesn't invite you to stop is a mall that doesn't provide for spending money, and that is a poor mall indeed.... Racial profiling rescinds this invitation to African-Americans. And of course, this was at the heart of the meeting between the guards and the African-American patrons: The assumption that the presence of too many African-Americans, and especially African-American males, would dampen the desire of other, potentially more affluent, patrons to make use of their invitations to stop and shop.

For further discussion on this particular operation of spatial profiling, see Edward Barnes, "Can't Get There from Here," *Time,* February 19, 1996, 33; Valerie Lynn Gray, "Shopping for EQUALITY: Tired of Racism in Retail, Black Shoppers Are Starting to Speak Up, and the Industry Is Being Forced to Listen," *Black Enterprise* (July 1998), 60; Tracy Mullin, "Cultural Diversity: Opportunity and Challenge," *Stores* (July 1997), 3; Clarence Page, "SWB: Just One of Many 'Crimes' Facing Blacks," *Chicago Tribune,* October 15, 1997, 21; Amy Trollinger, "Mall Security Under Fire for Racism," *Kansas City Business Journal,* August 14, 1998, 3–4; "Senator Watson Says 'Shopping While Black' Is No Crime!" *Oakland Post,* October 22, 1998, 2; and "ACLU Settles Race Discrimination Case Against Shopping Mall," ACLU press release, June 8, 1998. In addition, see Arnold Diaz, Hugh Downs, and Barbara Walters, *ABC 20/20 News Magazine* segment "Under Suspicion," initially aired on June 8, 1998, by the American Broadcasting Company.

Finally, one can also see this spatial profiling at work in the increased surveillance of people of Arab descent in public spaces since the tragedy of September 11, 2001.

34. Raúl Homero Villa, *Barrios Logos: Space and Place in Urban Chicano Literature and Culture* (Austin: University of Texas Press, 2000), 57.

35. Mohanram, *Black Body,* 31.

36. Ibid.: "Locke locates bodily identity as necessary to separate man from beast in the construction of civil society within liberal humanist thought and also provides the grounds for authorizing individuated identity, permeated with a consciousness and a sense of history. Nevertheless, notwithstanding his insistence on the importance of the body, he suggests that it is ultimately consciousness that must be valorized over the former."

37. Fanon, *Black Skin, White Masks*, 110, 117–20. Fanon, considered one of this century's most important theorists of the African struggle for independence from colonial oppression, joined the Algerian National Movement during its initial war for independence from France. He elaborates on the ways in which the colonizer/colonized relationship is normalized as psychology in such seminal tomes as *The Wretched of the Earth* and *Dying Colonialism*, as well as below: "As the other put it, when I was present, it was not, when it was there, I was no longer" (*Black Skin, White Masks*, 119–20).

Thandeka, "The Cost of Whiteness," *Tikkun* (May/June, 1999), 33–34, observes: "The adult motivation for this mini-tour of black America was to preempt a parental rebuke that would have occurred if Jay had indeed stared at 'them' while on vacation. Jay thus learned something about what to do with his own natural curiosity. Suppress it. The protocol associated with this new knowledge was self-evident: don't stare at them. The deeper implications of the message Jay received would develop over time: don't even notice they are there."

38. Mohanram, *Black Body*, 37, 39: "Like the animal, the body ultimately is used pejoratively; it functions only to give credibility to consciousness.... Only by keeping the racialized body or the sexed body in view can we read Locke's unmarked (normative/white) body, which grants identity to the individual" [parentheses mine].

39. Henry Shue, "Mediating Duties," *Ethics* 98 (July 1988), 687, as quoted by Goldberg in *Racist Culture*, 198.

40. Jordan, *White over Black*, 148: "[W]hite women were, quite literally, the repository of white civilization. White men tended to place them protectively upon a pedestal and then run off to gratify their passions elsewhere."

41. This important distinction is powerfully argued—in no particular order—by bell hooks, Hazel Carby, Angela Davis, Doreen Massey, Gloria Steinem, Rosalyn Deutsche, Judith Butler, Barbara Friedman, Janet Scott, Susan Taylor, and others.

42. I am hesitant to get into a debate on who is the most at risk in the Black com-

munity, males or females. In many instances I believe this to be a false dichotomy that keeps the Black community internally at odds. I also note that it assumes a particular type of male and female, exclusive of gays, lesbians, transsexuals, and transgendered people. Although I do realize that by setting up this hierarchy of circles I open myself up to a particular kind of criticism from, at the very least, Black feminists, this piece is theorized from the location of experience that requires me to spend a rather substantial portion of my time pursuing the "at risk" issues that are embedded in space that are particular to Black men. I trust that my concern will be understood not as exclusive, but specific. However, for a much more detailed explanation of my reasoning, please see the essay "Brothers/Others: Gonna Paint the White House Black" in *Anthology of Male Bodies*, Maurice Harington et al., eds. (Bloomington: University of Indiana Press, 2002).

43. Linda L. Ammons, "Mules, Madonnas, Babies and Bathwater: Racial Imagery and Stereotypes," in *Critical White Studies*, edited by Richard Delgoado and Jean Stefancic (Philadelphia: Temple University Press; 1997), 277. Ammons describes these conflicting images: "Scientists exploring stereotypes about African-Americans repeatedly find that blacks consistently receive the most unfavorable attributions. Among those that were created to keep black women marginalized were Mammy, the asexual nursemaid of white children; Aunt Jemima, the mammy-cook with a name; and Jezebel, the black seductive temptress. Modern caricatures include Sapphire, an emasculating, hateful, stubborn woman; the matriarch, the strong, single mother with no needs; and the welfare queen, the overbreeding, lazy, cheating, single black mother. These representations are so powerful that the sight of a woman of African Descent can trigger responses of violence, disdain, fear or invisibility."

Kate Rushin, *Black Back-Ups: Poetry by Kate Rushin* (Ithaca: Firebrand Books, 1980): "This is dedicated to all of the Black women riding on buses and subways back and forth to the Main Line, Haddonfield, Cherry Hill and Chevy Chase. This is for the women who spend their summers in Rockport, Newport, Cape Cod and Camden, Maine. This is for the women who open those bundles of dirty laundry sent home from those ivy-covered campuses.... At school in Ohio, I swear to Gawd there was always somebody telling me that the only person in their whole house who listened and understood them despite the money and the lessons was the housekeeper. And I knew it was true but what was I supposed to say.... This is for the Black Back-Ups ..."

44. Stuart Hall, "Cultural Identity and Cinematic Representation," *Framework: The Journal of Cinema and Media* 36 (1989), 70.

The Griffith reference is to filmmaker D. W. Griffith and his fictional, revisionist film propaganda *The Birth of a Nation*.

45. See John Edgar Wideman, "The Politics of Prisons: Doing Time, Marking Race," *The Nation* (October 30, 1995), 505. Wideman argues that: "Today, young black men are perceived as the primary agents of social pathology and instability."

See also Toni Morrison, *Sula* (New York: Plume/Penguin Books, 1982), 103. Morrison's Sula iterates what Wideman's observation illustrates: "Sula was smiling. 'I don't know what all the fuss is about. I mean everything in the world loves you. White men love you. They spend so much time worrying about your penis they forget their own. The only thing they want to do is to cut off a nigger's privates. And if that ain't love and respect I don't know what is. And white women? They chase you all to every corner of the earth, feel for you under every bed. I knew a white woman wouldn't leave the house after 6 o'clock for fear one of you would snatch her. Now ain't that love? They think rape soon's they see you, and if they don't get the rape they looking for, they scream it anyway just so the search won't be in vain. Colored women worry themselves into bad health just trying to hang on to your cuffs.'"

See also Farai Chideya, "Who's Making What News?" in *Don't Believe the Hype* (New York: Plume/Penguin Group, 1995), 241–52.

46. Herman Gray, "Black Masculinity and Visual Culture," in *Black Male: Representations of Masculinity in Contemporary American Art*, edited by Thelma Goldan (New York: Whitney Museum of American Art, 1994), 175.

47. Fanon, *Black Skin, White Masks*, 110.

48. Locke, *An Essay on Human Understanding*, 226.

49. The reference here is to Ralph Ellison's seminal work, *Invisible Man*.

50. Gray, "Black Masculinity and Visual Culture," 177: "This figure of black masculinity consistently appears in the popular imagination as the logical and legitimate object of surveillance and policing, containment and punishment. Discursively, this black male body brings together the dominant institutions of (white) masculine power and authority—criminal justice system, the police and the news media—to protect (white) America from harm."

The quotation in the text is from Stephen Nathan Haymes, *Race, Culture and the City* (Albany, N.Y.: State University of New York Press, 1995), 72.

51. Kenneth Jackson, "The Spatial Dimensions of Social Control: Race, Ethnicity, and Government Housing Policy in the US, 1918–1968," *Journal of Urban History* (August 1980), 423. The practice of Locke's theories—and its inherent "whiteness"—can also be traced in historical material constructions. As Jackson explains of the Emergency Relief Act that authorized the Home Owners Loan Corporation (HOLC) and the Federal Housing Administration (FHA) in 1934:

> Four categories of quality—imaginatively entitled *First, Second, Third,* and *Fourth,* with corresponding code letters of A, B, C, and D, and colors of green, blue, yellow, and red—were established. The *First* grade (also A and green) areas were described as new, homogeneous, and "in demand as residential locations in good times and bad." Homogeneous meant "American business and professional men" ... The *Second* security grade (blue) went to "still desirable" areas that had "reached their peak," but were expected to remain stable for many years. The *Third* grade (yellow) or "C" neighborhoods were usually described as "definitely declining," while the *Fourth* grade (red) or "D" neighborhoods were defined as areas "in which the things taking place in C areas have already happened." The HOLC's assumption about urban neighborhoods were based on both an ecological conception of change and a socioeconomic one. Adopting a dynamic view of the city and assuming that change was inevitable, its appraisers accepted as given the proposition that the natural tendency of any area was to decline—in part because of the increasing age and obsolescence of the physical structures and in part because of the filtering down of the housing stock to families of lower income and different ethnicity. Thus physical deterioration was both a cause and effect of population change, and HOLC officials made no real attempt to sort them out. They were part of the same process. Thus, [African-American] neighborhoods were invariably rated as *Fourth* grade, but so were any areas characterized by poor maintenance or vandalism. Similarly, those "definitely declining" sections that were marked *Third* grade or yellow received such a low rating in part because of age and in part because they were "within such a low price or rent range as to attract an undesirable element" [emphasis mine].

Fearing the loss of investment if racial separation was not reinforced, the *Underwriting Manual,* the handbook on proper appraisal procedures issued by the FHA to its appraisers, openly recommended "enforcing zoning, subdivision regulations and suitable restrictive covenants." In short, then, the FHA would not loan to African-Americans who wished to live in *predominantly non-African-American* neighborhoods; due to their subjective and highly questionable risk-rating system the FHA desired to keep sites segregated. But, in addition, the FHA would not lend to African-Americans who wished to live in *predominantly African-American* neighborhoods because those areas were "C" or "D" areas and not a good risk—because of the existing African-American presence.

So, in another example of the temporality of Black access to Lockean space, *African-Americans are both cause and effect* of neighborhood deterioration according to the FHA criteria. We are still trying to rid ourselves of this spatial dynamic decades later.

52. Tim Wise, "School Shootings and White America's Denial," *Afrique News-magazine* (March/April 2001), 6.

53. Goldberg, *Racist Culture*, 198.

54. The quotation is from Homi K. Bhabha, "Cultures In-Between," in *Questions of Cultural Identity,* edited by Stuart Hall and Paul Du Gay (London: Sage, 1997), 56.

See also Cameron McCarthy, et al., "Race, Suburban Resentment, and the Representation of the Inner City in Contemporary Film and Television," in *Off White,* edited by Fine et al., 232.

55. Goldberg, *Racist Culture*, 197, positions the pathology in much more succinct terms of crime and space: "So certain types of activity are criminalized—hence conceived as pathological or deviant—due to their geographical location in the city. Because of statistical variations in location, 'other kinds of crime are either not important, not widespread, or not harmful, and thus not really crimes at all.' This location of crime serves a double end: It magnifies the image of racialized criminality and it confines the overwhelming proportion of crimes involving the racially marginalized to racially marginalized space.... [Crime becomes] something 'they' (blacks) do."

This public perception is further exposed by Dana Canedy in the article "Boys' Case Is Used in Bid to Limit Trials of Minors as Adults," *New York Times,* October 6, 2000, 18. Quoting the conclusion of University of Washington sociology professor George Bridges concerning capital juvenile cases in Florida: "[R]ace was indeed a factor in public reactions to cases involving violent child offenders. Black children tend to be perceived as having committed crimes because they are weak in moral character, have bad attitudes and are incapable of controlling themselves, whereas white children accused of a crime are the result of environmental factors or external influence."

Finally, Neil R. Peirce, "Trapped in Suburbia," *St. Paul Pioneer Press*, June 6, 1999, 19, captures this notion of (white) America's belief in crime as something that happens in spaces of color when he states: "What has Americans puzzled is that the chilling armed attacks on defenseless students erupted so far from where popular culture would have predicted—the scorned ghettoes and barrios of troubled inner cities. Instead, the bloodshed hit affluent Littleton and such other 'nice' spots as Springfield, Ore.; Pearl, Miss.; West Paducah, Ky.; Jonesboro, Ark.; and most recently, Conyers, Ga."

56. Wise, "School Shootings and White America's Denial," 6.

57. Goldberg, *Racist Culture*, 188.

58. Chris Booker, "Combating Anti–African American Male Prejudice," *African American Male Research Project*, previously available at: http://www.pressroom.com/fflafrimale/antibias.htm.

59. bell hooks, *YEARNING: Race, Gender, and Cultural Politics* (Boston: South End Press, 1990), 148.

60. Brent Stapes, "Black Men and Public Space," *Harper's Magazine* (December 1996), 20.

61. Arthur Lee Symes, "Architecture and the Black Community: Towards the Development of a Relevant Architectural Education" (Ph.D. diss., University of Michigan, 1976).

62. Richard Sennett, "Theory," *GSD News* (Summer 1995), 4.

63. Whitney M. Young, Executive Director of the National Urban League, speech to the 1968 AIA National Convention in Seattle, Washington.

64. Bruno Zevi, *Architecture as Space: How to Look at Architecture* (New York: Horizon, 1957, 1974), 23.

65. Ibid.

66. Bradford C. Grant, "Accommodation and Resistance: The Built Environment and the African American Experience," in *Reconstructing Architecture*, edited by Thomas Dutton and Linda Mann (Minneapolis: University of Minnesota Press, 1996), 230.

67. Carrie Crenshaw, "Resisting Whiteness' Rhetorical Silence," *Western Journal of Communication* (Summer 1997), 255, 268.

2. Discipline—Person

1. Ellen Messer-Davidow, et al., *Knowledges: Historical and Critical Studies in Disciplinarity* (Charlottesville: University of Virginia Press, 1993), 8.

2. Ibid., vii–viii. In the authors' analysis: "[Disciplines] specify the objects we can study . . . and the relationships among them. They provide criteria for our knowledge . . . and methods . . . that regulate our access to it. Second, they produce practitioners . . . finally, they produce the idea of progress . . . and provide improve[d] explanations."

3. Judy Pearsall and Bill Trumble, eds., *Oxford Encyclopedic English Dictionary*, 3rd ed. (New York: Oxford University Press, 1996).

4. Leland M. Roth, "The Architect: From High Priest to Professional," *Understanding Architecture* (New York: IconEditions/HarperCollins, 1992), 111.

5. Thomas Dutton, "The Hidden Curriculum and the Design Studio," in *Voices in Architectural Education: Cultural Politics and Pedagogy*, edited by Thomas Dutton (New York: Bergin & Garvey, 1991), 168.

6. Sherry Ahrentzen and Kathryn H. Anthony, "Sex, Stars, and Studios: A Look at Gendered Educational Practices in Architecture," *Journal of Architectural Education* (September 1993), 14.

7. A definition from *Lawyers Title Ins. Corp. v. Hoffman*, 245 Neb. 507, 513 N.W. 2d 521 (1994); *Georgetowne Ltd. Part. v. Geotechnical Servs.*, 230 Neb. 22, 430 N.W. 2d 32 (1988). Available at: http://www.nebraskasurveyor.com/def-prf.html.

8. Barry Wasserman et al., *Ethics and the Practice of Architecture* (New York: Wiley, 2000), 74.

9. Dutton, "The Hidden Curriculum and the Design Studio," 171.

10. Madhu Sarin, *Urban Planning in the Third World: The Chandigarh Experience* (London: Mansell Publishing Limited, 1982), 8.

11. *Lawyers Title Ins. Corp. v. Hoffman* (1994); *Georgetowne Ltd. Part. v. Geotechnical Servs.* (1988).

12. Dutton, "The Hidden Curriculum and the Design Studio," 171.

13. Related disciplines include, but are not limited to: landscape design/architecture, interior design/architecture, planning, etc., all of which find their historical roots in the expertise of the architectural profession.

14. For a full discussion on "ideological state apparatuses," see Louis Althusser,

"Ideology and Ideological State Apparatuses (Notes Towards an Investigation)," in *Lenin and Philosophy and Other Essays* (New York: Monthly Review Press, 1971).

15. Sarah Wigglesworth, "The Crisis of Professionalization: British Architecture 1993," *Practices* 1.2 (Spring) (Cincinnati, Ohio: University of Cincinnati Printing Services, 1993), 14.

16. Sharon Sutton, "Architects and Power," *Progressive Architecture* (May 1993), 65.

17. Wigglesworth, "The Crisis of Professionalization," 14.

18. For a complete outline of this theory, please see, among others, Immanuel Kant, *Critique of Judgment* (Indianapolis: Hackett, 1987); Donald Crawford, *Kant's Aesthetic Theory* (Madison: University of Wisconsin Press, 1974); Paul Guyer, *Kant and the Claims of Taste* (Cambridge, Eng.: Cambridge University Press, 1997); and Salim Kemal, *Kant's Aesthetic Theory: An Introduction* (New York: St. Martin's Press, 1992).

19. Kemal, *Kant's Aesthetic Theory*, 70–71.

20. Ibid., 135: "Genius (1) 'is a talent for producing something for which no determinate rule can be given ... hence the foremost property of genius must be originality. (2) Since nonsense too can be original, the products of genius must be models, i.e. they must be exemplary ... (3) Genius cannot itself describes [*sic*] or indicate scientifically how it brings about its products."

21. It should be acknowledged that Kant recognized the difficulty—if not the impossibility—of applying this kind of aesthetic teleology to the practice of architecture. He specifically relegates architecture to the lower end of the arts because of its utilitarian element—its functionality—which on many levels negates its quest for a Kantian standard of beauty. So in a way, architecture foolishly strives to legitimize itself by invoking a framework in which its ultimate objective can never be obtained, ensuring a kind of professional schizophrenia.

22. Wigglesworth, "The Crisis of Professionalization," 14.

23. C. Greig Chrysler, "Critical Pedagogy and Architectural Education," *Journal of Architectural Education* (May 1995), 208.

24. Cornel West, *Keeping Faith: Philosophy and Race in America* (New York: Routledge, 1993), 47.

25. Ibid.

26. Chrysler, "Critical Pedagogy and Architectural Education," 208.

27. Thomas Dutton, "Introduction," in *Voices in Architectural Education*, x (see n. 5): "Within the last decade there has been growing concern among a number of scholars in a variety of disciplines with the notion of pedagogy. Refusing to reduce the concept to the practice of knowledge and skills transmission, the new work on pedagogical practice had been taken up as a form of political and cultural production deeply implicated in the construction of knowledge, subjectivities and social relations. In the shift away from pedagogy as a form of transmission, there is an increasing attempt to engage pedagogy as a form of cultural politics. Both inside and outside the academy this has meant a concern with analyses of the production and representation of meaning and how these practices and the practices they provoke are implicated in the dynamics of social power."

28. Kathryn H. Anthony, "Designing for Diversity: Implications for Architectural Education in the Twenty-first Century," *Journal of Architectural Education* (May 2002), 257. Anthony goes on to note: "[T]he late Ernest Boyer and Lee Mitgang in their seminal work, *Building Community*, based on extensive research with architectural practitioners, students, faculty, and administrators. They raise a deep concern: 'we worry about … the paucity of women and minorities in both the professional and academic ranks.' In a follow-up piece in *Architectural Record*, Mitgang calls for an end to 'apartheid in architecture schools,' and argues that 'the race record of architecture education is a continuing disgrace, and if anything, things seem to be worsening.'"

Anthony further mentions that these "[c]ontroversies about discrimination in architectural education occasionally have made headlines."

29. Ralph Wiley, *What Black People Should Do Now* (New York: Ballantine Books, 1993), 31–32 (emphasis mine).

30. Julia W. Robinson, "Architectural Research: Incorporating Myth and Science," *Journal of Architectural Education* (November 1990), 23. See also Roth, "The Architect."

31. Ahrentzen and Anthony, "Sex, Stars, and Studios," 14: These gatekeepers are defined as instructors, writers, and publishers, who, by virtue of what Sharon Sutton describes loosely as a limited knowledge paradigm, are free to define architectural history as *"what the 'masters' do."* The requirements for "Master" status are subjectively defined, and gratuitously granted by these "gatekeepers."

32. Llewellyn J. Cornelius et al. "The ABC's of Tenure: What All African-Ameri-

can Faculty Should Know," *Western Journal of Black Studies* (Fall 1997); Mitgang, "Saving the Soul of Architectural Education" (see preface, note 1), and the 2004 National Architectural Accrediting Board Statistical Report.

33. See also Mitgang, "Saving the Soul of Architectural Education," 125.

34. Wiley, *What Black People Should Do Now*, 25–26.

35. Among others, see particularly Alan Bloom, *The Closing of the American Mind* (New York: Simon & Schuster, 1987); Denish D'Souza, "Bogus Multiculturalism: How Not to Teach About the Third World," *American Educator* (Winter 1991) and *The End of Racism* (New York: Free Press, 1995); Gerald Early, "American Education and the Post-Modernist Impulse," *American Quarterly* (Spring 1993); Dick Ravitch, "A Culture in Common," *Educational Leadership* (1992), from *The Report of the New York State Social Studies Review and Development Committee, 1991*; Arthur Schlesinger, Jr., "The Disuniting of America," *American Educator* (Winter 1991) and the book by the same name.

36. Cornelius, "The ABC's of Tenure," 150.

37. Mitgang, "Saving the Soul of Architectural Education," 126.

38. Anthony R. Pratkanis and Marlene E. Turner, "The Proactive Removal of Discriminatory Barriers: Affirmative Action as Effective Help," *Journal of Social Issues* (Winter 1996), 114; Mitgang, "Saving the Soul of Architectural Education," 125.

39. Philomena Essed, *Understanding Everyday Racism: An Interdisciplinary Theory* (London: Sage, 1991), 267: "However, in the absence of effective institutionalized practices to prevent and to oppose racism, the struggle against racism becomes the sole responsibility of the Black [faculty]. 'So we have a tremendous job to do. . . . Not only do we service those student categories [who take Afro-American studies classes] but also the student categories confronting racial stereotypes, myths, etc. in other classes and helping them to cope with that.' "

40. Cornelius, "The ABC's of Tenure."

41. John F. Dovidio and Samuel L. Gaertner, "Affirmative Action, Unintentional Racial Biases and Intergroup Relations," *Journal of Social Issues* (Winter 1996), 52–53: "Aversive racism . . . has been identified as a modern form of prejudice that characterizes the racial attitudes of many Whites who endorse egalitarian values, who regard themselves as nonprejudiced, but who discriminate in subtle, rationalizable ways. . . . The feeling of aversive racists towards Blacks are characterized by mildly negative feelings, such as fear, disgust, and uneasiness, that tend to motivate avoid-

ance rather than intentionally destructive or hostile behavior, which is more likely to characterize the traditional, old-fashioned form of racism. Relative to the more overt, traditional racists ... aversive racists do not represent the open flame of racial hatred nor do they usually intend to act out of bigoted beliefs or feelings. Instead, that bias is expressed in subtle and indirect ways that do not threaten the aversive racist's nonprejudiced self-image. When a negative response can be rationalized on the basis of some factor other than race, bias against Blacks is likely to occur; when these rationalizations are less available, bias is less likely to occur."

Cornelius, citing a study done by Whicker, Kronefield, Strickland, Cornelius, et al. in "The ABC's of Tenure," speaks to the dangers of such subjectively defined criteria for tenure and promotions. Whicker et al. state that: "from a political point of view, 'academic excellence' is whatever the majority voting member of a tenure committee says that it is. This means that the tenure decision may very well be determined by the composition and disposition of the tenure committee, even when this is never explicitly expressed." Because of the dearth of African-American faculty at majority institutions, it almost goes without saying that the "composition and disposition of the tenure committee" will be white.

The impact that aversive racism can have when the evaluation criteria are subjective is disturbingly illustrated in another study documented by Dovidio and Gaertner that investigated the relationship between status and bias in the context of a university application process. Applicants were systematically varied: poorly qualified, moderately qualified, and highly qualified. In addition, the race was manipulated by photos attached to the application, in an attempt to discover the level of unconscious or unintentional racism and how it influences preference when the only difference between two choices is a difference of color. The study showed that: "Discrimination against the Black applicant occurred but, as expected, it did not occur equally in all conditions. Students rated the poorly qualified Black and White applicants equally low. They showed some bias when they evaluated the moderately qualified White applicant slightly higher than the comparable African-American candidate. Discrimination against the Black applicant was most apparent, however, when the applicants were highly qualified. This bias can also be interpreted as a pro-White manifestation of aversive racism.... Although White students evaluated the highly qualified Black applicant very positively, they judged the highly qualified White applicant—with exactly the same credentials—as even better. *Thus, a situation that appears to offer equal opportunity to very well-qualified applicants still favors Whites over Blacks because of subtle and pervasive biases*" [emphasis mine].

Further evidence of its operation can be seen in my own experience at my former institution, located in the upper Midwest. These decisions are made under the guise of being fair to everyone involved—but that is simply not the case. The status quo process is a thinly veiled justification for making no additional effort to recruit and diversify faculty. It allows a department to talk the talk of diversity, but when it comes to walking the walk, these same institutions claim they either can't find qualified personnel (a universal claim when faced with issues of diversity), or, in an exercise of "aversive racism," when faced with equally qualified candidates, hire the one who, the historical argument goes, just so happens to be white.

"If you do what you've always done, you'll get what you've always gotten"— seems to be the objective. When faced with having to act on its goals and objectives to diversify, my research and personal experience—in particular at the University of Minnesota College of Architecture and Landscape Architecture in the late 1990s— concludes that the failure of many African-American applicants, to echo an earlier quote, isn't a failure to *know* something, but a failure to *be* something.

42. Carolyn J. Thompson and Eric L. Dey, "Pushed to the Margins: Sources of Stress for African-American College and University Faculty," *Journal of Higher Education* (May/June 1998), 343.

43. Essed, *Understanding Everyday Racism,* 269: "As an academic there is an underlying edge of racism in what gets accepted as legitimate work in the [Afro-American studies] field. There would be the belief, I think, among most Black academics that the kind of work that most of us are interested in doing is not the kind of work that is acceptable in mainstream journals."

44. Lawrence J. Vale, *Architecture, Power and National Identity* (New Haven: Yale University Press, 1992).

Vale explores this notion in detail in the context of the principal seats of power in a number of postcolonial sites, both preexisting and newly developed after World War II. As he states frequently in this analysis, architecture, both building and site, often serves to "sanction the leadership's exercise of power and to promote the continued quiescence of those who are excluded."

45. Kim Dovey, *Framing Places: Mediating Power in Built Form* (London: Routledge, 1999), 38.

46. Essed, *Understanding Everyday Racism,* 271.

47. See Mitgang, "Saving the Soul of Architectural Education"; see also Linda Groat, "Architecture's Resistance to Diversity: A Matter of Theory as Much as Practice," *Journal of Architectural Education* (February 1993).

48. Mark A. Chesler, "Perceptions of Faculty Behavior by Students of Color," *CRLT Occasional Papers,* no. 7 (Ann Arbor: The Center for Research on Learning and Teaching, 1997).

49. Out of 112 disciplined experts selected to participate on juries across the country, studies report that not one African-American ever appeared on a jury. See Mark Fredrickson, "Gender and Racial Bias in Design Juries," *Journal of Architectural Education* (September 1993).

50. Gloria Joseph, "The Incompatible Menage a Trois: Marxism, Feminism, and Racism," as cited in bell hooks, *Feminist Theory: From Margin to Center* (Boston: South End Press, 1984), 51.

See also Essed, *Understanding Everyday Racism,* 271: "[D]ominant group members will be inclined to ignore racism ... thinking Blacks are unreliable as a source of information about race relations in society. Their suggestions to improve race relations are not accepted, which is rationalized with the argument that Blacks are 'partial.' "

51. Ahrentzen and Anthony, "Sex, Stars, and Studios," 14.

52. John Morris Dixon, "A White Gentleman's Profession," *Progressive Architecture* (November 1994), 59: "Differences of opinion along racial lines occurred in the perceived need for social relevance in the [architectural] program, with African-Americans giving it the greatest importance, followed in order by Latino/Hispanics, Asian-Americans and whites."

53. Symes, "Architecture and the Black Community," viii, 5 (see chapter 1, note 61): "In the great majority of architectural schools, there is no adaptation or accommodation which looks at or considers the uniqueness of [other] cultures, particularly Black culture.... There is *very little* (in most schools, zero) focus on the Black community: its *culture, problems, needs, desires, values and priorities*" [emphasis mine].

54. Anthony, "Designing for Diversity," 260.

55. Ibid.

56. Thompson and Dey, "Pushed to the Margins," 344.

3. Architecture—Thing

1. Craig L. Wilkins and Paolo Tombesi, "Introduction," *Journal of Architectural Education* (Winter 2005), 3: "[W]e ultimately chose to frame the specific terms of architectural globalization as a geographic growth in architectural practice and education markets due in large part to advances in both communication and information technology, supported by international trade agreements that open local markets to global competition and demands conformance of educational and professional qualifications among regions."

2. Leo Marx, "On Architectural Theory Today," *GSD News* (Summer 1995), 6.

3. Dovey, *Framing Places*, 68 (see chapter 2, note 45).

4. Marx, "On Architectural Theory Today," 6.

5. Thomas Dutton, "Architectural Education and Society: An Interview with J. Max Bond, Jr.," in *Voices in Architectural Education*, 92 (see chapter 2, note 5).

6. Dovey, *Framing Places*, 121: "It is the cultural and not the technical capacities of architects which make them indispensable to this market—using cultural capital to produce symbolic capital.... The market for new images requires imagination and architects are the imaginative agents of capital development."

7. Grant, "Accommodation and Resistance," 213 (see chapter 1, note 66).

8. Grant and Mann, *Directory of African American Architects*, 9 (see preface, n. 1).

9. Vincent Scully, "The Architecture of Healing," in *African American Architects in Current Practice*, edited by Jack Travis (New York: Princeton Architectural Press, 1991), 11.

10. Melissa Mitchell, "Research Project Spotlights African American Architects from U. of I.," available at: http://www.news.uiuc.edu/NEWS/06/0209architects .html: "In 'The Canon and the Void: Gender, Race and Architectural History Texts,' an article just published in the Journal of Architectural Education, [Professor Kathryn] Anthony and doctoral student Meltem O. Gurel document their examination of history texts assigned at 14 leading architecture schools. Despite lip service within the field regarding 'the importance of women and African Americans as critics, creators and consumers of the built environment,' Anthony noted, 'our analysis of these history texts revealed that contributions of women remain only marginally represented in the grand narrative of architecture. And for the most part, African Americans are omitted altogether.'"

11. bell hooks, *Art on My Mind: Visual Politics* (New York: New Press, 1995), 147.

12. Richard K. Dozier, *Community Design Centers Information,* edited by Richard K. Dozier, with Vernon A. Williams, coordinating ed. (Washington, D.C.: AIA Publications, 1972), 5.

13. Rex Curry, "The History of Community Design," in *The ACSA Sourcebook of Community Design Programs at Schools of Architecture in North America* (Washington, D.C.: ACSA Press, 2000), 53–54.

14. Dozier, *Community Design Centers Information,* 5–9.

15. *Principles for Inner City Neighborhood Design: Hope VI and the New Urbanism* (Congress for the New Urbanism and the U.S. Department of Housing and Urban Development), 4–5. Available at: http://www.cnu.org/sites/files/inner-city.pdf. As detailed in the document:

> The Inner City Task Force of the Congress for the New Urbanism has developed a set of design principles that have proven effective in inner city neighborhoods. These principles have been tested in several HOPE VI projects. They are proposed as a set of working principles to be further tested and refined through use.
>
> *Citizen and Community Involvement:* Engage residents, neighbors, civic leaders, politicians, bureaucrats, developers, and local institutions throughout the process of designing change for neighborhoods.
>
> *Economic Opportunity:* The design of neighborhood development should accommodate management techniques and scales of construction that can be contracted to local and minority businesses.
>
> *Diversity:* Provide a broad range of housing types and price levels to bring people of diverse ages, races, and incomes into daily interaction—strengthening the personal and civic bonds essential to an authentic community.
>
> *Neighborhoods:* Neighborhoods are compact, pedestrian-friendly, and mixed use with many activities of daily life available within walking distance. New development should help repair existing neighborhoods or create new ones and should not take the form of an isolated "project."
>
> *Infill Development:* Reclaim and repair blighted and abandoned areas within existing neighborhoods by using infill development strategically to conserve economic investment and social fabric.
>
> *Mixed Use:* Promote the creation of mixed use neighborhoods that support

the functions of daily life: employment, recreation, retail, and civic and educational institutions.

City-wide and Regional Connections: Neighborhoods should be connected to regional patterns of transportation and land use, to open space, and to natural systems.

Streets: The primary task of all urban architecture and landscape design is the physical definition of streets and public spaces as places of shared use. Neighborhoods should have an interconnected network of streets and public open space.

Public Open Space: The interconnected network of streets and public open space should provide opportunities for recreation and appropriate settings for civic buildings.

Safety and Civic Engagement: The relationship of buildings and streets should enable neighbors to create a safe and stable neighborhood by providing "eyes on the street" and should encourage interaction and community identity. Provide a clear definition of public and private realm[s] through block and street design that responds to local traditions.

Dwelling as Mirror of Self: Recognize the dwelling as the basic element of a neighborhood and as the key to self-esteem and community pride. This includes the clear definition of outdoor space for each dwelling.

Accessibility: Buildings should be designed to be accessible and visitable while respecting the traditional urban fabric.

Local Architectural Character: The image and character of new development should respond to the best traditions of residential and mixed use architecture in the area.

Design Codes: The economic health and harmonious evolution of neighborhoods can be improved through graphic urban design codes that serve as predictable guides for change.

16. Dozier, *Community Design Centers Information,* 5.

17. Interview with Charles Smith of Smith and Smith Architects, January 4, 2001, in Chicago, Illinois.

18. Dovey, *Framing Places,* 38.

19. Dutton, "Architectural Education and Society," 88.

20. Benjamin Forgey, "Breaking Down Washington's Glass Wall: Pepco's Downtown Building a First for Black Architects," *Washington Post,* March 30, 2002, C01.

21. Grant, "Accommodation and Resistance," 213 (see chapter 1, note 66).

22. Even when recognition occurs, it is typically not for any prowess in the area of design. For example, one of the few feature articles to focus on an African-American architect recently in *Architecture* magazine (July 2002, 39–40) highlighted the work of Mohammed Lawal, principal and principal designer for KKE Architects in Minneapolis. Despite his having won numerous awards for design work, the primary focus of this article was on Lawal's "community" work with the Architectural Youth Program (AYP); a program that works with underrepresented at-risk kids in Minneapolis in an effort to introduce them to the design professions. Ignoring the design expertise of KKE's Lawal to highlight his "social" work only serves to reinforce the notion that the importance and contribution of African-American architects is still essentialized in the area of "community service." In the same edition, the work of another African-American architect, Paul Bauknight, was mistakenly credited to another firm. The extremely rare emergence of African-American work in the popular media makes this carelessness even more problematic and, perhaps more important, endemic.

23. Jon Ruskin, *The Stones of Venice*, vol. 2 (New York: Hurst & Company, 1851), 162.

24. For more information on this architectural education process, please refer to Richard K. Dozier, "Tuskegee: Booker T. Washington's Contribution to the Education of Black Architects" (Ph.D. diss., University of Michigan, 1989). Also, extensive research has been conducted by Vinson McKenzie and Tulane University's architectural historian Ellen Weiss as well.

25. W.E.B. Du Bois, *Crisis* (August 1933). Excerpts from an address to the annual alumni reunion at Fisk University, June 1933.

26. National Architectural Accrediting Board (NAAB), *2004 Statistical Report*, formerly available at http://www.naab.org.

27. Essed, *Understanding Everyday Racism*, 187 (see chapter 2, note 39).

28. This, in fact, is already occurring, sanctioned, although indirectly, by the American Institute of Architecture's efforts to decrease liability. This pursuit of liability-free architecture has caused this architectural imbalance to be exacerbated.

29. Paolo Tombesi, "Super Market: The Globalization of Architectural Production," *Harvard Design Magazine* (Fall 2002/Winter 2003).

30. Ibid.

31. Robert B. Reich, *The Work of Nations* (New York: Alfred A. Knopf, 1991).

32. Tombesi, "Super Market."

33. Ibid., 7–8.

34. Harvey Gantt, as quoted by Dennis Alan Mann, "Making Connections: The African-American Architect," *Faith and Form: Journal of the Interfaith Forum on Religion, Art and Architecture* (Fall 1993), 23.

35. See Fredrickson, "Gender and Racial Bias in Design Juries" (see chapter 2, note 49); as well as Ahrentzen and Anthony, "Sex, Stars, and Studios" (see chapter 2, note 6).

4. Space—Action

1. Hubbard, *A Theory for Practice,* 65 (see On the Organization of This Book, note 1).

2. Henri Lefebvre, *The Production of Space* (Oxford: Blackwell, 1995), 84.

3. Social space, a relationship between nature and "activity which involves the economic and technical realms but extends well beyond them," is built upon a triad of spatial concepts—spatial practice, representations *of* space, and representational spaces—that require intersecting bodies to be produced.

Lefebvre goes on in some depth on the distinctions between these three types of spatial understandings that constitute social space. Spatial practice can be understood as the social activities that occur in a particular time and place that constitute—and are *specific* to—the establishment of a distinctive social order. Spatial practices, in Lefebvre's conceptual triad, can be observed or "perceived." *Spatial practice "presupposes the use of the body"* and presupposes, then, an *identity* for the body that is being used.

He sees representations *of* space as being, in their most basic form, "abstractions" of the perceived; a rational attempt at some logical ordering systems for space which Lefebvre recognizes are clearly ideological in their construction. For Lefebvre, representations *of* space are theorized, rational, logical, or "conceived" spatial understandings, informed by a particular world perspective and the place of the subject within it. Representations *of* space therefore grant a level of reflectiveness to the identity that spatial practices presuppose and in effect recognize, if not bestow, *subjectivity* to the body.

Finally, representational space is "space as directly lived through its associated images and symbols, and hence the space of 'inhabitants' and 'users.'" As "lived experience," *representational spaces "have their source in history—in the history of a people as well as in the history of each individual belonging to that people."* Representational space, which "is alive; [and] speaks," then, *affirms* the body's identity/subjectivity in speaking.

To further clarify these distinctions: for Lefebvre, spatial practices "ensure continuity and some degree of cohesion . . . [that] implies a guaranteed level of competence and a specific level of performance" over time within the social set. As a guide to expected role production and reproduction by individuals within particular social formations, and a measurement of social normalcy, *spatial practices* produce and reproduce space that has a history, but is specific to that particular time, place, and social formation. *Representations of space,* in turn, are "conceptualized space[s], the space of scientists, planners, [and] urbanists" applied to, rather than understood from, existing spatial uses. *Representational spaces,* while depending heavily on memory of that spatial use, is not necessarily logical or ordered, clearly distinguishing itself from representations of space.

This bodily triad of social space conflates to create "a social morphology; it is to lived experience what form itself is to the living organism," whose spatial markers are generated by and identified in the body's "gestures, traces and marks." This dialogue with history and memory indicates a spatial application of Lipsitz's notion of dialectal criticism, as it refers to space (discussed in chapter 1).

4. Michel Foucault, "Of Other Spaces," *Diacritics* (Winter 1986), 22.

5. Ibid., 23.

6. Ibid.

7. Ibid., 24.

8. Hurbert Muschamp, "Looking at the Lawn, and Below the Surface," *New York Times,* July 5, 1998, 32.

9. The author/poet David Muria has argued that the nationalist culture creates a veil of ignorance about the condition of marginalized cultures. The ideology of the nationalist culture allows only atomized bits of the histories of marginalized cultures to be heard. This ideological process not only works to keep marginal histories dispersed but also frames an acceptance of hegemony, as the marginalized choose fragments of their culture and history that will facilitate advancement and acceptance within the nationalist cultural program. This "fragmentation" is much worse in the

case of African-Americans simply because, unlike many marginalized cultures here in America, there has been a continued ideological negation of any cultural *origin*—a critical location of historical memory—for African-Americans.

In this passage from *Color and Democracy: Colonies and Peace* (New York: Harcourt, Brace, 1945), 91, 92, W.E.B. Du Bois illustrates two aspects of the nationalist culture's negation of African-American bodies that is embedded in our understanding of space: "[I]n the Immigration and Naturalization Service of the United States Department of Justice passengers arriving on aircraft are to be labeled according to 'race,' and are determined by the stock from which aliens spring and the language they speak, and to some degree nationality. But 'Negroes' apparently can belong to no nation: 'Cuban,' for instance, refers to Cuban people but not to Cubans who are 'Negroes'; 'West Indians' refers to the people of the West Indies 'except Cubans or Negroes'; 'Spanish American' refers to peoples of Central and South America and of Spanish descent; but 'Negro' refers to the 'black African whether from Cuba, the West Indies, North or South America, Europe or Africa' and moreover 'any alien with a mixture of blood of the African (black) should be classified under this [Negro] heading.'"

Du Bois points not only to the negation of Africa(n) by replacing it with the all-encompassing term "Negro"—neither a nation nor a place, but an *object* or *thing*—but also to the erasure of the cultural specificity of each of the diasporic identities now collected under the inadequate term "Negro." Illustrating the fragmentation that Muria outlines and that Homi K. Bhabha describes as partial cultures, "Negroes" now belong to "no-place," having been removed from their original location, stripped of their subjectivity, and relocated as objects according to a set of strategic hegemonic rules defined by the dominant culture, which effectively eliminated any historical claim to space.

10. In the 1870s and 1880s, thousands of black Americans settled in Kansas, Oklahoma, California, and other parts of the American West. Nicodemus, Boley, Allensworth, and other black towns were the products of a long-distance migration of blacks from the Deep South.

11. Haymes, *Race, Culture and the City*, 80.

12. Trica Rose, *Black Noise: Rap Music and Black Cultural Expression* (Hanover, Conn.: Wesleyan University Press, 1994), 2.

13. For example, the ritual of attending religious services on a communally

chosen weekday or holiday is understood as a social practice. It is a social activity (attending church, mosque, or synagogue) that is spatially defined (the place of worship is a space, there are particular relationships of people to artifacts, areas, and each other within the space of worship—you enter in a specific place, you are oriented to particular objects and symbols, you sit in a particular place, you pray in a particular place, etc.) that helps to define a particular social group (Christians, Muslims, or Jews).

14. Paul Gilroy, *The Black Atlantic: Modernity and Double Consciousness* (Cambridge, Mass.: Harvard University Press, 1993), 78.

15. Goldberg, *Racist Culture*, 205 (see chapter 1, note 12).

16. Lefebvre, *The Production of Space*, 84, states "Surely it is the supreme illusion to defer to architects, urbanists and planners as being experts or ultimate authorities in matters relating to space."

17. hooks, *Art on My Mind*, 151 (see chapter 3, note 11), notes: "Documentation of a cultural genealogy of resistance ... [a] [s]ubversive historiography [that] connects oppositional practices from the past with forms of resistance in the present, thus creating spaces of possibility where the future can be imagined differently."

18. Gilroy, *The Black Atlantic*, 102: "Black identity is not simply a social or political category ... it is lived as a coherent (if not always stable) experiential sense of self. Though it is often felt to be natural or spontaneous, it remains the outcome of practical activity: language, gesture, bodily significations, desires."

19. Greg Tate, "Preface to One-Hundred-and-Eighty Volume Patricide," *Black Popular Culture* (Seattle: Bay Press, 1992), 245.

20. Jordan, *White over Black*, 115 (see chapter 1, note 31).

21. Fanon, *Black Skin, White Masks*, 117 (see chapter 1, note 31).

22. Michel de Certeau, *The Practice of Everyday Life* (Berkeley: University of California Press, 1984), 117.

5. Discipline—State

1. Cornel West, "Notes on Race and Architecture," in *Keeping Faith* (see chapter 2, note 24); and Cornel West, "On Architecture?" *Appendx: Culture/Theory/Praxis* (1997).

2. James Mayo, "Political Avoidance in Architecture," *Journal of Architectural Education* (February 1985).

3. Ibid.

4. Linda N. Groat, "Rescuing Architecture from the Cul-de-Sac," *Journal of Architectural Education* (May 1992).

5. Some of the interdisciplinary pedagogical explorations that will be facilitated by this approach are:

- Reexamination and analysis of the frames of reference and methods by which land use policy decisions are reached.
- The class, gender, racial, and regional consequences of various policies as they relate to the politics of the city and the changing conception of urban crisis and urbanism—as opposed to suburbanism—as a way of life.
- Theoretical and empirical investigation of contemporary issues, especially economic and physical development and community power, with a special emphasis on the concept of "community," ranging from village, rural community, small town, and city subcommunities—ethnic village, city localities, etc.
- Issues of community development, planning, ownership, empowerment, and environmental racism.

6. Some of the interdisciplinary pedagogical explorations that will be facilitated by this approach are:

- Geographical aspects of micro and macro planning focusing on identifying patterns created by people in relation to natural and social environments.
- Concentration of poverty and diminishing services in residential areas and the effect on physical, child, family, and support structure development.
- Particular focus on the evolution and diffusion of cultural traits and habits in urban environments that are affected by socioeconomic problems in the built environment that include, among others, congestion and air and noise pollution.

7. Some of the interdisciplinary pedagogical explorations that will be facilitated by this approach are:

- Models for the comprehensive synthesis of the economic, political and social spaces of architecture.
- The spatial patterning and linking of national urban networks through architecture as well as the development and facilitation of the public life of individual cities.

• Principles of location and distribution of land use that reinforce or reinterpret the necessity and location of urban centers as we understand them as commercial, retail, and entertainment magnets.

8. Claus Seligmann, "Image, Imagination and Ethnocentrism," *Column 5: Journal of Architecture University of Washington* (February 1992), 69.

9. See my previous comments on Vale, *Architecture, Power and National Identity* (chapter 2, note 44).

The quotation is from Ahrentzen and Anthony, "Sex, Stars, and Studios," 14 (see chapter 2, note 6).

10. Nelson Goodman as quoted by Vale, *Architecture, Power and National Identity,* 4.

11. Dana Cuff, *Architecture: The Story of Practice* (Cambridge, Mass.: MIT Press, 1991), 65–66.

12. Shelby Steele, *The Content of Our Character: A New Vision of Race in America* (New York: HarperCollins, 1990), 6: "Both [cultures] instinctively understand that to lose innocence is to lose power (in relation to each other). To be innocent someone must be guilty ... it has never been easy for [the dominant culture] to avoid guilt where blacks [or other marginalized cultures] are concerned." The members of the dominant culture possess power. To bestow it upon someone else is to lose it yourself. The issue is therefore avoided.

13. Ibid., 12.

14. Derrick Bell, *Faces at the Bottom of the Well: The Permanence of Racism* (New York: Basic, 1992), 113.

15. Gloria Joseph, quoted in ibid., 113. Joseph is also cited by hooks, *Feminist Theory,* 51 (see chapter 2, note 50).

16. Kyle M. Yates, ed., *The Religious World—Communities of Faith* (New York: Macmillan, 1988); Leo Rosten, ed., *Religions of America—Ferment and Faith in an Age of Crisis* (New York: Simon & Schuster, 1975).

17. Derrick Bell, *Faces at the Bottom of the Well* (New York: Basic, 1992), 143.

18. hooks, *YEARNING,* 11 (see chapter 1, note 59).

19. Melvin L. Mitchell, *The Crisis of the African-American Architect: Conflicting Cultures of Architecture and (Black) Power* (New York: Writers Club Press, 2001), 105.

20. Du Bois, *Color and Democracy,* 91–92 (see chapter 4, note 9).

21. See Fredrickson, "Gender and Racial Bias in Design Juries" (see chapter 2, note 49).

22. Lani Guinier, "What I Would Have Said," lecture given at Southern University, Baton Rouge, Feb. 24, 1994.

23. Steele, *The Content of Our Character,* 130.

24. Craig L. Wilkins, "In the Muck and Mire, How Quickly We Tire: Pedagogical Paradigms Built on Sand," unpublished paper presented at the Tenth National Conference on Teaching the Beginning Design Student held at Tulane University, March 26–28, 1993.

25. Grant, "Accommodation and Resistance," 213 (see chapter 1, note 66).

26. Wiley, *What Black People Should Do Now,* 36–37 (see chapter 2, note 29).

27. Larry Rosenthal, "Comic-book Character Helping Artist Vent Rage," *Baton Rouge Advocate,* February 2, 1994, 15A. In this article, in which the columnist interviews and provides an analysis of marginalized cultures and artistic responses to institutionalized repression, Rosenthal quotes Dana Heller, assistant professor of American literature and gender studies at Old Dominion University: "It's a[n] . . . appropriation of a popular cultural form by a marginalized group that really has historically lacked the means of openly communicating (their) frustrations, and angers and fears." In this context, architecture also can be seen as an artistic expression of the marginalized culture, for the same purpose that Heller describes.

28. See Mitgang, "Saving the Soul of Architectural Education," 125 (see preface, note 1):"Lately, the thinking seems to be that a more inclusive curriculum is key: adding non-Western perspectives, promoting scholarship aimed at documenting how persons of color have shaped architecture here and abroad, and offering more studios that connect architecture to community concerns."

See also Seligmann, "Image, Imagination and Ethnocentrism," 70: "[A] pluralistic society such as ours encompasses many ethnocentrisms, many interpretive communities, and thus the primary challenge confronting us is one of devising an educational framework capable of responding to that multiplicity."

29. Symes, "Architecture and the Black Community," 5 (see chapter 1, note 61).

30. Dalton, "Admission, Retention and Support Service of African-American Architecture Students," 9 (see preface, note 1): "In its history and evolution towards becoming an independent discipline, architecture has sometimes been aligned with other areas of study. Some of these include: architecture and painting under a degree

program in the visual arts at Syracuse University in the 1870's; architecture and engineering at Cornell in the 1890's; architecture as a supplement to general education instruction in the fine arts at Harvard also in the 1890's; architecture and music at Columbia at the end of the 19th century; and architecture and the fine arts (interior decoration, painting, and illustration) at Carnegie Institute of Technology in the 1900's."

Such overtly humanistic or liberal arts programs continue to exist today at many institutions both here and abroad, including the University of Minnesota, the University of British Columbia, and the University of Pittsburgh, just to mention a few.

31. Essed, *Understanding Everyday Racism*, 74 (see chapter 2, note 39). "Through prolonged practice in dealing with racism, people become experts. This means that their general knowledge of racism becomes organized in more and more complex ways, while their interpretive strategies become more elaborate and effective."

32. Jimmy Lim is president of CSL Associates in Kuala Lumpur, Malaysia, and former editor of the architectural journal *Majalah Akitek*. He is currently a member of the Royal Institute of British Architects, the Malaysian Institute of Architects, and a fellow in the Royal Australian Institute of Architects.

33. Jimmy Lim, "Globalism of Architectural Education," abstract for Negotiating Architectural Education, symposium held at the University of Minnesota College of Architecture and Landscape Architecture, Minneapolis, May 7, 1999.

34. Conversation between Lim and author during the Negotiating Architectural Education symposium.

35. In response to the three-level model hypothesized by Lim, at the same colloquium I proposed an alternative organization of the architectural discipline's educational and professional knowledge boundaries designed to expand the definition of "Architect." Note that this configuration is subject to revision:

Generalist Degree (commensurate with the philosophy behind a bachelor of arts degree distinction)

Architectural Aesthetics:
- *Designer—macro, micro*
- *Theoretical—spatial, aesthetic*
- *Social / Behavioral—cultural, function*
- *Analyst / Critic—physical, aesthetic, performance*

Specialist Degree(s) (commensurate with the philosophy behind a bachelor of science degree distinction)

Architectural Technology:
- *Construction*
- *Production*
- *Management*

Architectural Development:
- *Policy Development and Consultation*
- *Public / Private Land Use Analyst—urban, rural, metro, regional*
- *Public / Private Education and Facilitation*

Architectural Research:
- *Aesthetic*
- *Technological*
- *Developmental*
- *Cultural*

36. Jacqueline C. Vischer, "Epilogue: Summing Up Opinions on Architecture and Social Change," *Design Intervention: Towards a More Humane Architecture* (New York: Van Nostrand Reinhold, 1991), 363–64.

37. Mitgang, "Saving the Soul of Architectural Education,"126 (see preface, note 1).

38. See Langston Hughes, "A Dream Deferred," *The Collected Works of Langston Hughes,* edited by Arnold Rampersad (Columbia: University of Missouri Press, 2001).

39. Rodner Wright, quoted by Mitgang, "Saving the Soul of Architectural Education," 126.

40. Lani Guinier, "What I Would Have Said."

41. Ibid.

6. Architecture—Motion

1. Fanon, *Black Skin, White Masks,* 206 (see chapter 1, note 31).

2. Hans van Dijk, "Architecture and Legitimacy: Styles and Strategies," in *Architecture and Legitimacy,* edited by Hans van Dijk (Rotterdam: Netherlands Architectural Institute, 1995), 8.

3. Greg Castillo, "Peoples at an Exhibition: Soviet Architecture and the Nationalist Question," *South Atlantic Quarterly* (Summer 1995), 722.

4. Greg Castillo, "Manufactured Proletariat: Constructivism and the Stalinist Company Town," in *Constructing Identities: Proceedings of the Association of Collegiate Schools of Architecture Annual Meeting and Technology Conference* (Washington, D.C.: ACSA Press, 1998), 657.

5. Ross King, *Emancipating Space: Geography, Architecture and Urban Design* (London: Guilford Press, 1996), 64.

6. For a dissenting view on this position, see Harries, *The Ethical Function of Architecture* (see chapter 1, note 7).

7. Matthew Smith, "Transforming Design: Architects and Social Responsibility," *Newark Review*, vol. 2, set 7. Available at: http://www-ec.njit.edu/fflnewrev/v2s7/msmith.html.

8. Wigglesworth, "The Crisis of Professionalization," 14 (see chapter 2, note 15).

9. Sennett, "Theory," 4 (see chapter 1, note 62): "Modern [architectural] theory ... tend[s] now to talk in code, and the circles of those who understand the code grow ever smaller."

10. DesignCorps, "A New Role for Today's Architect," formerly available at: http://www.designcorps.org/index1.html.

11. Peter Eisenman, "Architecture as a Second Language: The Texts of Between," *Threshold* (1988), 73.

12. Robin Burkhardt-Pennell, "The Schizophrenic Reaction to Society and Its Influence in Architecture" (Masters thesis, Miami University [Ohio] Department of Architecture, 1994), 46.

13. Marx, "On Architectural Theory Today," 6 (see chapter 3, note 2).

14. Thomas Fisher, "Three Models for the Future of Practice," in *Reflections on Architectural Practices in the Nineties*, edited by William S. Saunders (New York: Princeton Architectural Press, 1996), 37.

15. Wasserman, *Ethics and the Practice of Architecture*, 70 (see chapter 2, note 8). See also the definition given by the Professional Surveyors Association of Nebraska, "Definition—Profession," available at: http://www.nebraskasurveyor.com/def-prf.html (see chapter 2, note 7). In the cases of *Lawyers Title Ins. Corp. v. Hoffman* (1994) and *Georgetowne Ltd. Part. v. Geotechnical Servs.* (1988), professions were defined as "a calling requiring specialized knowledge and often long and intensive

preparation, including instruction in skills and methods as well as in the scientific, historical, or scholarly principles underlying such skills and methods."

See also similar definitions in Magali Sarfatti Larson, "The Historical Matrix of Modern Professions," in *The Rise of Professionalism: A Sociological Analysis* (Berkeley: University of California Press, 1977); Wilbert E. Moore, "The Formation of a Professional," in Wilbert E. Moore and Gerald. W. Rosenblum, *The Professions: Roles and Rules* (New York: Russell Sage Foundation, 1970); and Jeff Schmidt, *Disciplined Minds: A Critical Look at Salaried Professionals and the Soul-Battering System That Shapes Their Lives* (New York: Rowman & Littlefield, 2000).

16. Fisher, "Three Models for the Future of Practice," 37.

17. Margaret Crawford, "Can Architects Be Socially Responsible?" in *Out of Site: A Social Criticism of Architecture*, edited by Diane Ghirardo (Seattle: Bay Press, 1991), 40: "Venturi's unflinching realism led him to eliminate any possible technical and social aspirations in architecture since they appeared to be practically unrealizable under existing conditions . . . As defined by Venturi, the architect's 'own job' was an essentially formalist task."

18. Le Corbusier, *Towards a New Architecture* (New York: Dover, 1986; reprint of 1931 first publication in English), 288–89.

19. Crawford, "Can Architects Be Socially Responsible?" 43–44.

20. Jane Hobson, "New Towns, the Modernist Planning Project and Social Justice: The Case of Milton Keynes, UK and 6th October, Egypt," Working Paper No. 108, Development Planning Unit, University College London, 6. However, the CIAM views were infused by the problematic modernist Rorakian architect-as-hero image and that hero's desire to be unencumbered by past rules illustrated by the call of Le Corbusier to build on only cleared sites.

21. For an overview of the PRM, see Steven J. Eagle, *Policy Analysis No. 404: The Birth of the Property Rights Movement* (Washington, D.C.: Cato Institute, June 26, 2001).

22. Ibid., 4.

23. Ibid., 11, 13.

24. Ibid., 3.

25. Richard Ashcraft, "Locke's Political Philosophy," in *The Cambridge Companion to Locke*, edited by Vere Chappell (Cambridge, Eng.: Cambridge University Press, 1997), 242: "Man's Property in the Creatures, was founded upon the right he

had, to make use of those things, that were necessary or useful to his being ... any successive development or notion of property, Locke argues, presupposes this fundamental right."

26. Locke, "Second Treatise on Government" (see chapter 1, note 17): "But if either the grass of his enclosure rotted on the ground, or the fruit of his planting perished without gathering and laying up, this part of the earth, notwithstanding his enclosure, was still to be looked on as waste, and might be the possession of any other."

27. Joseph William Singer, *Entitlement: The Paradoxes of Property* (New Haven: Yale University Press, 2000), 31.

28. Ashcraft, "Locke's Political Philosophy," 242.

29. Singer, *Entitlement*, 37.

30. John W. G. van der Walt, as quoted by Singer, *Entitlement*, 140.

31. Ibid., 29.

32. Ibid., 17.

33. The most noticeable, effective, problematic, and dangerous methods for interrogating property and property rights are "squatting" and "spontaneous settlements/vernacular environments"—the difference between the two is loosely defined by whether the residents occupy existing structures (squatting) or appropriate unoccupied land for the purposes of constructing their own structures (spontaneous settlements/vernacular environments). The most organized and established movement of squatting is located in the Netherlands. Begun in earnest in Amsterdam in the 1960s, squatting changed from a desire for affordable housing into a bona fide sociopolitical movement when it began to respond to land speculation and the hoarding of property by Dutch landlords. It was supported by a custom of permitting legal squatting in the Netherlands—specifically allowing for occupation of buildings that had been left unoccupied for at least a year. In the 1970s and 1980s, squatting won public backing by exposing property speculation and governmental indifference to serious housing shortages. Once entrenched, squatters can't simply be evicted because in the Netherlands, they have rights.

Squatting and spontaneous settlements/vernacular environments have a long, sporadic, and unorganized history, but it has become more and more common, widespread, and concerted. Marjetica Potrc writes about the process and advantages of these developments in the *Centre on Housing Rights and Evictions (COHRE) On-*

line Newsletter Number 5 (November 2001) that these favela, shantytowns, or barrios follow "laws of an informal real-estate market, in which ownership of land is not particularly relevant, but homes are continually rented and sold, as well as improved by residents.... [Residents] have a strong sense of place and belonging, not frequently achieved in more formal areas of the city." Movements and squatting actions have been initiated in such diverse locations as London, Leeds, Newcastle-upon-Tyne, Manchester, Tunbridge Wells, Hackney, Bristol, Oxford, and Southampton, England; Montreal, Canada; Bialystok, Poland; Navarro and Barcelona, Spain; Dijon, France; Trastevere, Italy; Berlin, Germany; Santa Monica, New York, Baltimore, and Boston, United States; and the rural lands in Brazil. There are networks and organizations that share information and help coordinate efforts locally, nationally, and globally.

Some countries are addressing this in the law. The Brazilian constitution has a provision for unproductive estates to be taken over by the government and redistributed to landless agricultural workers. In the Turkish city of Narlıdere, an ordinance was passed stipulating that whatever homesteaders construct on unoccupied land within twenty-four hours is allowed to stay on that site. In Mexico, along the outskirts of Mexico City, similar incursions of property are occurring, while not with the explicit support of specific laws, certainly with the tacit agreement of the government. Currently in the United States, there are three of these informal developments that are of note: Dome Village in Los Angeles, established in 1993; Dignity Village in Portland, which has a commitment from the city to a one-year pilot project for the development and which has created architectural plans for its future; and Tent City in Seattle, which has employed a new federal law that gives churches the ability to disregard certain land-use regulations and zoning in the process of practicing religious and outreach services to remain in place and legitimize its presence. All three are actively engaged in challenging the current and widespread concept of property and property rights. In addition, international agencies such as the World Bank and the International Monetary Fund also support the policies that assist "self-help" housing strategies.

However, not all observers, critics, and participants in this housing process are so enamored, with the arguments against it ranging from the claim that supporters are romanticizing poverty and the agency of those who are impoverished, to the claim that support of these strategies alleviates the state's responsibility to provide basic services to its citizens, thereby reinforcing the unequal distribution of power within said societies, to the highly questionable aesthetic quality of these settlements, to, finally, the questionable claim of a universal applicability of these strategies.

For a more detailed description of these developments, please see Randy Gragg, "Guerrilla City," *Architecture* (May 2002), 47–51; Beth Kaiman, "Roving Tent City Can Build on Its Legal Foundation," *Seattle Times,* March 28, 2002; Carol Estes, "A Place for Dignity," *YES! A Journal of Positive Futures,* available at: http://www.futurenet.org/article.asp?id=490; and Peter Kellett and Mark Napier, "Squatter Architecture? A Critical Examination of Vernacular Theory and Spontaneous Settlement with Reference to South America and South Africa," *Traditional Dwellings and Settlements Review: Journal of the International Association for the Study of Traditional Environments,* 6, no. 2 (Spring 1995).

34. On average, 15 percent of an average city's land base was categorized as vacant by a recent Brookings Institute report; see Michael A. Pagano and Ann O'M. Bowman, *Vacant Land in Cities: An Urban Resource* (Washington, D.C.: Brookings Institution, Center on Urban & Metropolitan Policy, 2000), who note that "[t]his total includes widely varying types of land, ranging from undisturbed open space to abandoned contaminated brownfields."

However, in postindustrial cities like Detroit, this figure is outrageously higher; see the Kirwan Institute for the Study of Race and Ethnicity, The Ohio State University, "How Can a Land Bank Assist the City of Detroit? An Introduction to Land Bank Programs" (Columbus, Ohio: Kirwan Institute for the Study of Race and Ethnicity, 2004), 1: "Vacant land and abandoned structures are prominent throughout the City of Detroit. The City of Detroit currently owns approximately 38,000 parcels of land and 80% of these parcels are tax-reverted. The U.S. Census Bureau estimates over 26,000 housing units in the City of Detroit were vacant and not used seasonally, owned, rented or available for sale in 2002."

35. Kirwan Institute, "How Can a Land Bank Assist the City of Detroit?," 1.

36. This is also a critical point within the current intellectual property (IP) debate. Law professor and IP expert James Boyle asks if anyone could imagine Bill Gates's MS-DOS—a derivative and collaborative program indeed—being created if he did not have free access *(both materially and financially)* to the software codes of the time? Current IP advocates are aggressively attempting to destroy that sys-

tem—conveniently ignoring its own history in it—and establish another in which "Being Bill Gates" will become much more difficult, if not impossible.

37. For more information on the Favela/Bairro program, see among others: "3 Projects in Favelas," *Architecture Research Quarterly Santiago*, no. 55 (December 2003), 32–37; Robert Neuwirth, "Letter from Brazil," *The Nation*, July 10, 2000, 29–31, available at: http://www.islamamerica.org/articles.cfm/article_id/46; "Programa de Urbanizacao de Assentamentos Populares do Rio de Janeiro" [Program of Urbanization of Rio de Janeiro Squatter Housing], Inter-American Development Bank (September 1998); "Brazil: Rio de Janeiro Urban Upgrading Program," Inter-American Development Bank (November 1995); Patricia Pinho, "Urbanising an Informal Settlement of the City: Novos Alagados Project," Third International Conference on Social Integration and Security for the Urban Poor Towards Cities for All, International Forum on Urban Poverty (October 1999).

38. United States Department of the Interior, National Park Service, Homestead National Monument of America Web site at http://www.nps.gov/home/history culture/abouthomesteadactlaw.htm:

> The Homestead Act of 1862 has been called one the most important pieces of Legislation in the history of the United States. Signed into law in 1862 by Abraham Lincoln after the secession of southern states, this Act turned over vast amounts of the public domain to private citizens. 270 million acres, or 10% of the area of the United States[,] was claimed and settled under this act.
>
> A homesteader had only to be the head of a household and at least 21 years of age to claim a 160 acre parcel of land. Settlers from all walks of life including newly arrived immigrants, farmers without land of their own from the East, single women and former slaves came to meet the challenge of "proving up" and keeping this "free land". Each homesteader had to live on the land, build a home, make improvements and farm for 5 years before they were eligible to "prove up".... The Homestead Act remained in effect until it was repealed in 1976, with provisions for homesteading in Alaska until 1986.

See Kirwan Institute, "How Can a Land Bank Assist the City of Detroit?," 2: "A land bank authority is a public entity granted specific powers, with the goal of facilitating the reuse and redevelopment of vacant and foreclosed properties. A land bank authority can provide the legal and administrative framework to efficiently acquire and redevelop vacant land. The specialized function of a land bank allows a prolonged commitment of resources to redevelop properties. The land bank authority is also capable of comprehensively looking at the city's vacant land and adopting strategies for reuse that best fit community needs."

39. Grant, "Accommodation and Resistance," 212 (see chapter 1, note 66).

40. Vischer, "Epilogue," 364 (see chapter 5, note 36).

41. Ibid., 354, 364.

42. Wasserman, *Ethics and the Practice of Architecture*, 71 (see chapter 2, note 8): "Two cornerstones of professional standing are the duty to provide public service and to merit trustworthiness."

43. Sharon E. Sutton, "Reinventing Professional Privilege as Inclusivity: A Proposal for a Sustainable Praxis of Architecture," in *The Discipline of Architecture*, edited by Andrzej Piotrowski and Julia Williams Robinson (Minneapolis: University of Minnesota Press, 2001), 203.

44. Hannah le Roux, "Undisciplined Practices: Architecture in the Context of Freedom," in *Blank____: Architecture, Apartheid and After*, edited by Hilton Judin and Ivan Vladistavic (Rotterdam: Netherlands Architectural Institute, 1998), 356–57.

45. Ray Pratt, *Rhythm and Resistance: Explorations in the Political Uses of Popular Music* (New York: Praeger, 1990), 21.

46. Ibid., 266.

47. Brooke Gladstone, "Mainstreaming Urban Culture," National Public Radio Commentary, May 19, 2001.

48. Ken Gibbs, "Hip Hop, Napstar, and the New Music Industry," formerly available at: http://www.africana.com/DailyArticles/index_20000802.htm.

49. Ernest Allen, Jr., "Making the Strong Survive: The Contours and Contradictions of Message Rap," in *Droppin' Science: Critical Essays on Rap Music and Hip Hop Culture*, edited by William Eric Perkins (Philadelphia: Temple University Press, 1996), 164.

50. Mark Goldblatt, "On Being Whiteballed: Why My Novel Is Nowhere Near Your Bookstore," Guest Comment on National Review Online, April 24, 2002, available at: http://www.nationalreview.com.

51. Allen, "Making the Strong Survive," 160.

52. Michael C. Dawson, " 'Dis Beats Disrupts': Rap, Ideology, and Black Political Attitudes," in *Droppin' Science: Critical Essays on Rap Music and Hip Hop Culture*, edited by William Eric Perkins (Philadelphia: Temple University Press, 1996),
332–33.

53. Ibid. 319.

54. Allen, "Making the Strong Survive," 160.

55. Dawson, " 'Dis Beats Disrupts,' " 325.

56. Ibid., 319.

57. Houston A. Baker, Jr., *Black Studies, Rap and the Academy* (Chicago: University of Chicago Press, 1993), 58–59.

58. Dawson, " 'Dis Beats Disrupts,' " 335.

59. Ben Malbon, *Clubbing: Dancing, Ecstasy and Vitality* (London: Routledge,
1999), 98.

60. Simon Frith and Angela McRobbie, "Rock and Sexuality," in *On Record:
Pop, Rock and the Written Word*, edited by Simon Frith and Andrew Goodwin (New
York: Pantheon, 1990), 371.

61. Ibid., 373.

62. Ibid. Frith and McRobbie argue that while music is responsible for constructing gendered identities, rock is essentially a male form. Male-dominated positions
of power within the production and reproduction offer a *"variety of male sexual
poses"* (374) to young males, but for women in rock, "their musical appeal, the way
they were sold, reinforced in rock the qualities traditionally linked with female sing-
ers—sensitivity, passivity, and sweetness. For women to become hard aggressive
performers it was necessary for them, as Jerry Garcia commented on Janis Joplin, to
become 'one of the boys' " (377).

Frith and McRobbie summarize their position with the assertion that "Both in
its presentation and its use, rock has confirmed traditional definitions of what constitutes masculinity and femininity, and reinforces their expression in leisure pursuits."

Frith and McRobbie's argument demonstrates music's ability to form subjectivity/
identity—in this instance defining sexual positions by way of public activity—but, as
I will argue later, this is only one example of identity formation available via music.

63. George Lipsitz, *Time Passages: Collective Memory and American Popular Culture* (Minneapolis: University of Minnesota Press, 1990). Lipsitz applies the concept

of dialogical criticism as developed by literary critic Mikhail Bakhtin to the study of music. He posits that every instance of cultural production *"is the product of an ongoing historical conversation in which no one has the first or the last word"* (99). Lipsitz applies this theory of dialogical criticism to the study of music. He asserts that music is produced through, reflects, and affects the social and political context in which it evolves and is therefore inherently social and that the meaning of music emerges within the socio/historical context around its production by performers and its reception by listeners. In other words, Mozart might have written differently if he had lived in modern-day Brooklyn and had access to a tape player, MIDI machine, and a microphone. But he didn't. Like the music he produced, he was a product of his time—his history. Lipsitz's analysis equally argues that not only might Mozart have produced a different music, music would have greatly contributed to producing a different Mozart.

64. Ibid., 104.

65. Ibid., 105.

66. John Mowitt, "The Sound of Music in the Era of Its Electronic Reproducibility," in *Music and Society: The Politics of Composition, Performance and Reception,* edited by Richard Leppert and Susan McClary (Cambridge, Eng.: Cambridge University Press, 1987), 173.

67. Ibid., 181. To illustrate memory's fundamental and social influence on music, Mowitt gives an example from Maurice Halbwachs, "The Collective Memory of Musicians" (1939), in *The Collective Memory,* translated by Francis J. Ditter, Jr., and Vida Yazdi Ditter (New York: Harper & Row, 1980), that posits that when performing, many musicians find referring to their musical notations *(scores)* frequently unnecessary because they know their pieces "by heart," owing to many hours practicing, often with other musicians. This event "by heart" is a memory that is "exerted on a performer's brain by the 'colony' of other brains," those "other brains" belonging to fellow musicians. In other words, musicians play what they "remember" having *heard* being played previously, highlighting "a particular history and technology of reproduction [that] supplements the musician's memory." The sound is memorized by many players until a convention, a "normal" collective memory of the sound is realized. Thus, a collective "memory" defines the proper or "normal" way to listen and a community is produced.

68. Mowitt, "The Sound of Music in the Era of Its Electronic Reproducibility,"

179, succinctly summarizes and describes the idea of social order/community—complete with rules of conduct and various social categories (normal/abnormal, etc.)—with a quote from Jacques Attali: "All music, any organization of sounds, is then a tool for the creation or consolidation of a community, of a totality."

69. Albert Murray, *The Blue Devils of Nada: A Contemporary American Approach to Aesthetic Statement* (New York: Pantheon, 1989), 123.

70. Malbon, *Clubbing,* 86: "Dancing is a mode of behavior in which the relationship between movement and thought (or motion and emotion) is central.... As well as being a social, political, psychological, occasionally pharmaceutical and often economic activity, dancing is primarily a form of communication or body language and a mode of expression, a performance in which verbal communication can be supplemented and even temporarily superseded, either internationally or through compulsion."

Also, see de Certeau, *The Practice of Everyday Life* (see chapter 4, note 22).

71. Lefebvre, *The Production of Space,* 84 (see chapter 4, note 2).

72. For heterotopias, see Foucault, "Of Other Spaces," 23 (see chapter 4, note 4).

Lefebvre, *The Production of Space,* 86. In other words, for Lefebvre, the social space—perceived, conceived, and lived, generated and identified by the gestures, traces, and marks of the body—that delineates the space of home intersects with the gestures, traces, and marks that define the space of yard, penetrating into the gestures, traces, and marks that construct the space of neighborhood, that integrates into the gestures, traces, and marks that delimit the space of city, and so forth, ad infinitum.

73. De Certeau, *The Practice of Everyday Life,* 96.

For de Certeau, the pedestrian speech act is homologous to the verbal speech act in three ways: as "a process of appropriation" of an existing framework of meaning; as "a spatial acting-out of the place" from the existing framework in order to communicate meaning; and as "it implies relations among differentiated positions" by implying interaction between a speaker and listener to communicate meaning (97–98).

74. De Certeau further asserts that memory of experience *(social interaction/ historical dialogue)* constructs not only the language we use to communicate, but its *rhetoric*—the *way* we use the language to communicate: "[I]t is assumed that practices of space also correspond to manipulations of the basic elements of a

constructed order [and] it is assumed that they are, like the tropes in rhetoric, deviations relative to a sort of 'literal meaning' defined by the [constructed order]." Ibid.,
100.

For example, in verbal speech there is "proper" English, and all other uses are
a derivative of that proper form, from dialect to slang. He notes on page 100 that,
as with music and speech, space also lays claim to a "proper" form: "[I]t is assumed
that [other uses] are, like tropes in rhetoric, deviations relative to a sort of 'literal'
meaning: defined by the urbanistic system. There would thus be a homology between
verbal figures and the figures of walking (a stylized selection among the latter is already found in dancing) insofar as both consist in 'treatments' or operations bearing
isolatable units, and in 'ambiguous dispositions' that divert and displace meaning in
the direction of equivocalness. . . . In reality, this faceless 'proper' meaning (ce 'pro-
pre' sans figure) cannot be found in current use, whether verbal or pedestrian."

Implied in this understanding of space and its use is the fact that, again as in
verbal speech acts, there is a "correct" way to use the language by which all other uses
are measured. So too for the pedestrian speech act, where the "proper" use is the one
intended by the spatial organizer *(be it architect, landscape architect, interior designer,
etc.)* and all other uses, from shortcuts to avoidance, are derivatives of the "proper"
use; he argues that this "proper" use rarely, if ever, exists.

75. Ibid., 117.

76. Rose, *Black Noise*, 2 (see chapter 4, note 12): "Rap music is a black cultural
expression that prioritizes black voices from the margins of urban America. Rap music is a form of rhymed storytelling accompanied by highly rhythmic, electronically
based music. It began in the mid-1970's in the South Bronx in New York City as a
part of hip hop, an African-American and Afro-Caribbean youth culture composed
of graffiti, breakdancing, and rap music. From the outset, rap music has articulated
the pleasures and problems of black urban life in contemporary America." Purveyors of rap and its culture have taken something essentially powerless and made it
powerful.

77. Ibid., 96.

78. Ibid., 94. Rose presents a particularly rap version that builds on Mowitt's
theory of the social construction of music through technology. In discussing the
musical piece "Paid in Full" by the rap duo of Eric B. and Rakim, Rose identifies
and illustrates the primacy of Mowitt's studio in the production of the music by

highlighting from the piece's lyrics the acknowledgment by the duo of their location in the studio. Also, during the lyrical recorded "conversation" between Eric B. *(the producer)* and Rakim *(the rapper)*, there are specific, identifiable directions to the studio engineer as to the technical manipulation of the music for "effect," now that they have completed the lyrical "performance" portion of the piece. This acknowledgment of the power of studio technology over the music produced in the reproduction of the music itself "demystifies technology and its production . . . Eric B. and Rakim suggest that they are in control of what technology produces—including its on-site manager, Ely, the engineer" thereby confirming the primacy of the technology and its studio location.

79. Ibid., 82.

80. Mowitt, "The Sound of Music in the Era of Its Electronic Reproducibility," 182.

81. For instance, Gilroy in the *Black Atlantic* (see chapter 4, note 14) argues that it is difficult, if not impossible, to consider the musical traditions of the African diaspora as unbroken and universally traceable while positing that in their difference, these various strains of diasporic musics still recall a collective memory. Similarly, Rose in *Black Noise* argues—particularly with rap—that any focus on the possible legacy of the oral traditions of Africa to African-American expressions in diasporic music is to ignore the *music* itself. Gerald Early, in *One Nation Under a Groove: Motown and American Culture* (Hopewell: Ecco Press, 1995), argues that the development of R & B/Soul music—with Motown at its head—was a uniquely Black American experience. There are many more perspectives that at once question and reinforce a direct continuous historical link in the sonic traditions of Black music, but my point here is that there is a common point of departure from which these critics—and others—begin their investigations.

82. The nature of Black music is demonstrated through its focus on rhythm and repetition. As it concerns rap music, this focus has much to do with performance. I should make it clear that in this instance, I am using performance to refer to three individual, but wholly dependent, instances: *The performance of the music itself* (the production of the sound), *the performance of the musicians* (when producing the sounds), and *the performance of the listeners* (the reception of the sounds—as depicted in movement or dance). Gilroy, *The Black Atlantic,* 75, argues for a position where performance is a primary necessity for the emergence of memory in the Afri-

can diaspora: "This orientation to the specific dynamics of performance has a wider significance in the analysis of black cultural forms than has so far been supposed. Its strengths are evident when it is contrasted with approaches to black culture that have been premised exclusively on textuality and narrative rather than dramaturgy, enunciation and gesture—the pre- and anti-discursive constituents of black meta-communication."

The rhythm and repetition of African music facilitates the *invitation* to the performance. It is meant to be extended out in time, to flow beyond its immediate location. As music meant to be performed, it is cognizant of the limitations of the body and so calls to many performers to participate, creating an additional layer of flow and rupture—sometimes consistent, other times contradictory—to the music itself. These instances of performance illustrate not only the social aspect of music as it relates to the African diaspora, but also the construction of space *by* music, through the performances that are part of the music itself. As described by Lerone Bennett in *Before the Mayflower: A History of Black America,* 5th ed. (New York: Penguin, 1984), 25: "Before the coming of the European, music and rhythm were everyday things in Africa. Music was everywhere and it was grounded in two techniques which survived in the New World: polyrhythmic percussive technique and the call-and-response pattern (leader and chorus alternating). The poetry of tom-toms, the symphonies of synchronized bodies: these ebbed and flowed with the rhythm of life. Men and women danced because dancing had a social and religious meaning and because dancing was meaning, was life itself."

The technical nature of the (re)production of rap music, in particular the use of sampling, allows for an overapplification of the musical focus on the performance facilitators, the *break* or the *back beat* to become primary. In rap music, the beat is the king *(or queen),* and whether it is the beat/rhythm of the music or the voice that primarily drives the energy of the performance is, for all intents and purposes, unimportant. The fact that the rapper Guru of Gang Starr has alternately said, *"If the beat were a princess, I'd marry it"* and *"It must be the voice, that gets you up"* with equal conviction, illustrates this point. What is important is the memory that this use of rhythm awakens. It awakens the desire to perform—in answer to the call of the music. It is at once, immediate and historical, local and global, American and diasporic.

83. Black music's orality also has its presence in the memory of the diasporic community. Many black cultural critics and historians posit that the vocalese of rap

descends directly from the tradition of the storyteller/tribal historian—the *griot*—in African societies. This perspective rests in the understanding of the primacy in traditional African cultures of the spoken word and all of its communicative allies—dramaturgy and gesture *(performance)*. Others trace the orality of rap to a type of sonic phenomenon deeply embedded in the African tradition known as antiphony—call-and-response. Adapted to a specific interaction between two subjects, its appearance in African-American culture as *toasting,* also known as "crackin'," "boastin'," "playin' the dozens," "snappin'," or "signifyin'," is designed to come to a resolution only when one cannot answer the call *(toast, snap, crack, boast, etc.)* of another. (For more on this see Henry Louis Gates, Jr.'s *The Signifying Monkey,* which discusses the history of such techniques in African-American literature.) This position suggests that the development of the vocal pattern of toasting is, if not constituted by, certainly runs parallel to, the development of similar diasporic musical patterns in Africa and America. Others still, like Paul Gilroy quoting from Cornel West, "Black Culture and Postmodernism," in *Remaking History,* Discussions in Contemporary Culture, no. 4, edited by Barbara Kruger and Phil Mariani (New Press, 1998), propose yet another possibility, positioning rap music as "borrowing from the linguistic innovations of Jamaica's distinct modes of 'kinetic orality.'" This suggests an interesting "flip[pin'] of the script": instead of lyrical patterns being either separate from or influenced by music patterns, the vocal framework actually influences the musical patterns. The fact that the Jamaican "patois"—patterns of rapid vocalese bathed in distinct rhythmic tones, inflections, and enunciations—has heavily influenced the musics of the Caribbean supports such a position and suggests further investigation. However, for the purposes of this essay, it is not necessary—even if it were possible—to discern the truth of one perspective over the other. What is important is the acknowledgment by each perspective of its African diasporic foundation and the development of vocal historical frameworks and patterns as independent from the music itself.

84. The final segment of rap music's historical dialectic with the collective memory of the African diasporic social order is content. Highlighting rap music's connection with the diasporic collective memory, which is largely influenced by the postmodern condition of fragmentation that has rendered "tactical" the diasporic struggles for identity, I am using the term "tactic" here understood as defined by Michel de Certeau in *The Practice of Everyday Life.* While the tactics of diasporic

struggles for identity emerge in this manner, they are engaged in deconstructing each of the conditions that hold this understanding of "tactic" in place. So, as Early states in *One Nation Under a Groove*, 101: "It is, thus, no insignificant fact that ... some members of the black elite began to reinvent, in effect, the reinvention of an 'African' consciousness for black people in the 1950's—something that continues to this day, and something that black folk have been doing in this country since the 18th century."

The lyrical content of rap music recalls the "reinvention of an 'African' consciousness" and "continues to this day" to engage in the dialectic concerning marginality, location, agency, and the subject/object imbroglio. The lyrics of rap music are a form of aggressive agency, a reinterpretation of those conditions in an effort to reclaim *the person* from *the thing*. This distinctive Africentric *social practice* is at once recalled, produced, and enhanced in the music of the hip hop culture. As Rose points out (*Black Noise*, 27): "[H]ip hop has styles and themes that share striking similarities with many past and contiguous Afrodiasporic musical and cultural expressions. These themes and styles, for the most part, are revised and reinterpreted, using contemporary cultural and technological elements. Hip hop's central forms—graffiti, breakdancing, and rap music—developed in relation to one another and in relation to the larger society."

85. Gilroy, *The Black Atlantic*, 76. Also see Bennett, *Before the Mayflower*. Gilroy states: "Music, the grudging gift that supposedly compensated slaves not only for their exile from the ambiguous legacies of practical reason but for their complete exclusion from modern political society, has been refined and developed so that it provides an enhanced mode of communication beyond the petty power of words—spoken or written."

86. Ann Daly, "Conversations About Race in the Language of Dance," *New York Times*, December 7, 1997, 1, 44: "Choreographers are increasingly exploring the limits and possibilities of existing dance forms to address African-American [identity], as Mr. Lemon is doing with post-modern dance in 'Geography.'"

87. In other words, the various specific, individual ways of identity (re)defining that are developed by the members of the diaspora are homologous—having the same or relative position, if not necessarily identical—in function at any given moment in time across the membership.

88. *Bigger and Deffer* is the title of rap artist L. L. Cool J's 1987 album from Def Jam records.

89. Malbon, *Clubbing,* 147.

90. Mike Steele, "Bring It In," *Minneapolis Star Tribune,* December 14, 1997, 1, 18: "That beat has hung on from minstrel shows to the blues, jazz to rock to rap, ragtime to "Shuffle Along." It all began more than 250 years ago in the feet of [enslaved Africans] who created something out of nothing. Their drums were outlawed after [enslaved African] rebellions, but [they] found other ways to keep the rhythm flowing: They turned their feet into drums, conversing in rhythmic codes.... That's history in street rhythm carried by dancing feet."

91. For a highly informative, educational, and entertaining read of this history, see Katrina Hazzard-Gordon, *Jookin': The Rise of Social Dance Formations in African-American Culture* (Philadelphia: Temple University Press, 1990).

92. A few of rap music's identifiable *transnational capital* qualities are: Specific—*developed/grew out of the African-American experience;* Communicative—*speaks to common cultural experiences of people of African descent;* Identifiable—*symbolic;* Malleable—*revolutionary, inspirational, educational, etc.;* Economic—*control of the product and its distribution;* Culturally Authentic—*defining acceptable context in which it can be produced;* Redemptional—*reclaiming history.*

93. Venise Berry, "Redeeming the Rap Music Experience," in *Speculations: Readings in Culture, Identity and Values,* edited by Charles Schuster and William Van Pelt (Upper Saddle River, N.J.: Simon & Schuster, 1996), 191: "The power and promise of rap music rests in the bosom of urban America.... Years of degradation, welfare handouts, institutional racism, and discrimination have created a community where little hope, low self-esteem and frequent failure translates into drugs, teen pregnancy, and gang violence."

94. Haymes, *Race, Culture and the City,* 80 (see chapter 1, note 50): "[T]he reduced availability of inner-city housing for blacks, caus[es] them to live in very overcrowded housing conditions. In sum, the land use practices of city planners, real estate developers, and financiers contributed to the creation of overcrowded and deteriorated housing conditions, inflated rents, landlord neglect, abandonment of buildings and the curtailment of municipal services ... paired with the relocation of high paying unionized factory jobs to the suburbs, [and no means of transportation

to get to the relocated employment], was responsible for the formation of inner-city black ghettos."

95. *Palimpsestic* is understood here as a process of effacing the initial from a place or material to make room for the latest in the same place or on the same material.

96. Essential to this consciousness is the recognition that hip hop space flows, ruptures, and intersects with bodies. In hegemonic spatial structures, these things are viewed as discontinuations, accidents that were not planned *(both in the architectural and the organizational sense)*. This is antithetical to the spatial organization inherent in hip hop. As a space formed by sound, such "accidents" are designed and expected and are considered not only as continuous, but invitations to perform.

97. Lefebvre, *The Production of Space,* 87.

98. Suzanne Preston Blier, *The Anatomy of Architecture: Ontology and Metaphor in Batammaliba Architectural Expression* (Chicago: University of Chicago Press, 1994), 118.

99. Ibid., 119 (emphasis mine).

100. The intersection of several subject positions that are part of the world of people of color is discussed by Gilroy in *The Black Atlantic* when he speaks about the double consciousness of the diasporic experience, while W.E.B. Du Bois speaks of a "twoness," and James Baldwin speaks about duality. Lefebvre, *The Production of Space,* 183, hints at this intersection of subjectivity and space as being "space contain[ing] opacities, bodies and objects, centers of efferent actions and effervescent energies. On the other [hand], it offers sequences, sets of objects and concatenations of bodies." For simplicity's sake, I have referred to these similar themes as "simultaneity."

101. Blier, *The Anatomy of Architecture,* 200.

102. See Upton, ed., *America's Architectural Roots* (see preface, note 1); Dozier, "Tuskegee" (see chapter 3, note 24); and Susan Deyner, *African Traditional Architecture* (New York: Africana Publishing Company, 1978).

103. hooks, *Art on My Mind,* 157 (see chapter 3, note 11).

104. Forman, *The 'Hood Comes First,* 13 (see chapter 1, note 4): "The articulation of experience and the influences of contemporary conditions that inform cultural identities frequently emerge within the arena of hip-hop culture as a series of counterdiscourses, representing an attempt to circumvent constraining and outdated programs for social empowerment."

105. Carl Boggs, *Social Movements and Political Power* (Philadelphia: Temple University Press, 1986), 49.

106. Simon Sadler, *The Situationist City* (Cambridge, Mass.: MIT Press, 1999), 107.

107. Rose, *Black Noise*, 17, as quoted from Andrew Ross.

108. Melvin Mitchell, "Black Boxes—A Yale Symposium: A Critical Review," *African American Architect: Magazine of the National Organization of Minority Architects* (Spring 2004), 29–30.

Precis

1. Crawford, "Can Architects Be Socially Responsible?" 43, 44 (see chapter 6, note 17).

2. David Harvey, "Poverty and Greed in American Cities," in *Reflections on Architectural Practices in the Nineties*, edited by William S. Saunders (New York: Princeton Architectural Press, 1996), 104.

3. For a discussion on planning and architectural methods of spatial marginalization of communities, see Marshall Berman, *All That's Solid Melts into Air* (New York: Simon & Schuster, 1988); Peter Hall, *Cities of Tomorrow* (Oxford: Blackwell, 1994), chapters 2, 3, and 11; Peter Kivisto, "Changes in Public Housing Policies and Their Impact on Minorities," in *Race, Ethnicity and Minority Housing in the United States*, edited by Jamshid A. Momeni (New York: Greenwood Press, 1986); Jackson, "The Spatial Dimensions of Social Control" (see chapter 1, note 51); John Mollenkopf, *The Contested City* (Princeton, N.J.: Princeton University Press, 1983); Douglas Massey and Nancy Denton, *American Apartheid* (Cambridge, Mass.: Harvard University Press, 1993); and Le Corbusier, *The Radiant City*, among others.

4. Rose, *Black Noise*, 36, Interview with filmmaker, artist, and cultural critic Arthur Jafa.

5. Linda Kafka, "Your Work and Who Owns It," *New Architect* (May 2001), formerly available at http://www.newarchitectmag.com/archives/2001/04/kafka, provides a brief working definition of intellectual property sufficient for the purposes of this discussion: "Lawyers have a name for the relationship between people and their creative output: intellectual property ... The term suggests two very important and abstract notions. The first is that there's a type of property that may not have a physical presence. And the second is that this "something" without a physical presence

can be owned.... Because intellectual property deals with the content of thoughts, and not their embodiment—the precise way that Ferlinghetti strings his words together, rather than the physical paper and ink edition of his poems—some lawyers have labeled this area of practice the metaphysics of law."

A more through examination of this concept is beyond the scope of this work, but for an excellent discussion on this topic, please see Siva Vaidhyanathan, *Copyrights and Copywrongs: The Rise of Intellectual Property and How It Threatens Creativity* (New York: New York University Press, 2001).

"Sampling" is the practice of digitally copying or transferring snippets or portions of a preexisting record to make a new composition. An artist will take a piece of a preexisting recording and use that piece *(sample)* to create a new, collaged recording. The industry prominence of sampling is owed to hip hop and rap music, which in a large measure takes its approach to music from its ancestors *(blues, ska, reggae, jazz, etc.)*, which have a long history of considering music and experience "common material," and the performance of that common material "original." Vaidhyanathan discusses why sampling is so disruptive to the concept of property ownership and indicates that such tension was, at least in part, born of cultural differences that are at the core of hip hop/rap music: "While the cultures of West Africa are diverse and complicated, some cultural forms helped form a 'cultural commons' that exists today across the Atlantic, linking many of those in the West African diaspora to those on the continent through a web of familiar signs and tropes. Anthropologists and musicologists have emphasized the importance of the 'circle' as the site of both creativity and community in African cultures.... This has created a cultural value system among West African–derived traditions that differs from the 'progressive' value system that emanates from the European artistic tradition and informs European and American copyright law....

"[T]he concepts of copyrights have been deeply entrenched in western literary traditions for centuries, but do not play the same role in African, Caribbean, or African-American oral traditions.... Sampling seemed to undermine the very definitions of 'work,' 'author,' and 'original'—terms on which copyright law rests."

6. Forman, *The 'Hood Comes First,* 13 (see chapter 1, note 4).

Gladstone, "Mainstreaming Urban Culture" (see chapter 6, note 47): "There's a kind of cultural alchemy that transforms street corner hip hop and graffiti into platinum watches and billion dollar deals. The marketers call the result urban culture. Urban I.Q., an urban media research firm, says there are 45 million consumers of urban culture, fully two thirds of Americans between the ages of 18 and 35. More than half live outside major urban centers. More than 60 percent are white. Thus the urban culture consumer, like any consumer, is not defined by who he is but by what he buys.... Urban culture may be fueled by a rainbow coalition of cash money, but it is still a commodity based on racial difference, on the general perception that black urban style, its agility, its ineffable cachet is what everybody wants to buy.... Artists have a tendency to live on the margins, but when the sums are this large, there seems to be no choice but to follow the money into the mainstream."

7. Those who believe that the future of wealth in this society lies with information and information technology—which does not require landed property as we know it—will find my declaration a bit dubious. Law professor and IP legal expert James Boyle, "A Politics of Intellectual Property: Environmentalism for the Net?" *Duke Law Journal*, 47 (1997): 89–90, states: "It is intellectual property ... that provides the key to the distribution of wealth, power and access in the information society.... In terms of ideology and rhetorical structure, no less than practical economic effect, intellectual property is the legal form of the information age."

8. Singer, *Entitlement*, 13 (see chapter 6, note 27).

9. Sadler, *The Situationist City*, 54 (see chapter 6, note 106).

To be even more specific about how this phenomenon has been specifically applied to control the social tensions between the African-American community and white America, Massey and Denton conclude in *American Apartheid*, 2, 11, 18–19, that "The residential segregation of blacks is viewed charitably as a 'natural' outcome of impersonal social and economic forces.... But black segregation is not comparable to the limited and transient segregation experienced by other racial and ethnic groups, now or in the past. No group in the history of the United States had ever experienced the sustained high level of residential segregation that has been imposed on blacks in large American cities for the past fifty years. This extreme racial isolation did not just happen; it was manufactured by whites through a series of self-conscious actions and purposeful institutional arrangements that continue today....

"The urban ghetto ... represents the key institutional arrangement ensuring the continued subordination of blacks in the United States.... Through its actions and inactions, white America built and maintained the residential structure of the ghetto ... which provides a firm basis for a broader system of racial injustice."

10. Michel Foucault, "Space, Power and Knowledge," in *Rethinking Architecture*, edited by Neal Leach (London: Routledge, 1997), 371–72.

11. Singer, *Entitlement*, 138.

12. Karsten Harries, "The Ethical Function of Architecture," in *Theorizing a New Agenda for Architecture: An Anthology of Architectural Theory 1965–1995*, edited by Kate Nesbitt (New York: Princeton Architectural Press, 1996), 396.

13. Le Corbusier, *Towards a New Architecture*, 251 (see chapter 6, note 18).

14. Rose, *Black Noise*, 61.

15. Queen Latifa, "Come into My House," on *All Hail The Queen* (New York: Tommy Boy Music, 1989).

INDEX

AAAE. *See* Asian American Architects and Engineers

Abele, Julian, 67, 143

ACD. *See* Association of Community Design

ACSA. *See* Association of Collegiate Schools of Architecture

ACSA News, 62

ADPSR. *See* Architects/Designers/Planners for Social Responsibility

Africa, 189

African American architects: design exhibitions, 77; obstacles to professional advancement, 71, 78–83, 85, 86, 90; perceptions of, 81, 82–83; professional history of, 67–68, 69–76, 77–78, 80; professional visibility of, 64–66, 68, 77, 80–81

African American Architects, A Biographical Dictionary, 1865–1945 (Wilson, Henderson), 76, 145

African Americans: architectural resistance to, xi–xii; disciplinary practices specific to architecture students, 51–52; disciplinary practices specific to faculty, 48–51; female, 20; history in architecture, 143–44; identity, xvii; identity construction, 205; importance of faculty, 48; male, 20–21; participation in architecture,

53–54; as percentage of faculty, 47; spatial strategies of, xvii; support for architectural student, 124–25, 126–27, 128–30, 131–35, 144. *See also* Black; spatial practices

AfriCobra, 70

Afro-American Association, 71

agency, 104–5, 109–10

Age of Reason, 32. *See also* Enlightenment

Ahrentzen, Sherry, 52

AIA. *See* American Institute of Architects

Allen, Ernest, 176

Althusser, Louis, 38, 226–27

American Institute of Architects (AIA), 73, 77, 145; AIA National Diversity Committee, 145; AIA Task Force on Equal Opportunity, 73

American Institute of Architecture Students, 116

American Quarterly, 9

Amsterdam, the Netherlands, 248

Anthony, Kathryn, 52

Appendx, 145

Appiah, K. Anthony, 65

ARCH. *See* Architect's Renewal Committee of Harlem

architect: as aesthetic expert, 63, 64, 81; African American, professional

CRAIG L. WILKINS

is the director of the Detroit Community Design Center at the
University of Michigan Taubman College of Architecture and
Urban Planning. In 1991, he helped establish the collaborative
BAKARI Design, and he has worked as a designer, project architect,
and urban consultant in Washington, D.C., New York, Houston, and
Minneapolis. He has served as a research fellow at the University of
Minnesota Design Center for the American Landscape, University
of Illinois Chicago City Design Center, and the U.S. Department of
Housing and Urban Development.